Boundaries of Obligation in American Politics
Geographic, National, and Racial Communities

This book shows how ordinary Americans imagine their communities and the extent to which their communities' boundaries determine who they believe should benefit from the government's resources via redistributive policies. By contributing extensive empirical analyses to a largely theoretical discussion, it highlights the subjective nature of communities while confronting the elusive task of pinning down "pictures in people's heads."

A deeper understanding of people's definitions of their communities and how they affect feelings of duties and obligations provides a new lens through which to look at diverse societies and the potential for both civic solidarity and humanitarian aid. This book analyzes three different types of communities and more than eight national surveys. Cara J. Wong finds that the decision to help only those within certain borders and to ignore the needs of those outside rests, to a certain extent, on whether and how people translate their sense of community into obligations.

Cara J. Wong is Assistant Professor in the Department of Political Science at the University of Illinois, Urbana-Champaign. She holds a PhD in political science from the University of California, Berkeley, and has taught previously at the University of Michigan and Harvard University. Her research interests include American government and politics; political psychology; and race, ethnicity, and politics. She has published numerous articles on racial and ethnic politics, voting behavior, citizenship, social capital, and multiculturalism in edited volumes and in the following journals: *Journal of Politics, British Journal of Political Science, Public Opinion Quarterly, Political Behavior, Political Psychology,* and the *Du Bois Review.*

CAMBRIDGE STUDIES IN PUBLIC OPINION
AND POLITICAL PSYCHOLOGY

Series Editors

DENNIS CHONG, *Northwestern University*
JAMES H. KUKLINKSI, *University of Illinois, Urbana-Champaign*

Cambridge Studies in Public Opinion and Political Psychology publishes innovative research from a variety of theoretical and methodological perspectives on the mass public foundations of politics and society. Research in the series focuses on the origins and influence of mass opinion; the dynamics of information and deliberation; and the emotional, normative, and instrumental bases of political choice. In addition to examining psychological processes, the series explores the organization of groups, the association between individual and collective preferences, and the impact of institutions on beliefs and behavior.

Cambridge Studies in Public Opinion and Political Psychology is dedicated to furthering theoretical and empirical research on the relationship between the political system and the attitudes and actions of citizens.

Books in the series are listed on the page following the Index.

Boundaries of Obligation in American Politics

Geographic, National, and Racial Communities

CARA J. WONG

University of Illinois, Urbana-Champaign

CAMBRIDGE UNIVERSITY PRESS
Cambridge, New York, Melbourne, Madrid, Cape Town, Singapore,
São Paulo, Delhi, Dubai, Tokyo

Cambridge University Press
32 Avenue of the Americas, New York, NY 10013-2473, USA

www.cambridge.org
Information on this title: www.cambridge.org/9780521691840

First published 2010

Printed in the United States of America

A catalog record for this publication is available from the British Library.

Library of Congress Cataloging in Publication data
Wong, Cara, 1970–
  Boundaries of obligation in American politics : geographic, national, and racial
  communities / Cara J. Wong.
    p. cm. – (Cambridge studies in public opinion and political psychology)
  Includes bibliographical references and index.
  ISBN 978-0-521-87132-7 (hardback) – ISBN 978-0-521-69184-0 (pbk.)
  1. United States – Politics and government – 1989– 2. Political obligation.
  3. Distributive justice – United States. 4. Community power – United States.
  I. Title. II. Series.
  JK1726.W68 2009
  307.0973–dc22   2009014995

ISBN 978-0-521-87132-7 Hardback
ISBN 978-0-521-69184-0 Paperback

Additional resources for this publication at http://carawong.org/
Boundaries-Appendix.pdf

Contents

Acknowledgments

Books gather debts like snowballs rolling down hills – the longer the hill, the bigger the snowball. A book that began as a dissertation eons ago is like a tiny pebble at the center of an immense avalanche. Gratitude and joy overwhelm me when I think about the many people who lavished support while I worked on this project. However, this gratitude comes with guilt; as I step back and take stock, I wonder, "How does one have the help of such an amazing community and not produce a weightier, more substantial tome?" *Mea culpa.*

I first want to thank the many people who enabled me to complete the dissertation, particularly my committee of Jack Citrin, Laura Stoker, Bruce Cain, Tom Tyler, and Martín Sánchez-Jankowski. Jack was my ideal teacher, mentor, co-author, and dissertation chair, and he has continued to be a great friend, colleague, and advisor; few are able to play so many important roles with such wisdom, kindness, and honesty. Laura's intense engagement with my writing and ideas improved the quality of every piece of my work that she read; I greatly appreciate both her friendship and her insight. Bruce advised and guided me throughout my time at Berkeley, and I am grateful for his encouragement and pragmatism. Besides the members of my committee, I also owe thanks to a number of other professors from graduate school, especially Henry Brady, Nelson Polsby, Paul Sniderman, and Ray Wolfinger. The friends and colleagues I met while at Berkeley have made both my work and my life better; I want to thank Jake Bowers, Arthur Burris, Andrea Campbell, Brian Duff, Ben Highton, Anna Law, Sam Luks, Mike Metelits, Chris Muste, Eric Oliver, Nate Persily, Sharon Pinkerton, and especially Mark Walker. Mark was a comrade, colleague, coconspirator, and very dear friend. At UC-Berkeley,

ix

the Political Science Department, Institute of Governmental Studies, and Survey Research Center all contributed to a fantastic graduate school experience.

The Political Science Department at the University of Michigan gave me multiple opportunities to benefit from the wisdom and kindness of wonderful colleagues. While I was in graduate school, I was fortunate to meet Adam Berinsky and Kathy Cramer Walsh at the ICPSR summer program. Later, as a faculty member, my ideas were greatly improved by conversing with and getting feedback from Jake Bowers, Ted Brader, Ron Brown, Nancy Burns, Tony Chen, Anna Grzymala-Busse, Don Herzog, Vince Hutchings, James Jackson, Orit Kedar, Don Kinder, Ken Kollman, Mika LaVaque-Manty, Ann Lin, Skip Lupia, Rob Mickey, Mark Tessler, Nick Valentino, Hanes Walton, and Liz Wingrove. In particular, I want to thank Don Herzog for commenting on portions of the book; Kathy, Nancy, and Don Kinder for reading a very early version of the book in its entirety; and James, Vince, and Ron for collaborating with me on the National Politics Study. I also want to thank Grace Cho and Katie Drake for their excellent research assistance.

Harvard University provided a home when I moved to Cambridge for family reasons. (I thank Jake Bowers for giving me the opportunity to spend two years with old friends and new.) I thank Eric Schickler for making my visit possible. I greatly benefited from my discussions with Claudine Gay, Yoi Herrera, Jennifer Hochschild, Dan Hopkins, Maggie Penn, and Bob Putnam. I also want to thank Dan Carpenter and the Center for American Political Studies for the unexpected generosity of funding a book manuscript conference while I was there. I am deeply indebted to Dennis Chong, Claudine Gay, Taeku Lee, Tali Mendelberg, Lynn Sanders, and Rogers Smith, who were willing to tackle a penultimate draft of the book in its entirety for the conference. The exchange of ideas by these profound scholars was one of the most exciting and intellectual engagements of my career, and it reminded me of everything I admire and love about the academic profession.

My colleagues at the University of Illinois, Urbana-Champaign, have provided the intellectual and personal support required to complete the book; Bill Bernhard, Jake Bowers, José Cheibub, Wendy Tam Cho, Sam Frost, Jim Kuklinski, Peter Nardulli, and Gisela Sin deserve special thanks. I also want to thank Tarah Williams for her excellent proofreading help.

The National Science Foundation provided three years of support in graduate school, and then helped to fund the National Politics Study, along with the Carnegie Corporation and the Office of the Vice President of Research at the University of Michigan. The book uses many different datasets, and I am very grateful to the National Election Studies, the National Opinion Research Center, the Public Policy Institute of California, the ICPSR, and the Roper Center for making these data publicly available. I particularly want to thank the National Election Studies Board for being willing to incorporate my proposal in the Pilot Study in 1997. The staff at the Rare Book, Manuscript, and Special Collections Library at Duke University went above and beyond the call of duty in making the *Indivisible* interviews available to me in an electronic format. I also want to thank Lew Bateman, my exceedingly patient editor at Cambridge University Press, for his enthusiasm about the manuscript. I greatly appreciate the careful copyediting and editing help of Mary Cadette and Kathryn Ciffolillo. I cannot thank Jake Bowers enough for all his work in helping me (find and) replicate in R all the analyses I had done over a decade using a variety of programs, formats, and computer platforms (all with minimal documentation), and for helping me create figures from the infinite number of tables I wanted to include. I also want to thank Dennis Chong and Jim Kuklinski for their sage advice and comments as the editors of the Cambridge Studies in Public Opinion and Political Psychology series. I feel honored that my book is part of this excellent series.

I am extremely lucky in the friends I met before graduate school: Abigail Cheever, Greg Chen, Hanley Chew, Tony Shen, Shirley Su, and Vicki Wong have all provided unstinting support over the years. I owe a tremendous debt to my parents, John and Joy Wong, who fostered my interest in research, and who provide models for how love, courage, and the pursuit of excellence are expressed in everyday life. My brother and sister-in-law, Eric and Luella Wong, have given me years of invaluable advice, help, understanding, and fun. My family expanded exponentially when I met Jake Bowers, and I thank the Bowers, the DeFilippos, the Hammans, the Lutzers, the McGoughs, and the Sunnyside folks for their encouragement and support. In particular, I want to thank Vicki Lutzer for commenting on the book prospectus and reminding me of the movie *Boys Town*, which I had enjoyed as a child. My daughter Mari provided the only really good reason for why it took me so long to finish the book; she inspires me everyday to do better.

Jake Bowers is a colleague, coauthor, friend, and partner in all matters of my life. This book is dedicated to him.

Preface

> "... [T]hese children are ours now, and we don't look at them any other way."

In August 2005, Hurricane Katrina damaged and destroyed homes along the Gulf Coast of the United States, from Florida to Texas. The storm forced hundreds of thousands of residents of New Orleans to leave the city, many of whom went to Baton Rouge and Houston. Kip Holden, the mayor of Baton Rouge, described the evacuees from Hurricane Katrina as "New Orleans thugs," and gun sales increased sharply in his city. At the same time, however, a spokesperson for the Houston Independent School District called the thirty thousand largely poor and black children from New Orleans who suddenly appeared in Houston schools "ours." Why would the black elected leader of a city only 80 miles from New Orleans worry about "thugs" and violence from the newcomers while a white spokesman (Terry Abbott) of a white- and Latino-led school district in a Texas city 280 miles from New Orleans welcomed the children?[1] Why were the reactions so different?

This book will help provide a framework for understanding how it could happen that people in Houston might see those children as a part of their community. It will also help us understand why many citizens of neighboring Baton Rouge sharply circumscribed the help that they offered to fellow Louisianans in need. For example, the law school at Louisiana State University absorbed Tulane's law students but did not

---

[1] In the book, I will use the term "white" as a shorthand for "non-Hispanic white," and "Hispanic" and "Latino" are treated as synonyms. I also use the terms "African American" and "black" interchangeably, as both are almost equally chosen for self description (Sigelman et al. 2005).

otherwise organize to house or feed or help non-law students. The black population of Baton Rouge worked through churches to help black evacuees and often avoided contact with FEMA, which many distrusted. This book offers a theory that encompasses both hard-to-understand hostility (why buy guns when people from a nearby city – many of whom have ties to your family and friends – arrive in distress?) and compassion (why absorb tens of thousands of new children into your schools when the education of your own children could be compromised by this action?).

In many ways, Houston's reaction to the Katrina refugees is difficult to understand for social scientists. In contrast, there are a number of theories to explain the opposite response, including emphases on self-interest and group interest, intergroup conflict, prejudice, contact between groups under conditions of competition and stress, and rapidly changing environments. When a choice is to be made to benefit oneself and one's family or to benefit someone else, self and group interests drive the decision toward helping oneself; given that property taxes are used to fund public schools, sharing a finite number of resources could be at the expense of one's own schoolchildren. Similarly, "not in my backyard" (NIMBY) and related concerns would dictate that Houston residents consider the problems arising from the levees' destruction by Katrina as New Orleans's problems, not Houston's. In a zero-sum situation with finite resources and overcrowding, visible group boundaries can also compound competition with prejudice and discrimination; many of the children from New Orleans were African American – in contrast to the more diverse mix of white, Latino, and black schoolchildren in Houston – and even if there were no preexisting racial prejudice (or anti-Louisiana prejudice) in Houston, competition could certainly stimulate favoritism of Us and denigration of Them (Sherif and Sherif 1979; Tajfel 1982). The New Orleans schoolchildren who were relocated to Houston were also, relatively speaking, poorer than the average New Orleans child; many of the wealthier children had not needed to be evacuated en masse by FEMA. Furthermore, media stories of the "refugees" exaggerated their violence and criminal behaviors, fanning the flames of fear gripping host populations about marauding invaders (Davis 2005; Fox News 2005). Distorted visions of rape and pillage by the homeless black poor of New Orleans drove up sales of firearms across Louisiana, prompting the mayor of New Orleans to ban and confiscate guns.

Above and beyond the effects of interests and competition, Katrina produced a situation where prejudice could easily overcome rationality, let alone fellow-feeling and humanitarian values. Evacuations – both voluntary and assisted – had the greatest and most immediate impact on nearby cities such as Baton Rouge. New Orleans residents originally hoped they would be able to return to their homes soon after the storm, and FEMA also concentrated initially on relocation nearby. This type of rapid influx of outgroup members is exactly what researchers have found to bring prejudice to the fore (Green et al. 1998). Diversity alone is not necessarily a predictor of prejudice and resulting discrimination; large changes in a short period prompt negative attitudes about and actions against the newcomers in ways that go beyond material self-interest. So, even in a racially diverse city like Houston, the sudden appearance of more than a hundred thousand people could have sparked conflict even in the absence of explicit threats to the self-interest of the community, such as increasing the class sizes at public schools. Although social scientists have also found that contact between ingroup and outgroup members can lead to a diminution of prejudice, this positive outcome occurs in situations where the groups have equal status and have a common goal that can only be achieved by intergroup cooperation (Allport 1954; Sherif and Sherif 1979). The post-Katrina situation did not lend itself to such conditions, given the straitened circumstances of the evacuees in contrast with the native residents.

Given all the reasons to expect Houston residents to expel or attack rather than embrace the newcomers, one would think that such a terrible outcome would have been inevitable. And yet, despite all these conditions working in the direction of *not* helping, fueling potential competition and negative feelings, there was outreach: the city of Houston extended a helping hand to the victims of Katrina.

Of course, such help might have arisen merely out of fear and a desire for social control (Piven and Cloward 1971). Hungry hopeless people fleeing a city already associated with crime and poverty could as easily be seen as potentially violent as they could be seen as pitiful. Therefore, receiving cities could choose to help the victims of Katrina in order to placate them. Of course, if these fears were great enough, one would assume the cities would have refused to open their doors altogether. Alternatively, Houston did not have to open its doors to as many evacuees as it did and would have been less likely to do so if it had been motivated by fear. The city also could have limited social support to policies that would ensure temporary residence, rather than longer-term investments and community incorporation such as schooling; and it could have segregated the New Orleans residents in Houston stadiums or concentrated them in certain housing projects if social control had been of paramount concern. In fact, such segregation did not happen in Houston. In Baton Rouge, where fear of violence was in the forefront of the public imagination, many of the evacuees stayed with relatives and friends because the social networks between Baton Rouge and New Orleans are much denser and tighter than between New Orleans and Houston. More than six thousand people who did not have family or friends in Baton Rouge were concentrated in the Baton Rouge civic center.

A much less cynical explanation for Houston's response is altruism. The citizens of Houston helped the tragic victims of Katrina, not because of calculations of interest, but because of a simple desire to help. Certainly there were individuals across the region, the country, and even worldwide who provided aid and solace. People's values and religions advocate helping those in need, including strangers; the story of the Good Samaritan is only one example of helping in times of crises. And research has shown that helping hands are extended more readily when the miserable circumstances or disasters suffered are not of the victims' own making (Skitka and Tetlock 1992, 1993). Clearly, the evacuees from New Orleans were not responsible for the hurricanes. However, research has also shown that helping behavior in response to a natural disaster depends on characteristics of the potential recipients of the aid, all of whom are located in the same area. Whites are more likely to help white victims of a hurricane, and blacks are more likely to help black victims (Skitka 1999). Nature may wreak havoc across racial boundaries, but humans – consciously or unconsciously – are not so blind when they choose whom to help.

It is common knowledge among philanthropic organizations that giving is consistently greater for domestic causes than international ones. So, while Katrina was disastrous in 2005, killing about two thousand people and damaging homes along the Atlantic coastline, the Indian Ocean tsunami of 2004 killed about three hundred thousand people and wiped out entire villages across multiple countries. Nevertheless, $1.8 billion was donated in the United States for aid to the victims of Katrina, compared with $1.3 billion donated in the United States by October 2005 for aid to victims of the Indian Ocean tsunami (Strom 2005). The scale and scope of devastation caused by the tsunami was much, much worse, in both deaths and monetary costs of the damages, yet much more money was given for Katrina; the fact that people gave differentially means that something else matters, something more than simply the need of those receiving aid or the altruistic values of those who give aid.

Why should Americans privilege the victims of the hurricane over those of the tsunami? Is it because of the potential effect of their contributions?

This cannot be the case, because a U.S. dollar in Indonesia has much greater buying power than the same dollar in New Orleans.[2] Is the reason behind the domestic bias a fear of corruption by international aid organizations? During the years preceding these natural disasters, it was not uncommon to read about aid dollars ending up in Swiss bank accounts. Thus, perhaps more money was given to the victims of Katrina by U.S. citizens because they worried about whether a dollar donated would result in even a dime for its intended beneficiaries. In this case, however, many of the same organizations that were working on the U.S. Gulf Coast post-Katrina were also working around the Indian Ocean post-tsunami, and stories about government corruption in New Orleans and along the Gulf Coast in general were probably just as available as stories about problems in Thailand or Indonesia; therefore, the degree of efficiency and corruption was largely held constant. So why would Americans donate more money to help the victims of Katrina?

The answer is that more Americans chose to express their generosity and compassion to other members of their national community, helping those at home before helping others. Even if Americans considered victims of the tsunami to be members of their global community, it is clear that members of their national community received priority. We often think of charity as giving above and beyond any sense of obligation or duty; it is a manifestation of compassion and sympathy for the recipients, rather than a moral duty. Even if one accepts this distinction, however, the question still exists: why was there greater compassion and sympathy for victims of this particular hurricane than for the victims of a more devastating tsunami.

The answer in this case is that interest, altruism, and values must all operate within boundaries. If someone motivated by material interest asks, "Do my costs outweigh my benefits?" even a simple tit-for-tat calculus is made with reference to a particular context: refusing to help a neighbor could be Pareto suboptimal, but if someone is too distant, the equilibrium is not to interact strategically with an individual from whom no benefits could flow. If someone motivated by humanitarian values or who is otherwise altruistic is asked to help, they may ask themselves, "Would I be able to live with myself if I refused? How badly would I feel about refusing?" The answers to these questions again depend crucially

---

[2] In addition, Van de Kragt et al. (1988) conducted experiments to determine reasons for altruistic cooperation, and found that the magnitude of the external benefit and the cost to the subjects did not predict acting for the benefit of others.

on the existing relationship between the helper and the person needing help under the assumption of finite resources. Contributing help to ease distant suffering, such that little time or money remains to help a neighbor, would be strongly sanctioned by most of the most common value systems.

In this book I talk about the process of defining the boundaries within which interest, values, or other helping-relevant motivations operate as the process of defining a "community." The community of a person (as understood by that person, and as defined with reference to a particular set of relationships in a given moment of time) is the set of people for whom questions about helping are most meaningful. At the limit, the suffering of certain beings is not of concern even for the more altruistic among us (say, the extinction of a species of bugs). And even the person with the very least fellow-feeling may calculate that helping a neighbor is worthwhile. This book shows that the boundaries of community matter.

The adoption of New Orleans children into the Houston school system is a case where people redefined the bounds of their local community. Terry Abbot, a spokesperson for the Houston Independent School District, redrew the community to include these new schoolchildren from New Orleans when he said,

We have asked the state government for resources to get them up to speed. That will be a concern, *but these children are ours now, and we don't look at them in any other way.* (Steinhauer 2006, emphasis added)

The New Orleans students, in other words, were now seen as part of the Houston community of schoolchildren, and Houston was willing to fight to get resources for all their community members, new and old. Where people draw their community boundaries helps us explain phenomena such as reactions to Hurricane Katrina (and the Indian Ocean tsunami), above and beyond what self-interest, humanitarianism, or patriotism would predict.

A NOTE ON THE MODELS

This book has a short appendix with the data that are most central to my arguments. The full statistical models and results can be found at http://carawong.org/Boundaries-Appendix.pdf.

Boundaries of Obligation in American Politics

Geographic, National, and Racial Communities

I

Community and Special Obligations

The 1938 movie *Boys Town* tells the story of how the young hoodlum Whitey Marsh learns about democracy, authority, fair play, and friendship from the other boys in the town and from its head, Father Flanagan.[1] *Boys Town* was based on the founding of a real Nebraska orphanage, whose iconic statue shows one boy carrying an even younger orphan child on his back. The motto of Boys Town, which accompanies this image, is "He ain't heavy, he's my brother." The articulation of "my brother" helps outsiders see the act of lifting another boy (physically or metaphorically) as an obligation to be embraced, rather than as an encumbrance to be avoided. More generally, the answer to the question of "who counts as my brother?" or "who is a member of my community?" is central in a democracy where citizens debate about to whom the government should allocate resources.

This book provides empirical evidence for what has largely remained a theoretical discussion, showing how ordinary Americans imagine their communities, and the extent to which their communities' boundaries determine who they believe should benefit from the government's resources via redistributive policies. How do people draw the boundaries dividing Us and Them, and how do they represent these "pictures in [their] heads" (Lippmann 1965)? Where the boundaries of communities are drawn depends on who someone believes to have a quality in common. This quality in common may be locality, nativity, belief, or activity, among others, and individuals may have multiple communities. The decision to help only those within certain borders and ignore the needs

---

[1] Spencer Tracy, who played Flanagan, won an Academy award for the role.

I

of those outside rests, to a certain extent, on whether and how people translate their sense of community into obligations.[2] A man can feel that he belongs in a community, for example, without necessarily feeling that he has any duties to fulfill as a result of his membership; even if he does feel a sense of obligation to others in his community, he may still choose not to act on their behalf (and, instead, deal with any feelings of guilt that may arise from his inaction).

Questions about political obligation and entitlement are key to understanding the motivations behind the stability of and relationships within political entities: what duties does a citizen owe to his or her state, and conversely, what does a government owe its citizens, as a result of their implicit social contract (see, for example, Klosko 2004)? Despite the importance of these questions, there has been little empirical research on individuals' sense of responsibility toward one another. On the one extreme, individuals cannot kill one another indiscriminately; yet at the other extreme, being a Good Samaritan, although praiseworthy, is not legally required. Within the bounds established by a state's laws – and in the large, gray expanse between narcissism and altruism – whom people choose to help is left to their discretion. Although a sense of morality certainly does not require the presence of a sense of community, it is more likely that a man will risk jumping into a river to save his drowning friend than to save a stranger. Attitudes about redistributive policies are also, in essence, attitudes about who should be helped.

Social scientists tend to rely on concepts such as self-interest, group interest, and ideology in their models for explaining how people decide on whose behalf they should act and who has a right to public services and shared resources. In essence, current understanding about what motivates redistributive behavior boils down to three statements: (1) we want to help ourselves, (2) we want to help those in our groups, and (3) we want to apply our values – such as egalitarianism or individualism – and ideas about the role of government widely, not just to a small subset of the population. In this book, I argue that these distinctions are not as clear as they appear to be because the applicability of each depends on boundaries that are subjective and blurred. Self-interest may include one's immediate family, but it could also apply to one's more distant relatives and friends. Group interest – whether it is used as a

---

[2] Theorists often assume that obligations are derived from membership (Macedo 2008). However, because reality does not always live up to theory, it is an empirical question whether people do, in fact, believe that membership automatically implies obligations.

proxy for self-interest or as a spur for action irrespective of one's own desires – also depends on how one imagines the boundaries of one's group or groups; does a white man, for example, really want to help *all* white men and *only* white men? Even ideology, which often encourages individuals to apply a set of beliefs broadly, is almost always constrained in practice by boundaries: egalitarians seek equality of opportunity (and often equality of outcome) for all Americans, but it is rare that they seek an adjustment of the American standard of living that would match that of Malawi or Yemen. Thus, while the concepts of interest and ideology have utility, underlying these political motivations is the drawing of community boundaries.

WHAT IS A COMMUNITY?

The definition of "community" has always been contested. Beginning ostensibly with Aristotle (Friedrich 1959; Yack 1993) and continuing in contemporary works, scholars have used the term to describe entities that vary so much that no common set of necessary and sufficient characteristics of community can be found (Ladd 1959). Much like the debate over the meaning of "self-interest," "community" is either defined so broadly that it encompasses everything and everybody, or so narrowly that many commonly recognized communities are excluded. Not surprisingly, then, debates over the role of community in politics often come back to disagreements over its definition. For example, in a critique of communitarianism, Jeremy Waldron writes, "What is this community and who is this 'we' we keep talking about?" (1993, 193).

Rather than adding to the already voluminous debate among political theorists about communitarianism (see, for example, Chapman and Shapiro 1993, Corlett 1989, Sandel 1982,), this book responds to Waldron's question by using data to explore the meaning of "community" as it exists in the minds of ordinary Americans. Social scientists study concepts such as anomie, symbolic racism, and constructivism with little expectation that average citizens think of their lives, attitudes, or actions in those terms. These concepts are unlikely to show up in everyday conversations. However, "community" *is* a part of ordinary language, and it is unclear how its common usage is related to its role in social science research. Whether liberals or communitarians are "right" is a separate question from the empirical question of how citizens perceive their own communities.

The definition of community that I use in this book draws on the classic work of Benedict Anderson on nationalism, stressing the subjectivity

of the concept. Anderson describes a nation as an imagined community: "It is *imagined* because the members of even the smallest nations
will never know most of their fellow-members, meet them, or even hear
of them, yet in the minds of each lives an image of their community"
(italics in original) (1983, 6). This definition of an imagined community
can be applied much more broadly. Although it may apply to a nation,
it can also be used to describe many other geographic entities, such as
one's state or city. Even one's neighborhood is an imagined community.
While it may be possible for someone to have met and even know all the
individuals who live in the many blocks surrounding her own home, she
will have a particular image of her neighborhood community. This image
probably does not coincide with how the local city council officially
defines her neighborhood, and the image almost certainly is not the same
image that her neighbors have of their neighborhood community. One
neighbor may imagine her community to fall within the confines of major
thoroughfares around her home; another's image may be restricted to the
circle of neighbors with whom he is acquainted; and yet another may
think of her neighbors as individuals who live close to her in proximity
but with whom she does not imagine any sense of community (Wong
et al. 2005).

Anderson's definition of imagined community can also apply to social
units or groups. For example, when one thinks of the African American
community or the Chinese American community, it is very clear that
members will never meet most of the others in their community. And
one Chinese American's image of this community is unlikely to overlap
perfectly with the image in another's. One member's image may include
anyone who would describe themselves as Chinese; another's imagined
community may only include those individuals who are "culturally"
Chinese (e.g., individuals who are fluent in a Chinese dialect and eat
Chinese cuisine); and yet another's may be restricted to those who are
American citizens.

This definition of imagined community can include families – because
an individual may not have met all the members currently alive, much
less have full information about generations past – and even a university,
where a professor will probably not have face-to-face interactions with
all the faculty, staff, and students present (Tamir 1995).[3] The important

---

[3] Tamir provides these examples as reasons why Anderson's definition of the nation as
an imagined community is too broad. Her argument about the overly broad applicability of the notion of an "imagined community" to a nation underscores its suitability

feature of any community is the image that individuals carry in their heads, not the issue of acquaintance with all other members. Tamir writes "If the condition for a community to be considered imagined is that the only way to perceive it as a whole is to refer to its image, then all social groups, even the smallest, are imagined communities" (421). She refines this definition by arguing that it should not be applied to communities for whom the distinguishing characteristics are

...independent of the feelings and perceptions of the agents – age, gender, race, income, or place of birth...[Instead, a nation's] existence cannot be deduced from certain objective features, but rather from the feelings of communion among its members, as well as from the existence of a shared national consciousness. (1995, 422)

I would revise this definition to state that all social groups *could be* imagined communities. Even the borders of groups defined by age, gender, race, income, and place of birth are fuzzy, and members of these groups may have an image of a community based only loosely on these characteristics: one's image of a community of senior citizens may include individuals below retirement age (Koch 1993); one's image of a feminist community may include only some women and not others (Lorde 1984); one's image of the Chinese American community is complicated, as I mention above; membership in a community of middle-class Americans is claimed by many whose objective income would place them well below or above the median income (Walsh et al. 2004); and while birthright citizenship is the law in the United States, it is not the case that all Americans would include anyone born on U.S. soil as a member of the national community (Citrin et al. 2001; Pear 1996).

I have one final distinction to make. What Anderson and Tamir seem to assume, at least with the nation as an imagined community, is that the community's members all share the same image and feelings. I would argue this assumption is both unlikely and unnecessary. An imagination is not shared. In the case of a nation, it is very likely that a Jew residing in a West Bank settlement does not have the same image of or feelings about her nation as does a Jew residing on the Upper West Side of Manhattan, even if both were born in Israel. Similarly, Americans residing in Guam, the Fond du Lac Reservation, and Boston will very likely have different notions of their nation as well. And individuals who hold the very same

---

as a concept that can be applied to a wider variety of social groupings. Similarly, her argument that "deliberate forgetfulness and misrepresentation of historical facts" are inherent in nation building can be applied to other types of communities as well.

image of their nation may have vastly different feelings of communion with other members: some would die to protect their nation, while others would fail to see why it is worth defending.

This does not make the nation or any other community any more or less "imagined"; if anything, it is more realistic and accurate to assume images of communities will vary from individual to individual, even those claiming membership to what they believe is the same community. After all, while we can share the fruits of our imagination, we are now – outside the arena of science fiction fantasy – unable literally to share our imaginations and consciousnesses completely with each other.

Therefore, I use the following definition for community: *it is an image in the mind of an individual, of a group toward whose members she feels a sense of similarity, belonging, or fellowship.* This definition does not assume that these imagined communities will have political outcomes; feelings of comradeship or fraternity do not necessarily translate into any particular attitudes and actions. What I test and show in this book is that self-defined membership can lead to an interest in, and a commitment to, the well-being of all community members (and only community members), regardless of one's own interests, values, and ideology.

THE "GLUE" AND BORDERS OF IMAGINED COMMUNITIES

At their core, all discussions of "community" emphasize a shared place or spirit as the "glue" that holds its members together. And, as Toennies writes in his classic *Gemeinschaft und Gesellschaft*, geography and social ties are often intertwined:

Community by *blood*, indicating primal unity of existence, develops more specifically into community of *place*, which is expressed first of all as living in close proximity to one another. This in turn becomes community of *spirit*, working together for the same end and purpose. Community of place is what holds life together on a physical level, just as community of spirit is the binding link on the level of conscious thought. (Toennies 1957, 27, emphasis in original)

Whether both locality (geography or Toennies's "place") and social relations (sentiment or Toennies's "spirit") are necessary is contested. MacIver and Page (1952), for example, note that "the mark of a community is that one's life *may* be lived wholly within it" and that "the basic criterion of community, then, is that all of one's social relationships may be found within it" (8–9, emphasis in original). Their clear definitions, however, become problematic when the discussion moves from more abstract arguments about theoretical communities to concrete applications.

Churches and business organizations, MacIver and Page argue, are not communities, but prisons and immigrant groups are. It is not obvious how one's entire life can be lived in an immigrant group – unless one pictures a completely segregated and self-sufficient immigrant ghetto – and one could imagine nuns in a convent, for example, living with all of their social relationships within the church. Nevertheless, although their particular configuration of requirements is problematic, I want to underscore that MacIver and Page emphasize both the geographic and relational aspects of the concept.

This dual emphasis appears in more recent scholarship as well. Spurred by the growth of planned communities and the concerns expressed by scholars of "New Urbanism," a new discussion of community is taking place in the field of city and urban planning (Duany et al. 2000). In their book on gated communities, for example, Blakely and Snyder delineate five separate elements of community: shared territory, shared values, shared public realm, shared support structures, and shared destiny (1997, 33). These elements can also be grouped by their focus on place and spirit: shared territory and public realm reflect the borders and interior space of a place, while shared values, support structures, and destiny reflect a community of spirit or relations.

Not all scholars insist that both shared locality and shared sentiment are necessary and sufficient conditions for community. However, no one would argue that these two broad categories – geographic and relational communities – are mutually exclusive. In research where community is explicitly conceived of as simply territorial or geographic, scholars often focus on how neighborhoods, towns, cities, or regional characteristics affect individuals (Baldassare 1992; Frug 1996; Keller 2003; Oliver 2001; Putnam 1993). Nevertheless, in their discussions, what would make a city a vibrant "community" – and not simply a municipality of solitary TV addicts burrowed deep in their dens – would be the presence of relational ties among its residents. When scholars understand community as "concerned with quality of human relationship, without reference to location," the focus shifts to groups like professional or religious organizations, or to social networks (Bellah et al. 1985).[4] However, the "habits of the heart" that Bellah and his colleagues describe are commonly exhibited by people who share a geographical area, such as a neighborhood or

---

[4] Although trying to separate sentiment from place is difficult in practice, it is a necessary distinction in order to avoid "reducing communities of all kinds to instrumental associations" (Miller 1995, 66).

a local church. Finally, a community may consist of a grouping of people who share common interests and who may never physically encounter one another (see, for examples, Meyrowitz 1985 and Smith and Kollock 1999 on electronic or virtual communities). One might argue that this community is located literally at one's fingertips, although this is clearly not the same notion of proximity that Toennies had in mind. The purpose of this brief discussion was not to provide a comprehensive review of the literature. Hillery (1955) identified 94 definitions of community, and the count can only have increased dramatically over the past fifty years. Instead, the snapshots of past research simply highlight the importance of both a shared locality and a shared spirit as the possible glue of community.

Just as there are contrasts between geographic and relational communities, both types can be objective (aligned with official, fixed demarcations or categories) or subjective (existing only in the minds of individuals). Although borders between cities or census race categories can be seen as objective, or at least commonly recognized, there is also a great deal of subjectivity in people's images of towns and races.[5] New York City, with its limits legally defined by maps drawn by City Hall, is a different community from the "New York City" depicted in Saul Steinberg's "View of the World from Ninth Avenue," with New York forming both the center and the bulk of the entire country. However, the latter community exists only in Americans' imaginations (and on the cover of the *New Yorker*) and cannot be found on any map; where "New York City" begins and ends is in the mind of the viewer. Similarly, for some Americans, the "black community" is a relational community composed exclusively of African Americans as defined by the census; for other Americans, the boundaries of the "black community" are drawn to include only those individuals who adopt "black culture," who engage in "black politics," or who "look black."

The American national community straddles all four possible combinations: objective-geographic, subjective-geographic, objective-relational, and subjective-relational. Its land is geographically defined by fixed boundaries drawn on maps and defended by force when necessary; it is also a community with a protean outline, depending on whether territories, commonwealths, and states not part of the continental United States

---

[5] Although I do not place quotation marks around the word "objective" every time it appears in the text, the quotes are always implied, especially when "objective" is applied to group membership.

are part of the picture of the nation in people's imaginations. The national community is relational, with officially recognized citizens composing the community's formal membership; it is also a subjective relational community, founded on shared American ideals, hopes, and dreams, with boundaries drawn in the minds of its residents as to who belongs as part of the American community. An American-born citizen who burns the flag may be seen as un-American, for example, while a foreign-born permanent resident – like the record-breaking baseball player Sammy Sosa – may be welcomed with a ticker-tape parade into the fold of the American community as one of Us.

Of course, subjective communities can overlap with objective lines, and I do not assume that they have to be different. One reason for why people's imagined communities may coincide with objective communities is socialization and norms, often instilled from childhood. Although the definition of communities as imagined emphasizes the role of the individual as the imaginer and agent, it does not therefore diminish the importance of states, institutions, and politics. Obviously, how the state defines geographies, members of the nation, and races will affect how people imagine these groups as potential communities. Furthermore, political parties, unions, churches, and other civic organizations also affect people's perceptions of who is similar, or with whom else they belong. Nevertheless, the ultimate decision will be made by an individual, at least when it comes to deciding how certain community boundaries may or may not play a role in affecting judgments to help others. Current social science research overemphasizes the political effects of membership in objectively defined groups – e.g., African Americans, Southerners, and first-generation immigrants – by ignoring the effects of imagined communities.

While governmental policies often deal with objective community boundaries – including district lines, definitions of race laid out by the Office of Management and Budget, and constitutional and congressional definitions of citizenship – people themselves use the pictures in their heads to make decisions about who should benefit. The average American cannot name the chief justice of the Supreme Court (Delli-Carpini and Keeter 1996), much less what the OMB's Directive 15 says about race or what the phrases *jus soli* and *jus sanguinis* represent. Nevertheless, most Americans are able to express strong views about who should benefit from affirmative action or what makes someone "truly American." In other words, people's perceptions of community boundaries are probably more important than objectively defined borders for determining how individuals make decisions about who should benefit from government resources.

There is no assumption that an individual must like all the other members of her imagined community, although obviously it would be quite common to like them. After all, that would make the decision to spend effort and energy improving the lives of community members much easier. A family is a relevant analogy: I may not like all my relatives, but because they are family, I may feel some special obligation to them. I can, of course, choose to redefine my family so that a black sheep uncle, for example, is dead to me. And I may only reluctantly agree to let a disliked aunt borrow my money or car. But as long as I imagine a relationship with a person, then I may feel some tie and pull. So, although I will distinguish likeability from community in the empirical analyses as an impetus for acting on behalf of another individual, I also assume that likeability can be expressed commonly about the members of an individual's community.

One final implication of my particular definition of community is how members of a community are defined. Who belongs as a member is all seen from the perspective of the imaginer, be it the state or an individual. The state's perspective is oftentimes interpreted as the "objective" definition of community membership, but it is, nevertheless, simply a product of the imagination of the state, embodied as anything ranging from a single bureaucrat to the explicitly shared mind of Congress. Although the state's definitions of who belongs as a member of a community have the backing of laws (and force), they are no more "natural" or "right" than the definitions of any ordinary American.

POLITICAL EFFECTS OF COMMUNITY BOUNDARIES: EXAMPLES

Because communities are not simply descriptive units of organization, they may have tangible effects on their members and nonmembers. They matter in politics because they are not simply containers; the glue that a person believes holds him in a community leads to different attitudes and behaviors than would prevail if this same individual were unencumbered by membership. Marshall's (1973) classic trichotomy of citizenship into civic, political, and social rights highlights the varying benefits granted to different members of the same national community; only by achieving all three sets of rights does a legal citizen become a full citizen or a full member of the community. Where community boundaries are drawn determines who is considered a member and who is not, and these boundaries may lead the imaginer to want to help members, to want to deny aid to nonmembers, or even to want to harm nonmembers.[6]

The political effect of these community definitions can be seen across a number of arenas, ranging from national to local politics. For example, in the area of immigration politics, precisely where boundaries of inclusion are drawn by policy makers can affect who will benefit from social services. As part of the 1996 welfare reform, the federal government left it up to the states to decide whether to pay for certain benefits for legal residents out of state coffers.[7] Since then, state fiscal problems often have led to budget cuts, and as a result, legal residents in a number of states have lost their health care benefits. Immigrants who were legal residents in Colorado, for example, lost access to Medicaid in 2003. Although advocates for these elderly immigrants argued that Medicaid eligibility was a matter of life and death, some state representatives defended their vote as a difficult choice between citizens and noncitizens (Austin 2003). Those who were considered to be members benefited, while nonmembers were neglected.

The location of community lines also drives local politics. For example, in recent years, residents of gated communities have been pushing for tax relief with some success. They pay entry and maintenance fees to their homeowners' associations for services that often include trash removal, police-like security forces, and maintenance of grounds and roads. As a result, they ask why they should be taxed twice, paying additional local

---

[6] I want to clarify what I mean by obligation or a willingness to help others. Researchers who study prosocial acts and altruism distinguish between helping behavior that is spontaneous and nonspontaneous (Clary and Snyder 1991). Many psychology experiments, including some addressing social identity, focus on spontaneity, which by definition means that individuals do not have time to contemplate all of the potential trade-offs of their actions. This book is about redistributive politics, however, and so my focus here is on attitudes and behaviors that are not quite so spontaneous. I examine support for public policies and political participation in order to determine if these particular politically relevant "helping behaviors" are restricted to benefiting other members of one's self-defined community.

Trade-offs are also made, of course, for spontaneous acts. Many of the bystander studies showed that considerations about how helpful one's actions would be (e.g., how many other people were witnesses, how much of a rush one was in, how much personal distress not helping would cause) were factors in determining whether an individual would act or not (Darley and Batson 1973; Latane and Darley 1969). However, if they had been given some more time to think about their choices – to act or not to act – the subjects in these studies might have come to different conclusions.

[7] The 1996 legislation also banned outright some kinds of state assistance to immigrants.

city taxes for services they do not use. If their children attend private schools and swim in the gated community's pool, for example, why should they support bond issues for public schools and parks? Some urban studies scholars, such as Pivo, note the costs and benefits of these walls and gates: "People probably would report a greater sense of neighborliness and so forth inside gated communities. But gated communities also give people an excuse or an opportunity to turn inward and recognize that that's their tribe, more so than their city is or their region is" (quoted in Lang and Danielsen 1997, 882). Again, members of the imagined community benefit while nonmembers are beyond the sphere of concern.

How people perceive their racial communities also affects local politics. For example, governmental attempts to redraw educational boundaries between whites and blacks unintentionally forced a choice between integrated schools and integrated neighborhoods. Busing and other strategies for ending segregation of white and black children in schools often spurred "white flight," as white parents chose to move away from districts that were under court-mandated busing plans so that their children could attend neighborhood schools they believed to be better and safer (Orfield et al. 1996). According to the census, schoolchildren remained as racially segregated in 2000 as in 1990, despite the increases in ethnic diversity in the nation as a whole (Logan et al. 2001). And, in 2007, the Supreme Court again heard cases about the constitutionality of desegregation plans – voluntarily chosen by the cities – in Louisville and Seattle, revisiting how exactly the *Brown v. Board of Education* decision of more than 50 years ago should be interpreted.

The physical separation of blacks and whites into different neighborhoods adds a twist to policies that are voted on by the general public. In a study in Mississippi, Glaser (2002) found that in counties with larger percentages of black residents, whites – who still made up the majority of voters – were much less willing to support school bonds. It would be difficult to argue that whites and blacks in these counties see themselves as part of the same community, given their isolation from one another and their disparate interests and goals. However, these are counties with schools that are disproportionately filled with black schoolchildren, so in essence, one "community" may be deciding on the school funds to benefit another.

POLITICAL EFFECTS OF COMMUNITY BOUNDARIES: THEORIES

In the simplest form, it seems intuitive to most Americans that redistributive policies should privilege the needs of people living in the United

States over people living in other countries. Consistently over the past three decades, three out of four Americans have stated in surveys that spending on foreign aid should be lower (General Social Survey 1972–1998). Attitudes about spending on education and defense programs have fluctuated over time, but sentiment about whether we should spend less on helping people in other countries has remained steady.[8] This intuition illustrates the power of a group boundary – in this case the nation – in the assessments of obligation by individuals.

The phrases "charity begins at home" and "compatriots take priority" refer to the idea or intuition that helping others should occur only after one's own – defined here at the national level – have been fed and nurtured (Dagger 1985, 436). Dagger calls this intuition "moral parochialism" and explains it in the following manner:[9]

> To say that compatriots take priority is to say that we stand in a special relationship to those men, women, and children who share with us membership in a political community. This relationship is special because it requires us to attend to the needs and interests of our compatriots before we attend to the needs and interests of foreigners. (1985, 436)

However, the sphere of concern may be even smaller than the nation: people's "special relationships" may be limited to the needy of "our own neighborhood" or "our race" or more generally, "people like us." Such particularism could pose problems for a democratic welfare state that purports to treat its citizens equally.

Politics in the United States has been described by Nelson and Kinder (1996) as "group-centric," yet it is unclear how people circumscribe their sphere of concern to narrow subgroups within the nation. Of the numerous available possibilities, which groups matter? For example, while the American public expects its various political leaders to have clear geographical loyalties to the local constituencies they were elected to represent – with pork barrel politics as one result – there is little evidence for

---

[8] This constancy is independent of the fact that, on average, Americans have little idea of the actual amount being spent at the moment.

[9] Miller calls this same phenomenon "ethical particularism" (1995). I believe these are basically equivalent names, although "parochialism" may be seen in a more pejorative light than "particularism." I use both interchangeably, and also use the term "bounded morality," borrowing from the work on bounded rationality. However, I want to distinguish this idea of bounded morality from other work on "bounded ethicality," which is defined as "... the unintentional ways in which managers, leaders, and other hurried decision-makers are unethical, despite their intention not to be ..." (Chugh 2006). I would not argue that prioritizing one's compatriots is unethical, nor do I think it is a result of cognitive errors.

what kinds of obligations people believe they themselves have. Does a community have ethical significance? Should a Californian privilege the needs of other Californians over Oregonians? When Pete Wilson, governor of California in the 1990s, argued for a residency requirement for welfare recipients in order to prevent out-of-state migrants from taking advantage of California taxpayers, he clearly thought so; however, we do not know how ordinary Californians (or Oregonians) would answer the same question, normatively or empirically.[10]

That special relationships created via communities could invoke unique duties is a plausible empirical outcome, especially if the community in question is the nation or one's family. Theoretically, this link between relationships and obligations is made explicit in the philosophical category called "special obligations." These are

> ...obligations owed to some subset of persons, in contrast to natural duties that are owed to all persons simply *qua* persons. Common sense morality seems to understand us as having special obligations to those to whom we stand in some sort of special relationship, e.g., our friends, our family members, our colleagues, our fellow citizens, and those to whom we have made promises or commitments of some sort. (Jeske 2008)

The challenge for philosophers is to justify these common sense intuitions with notions of consequentialism and natural duties. Ordinary citizens rarely confront this challenge as they make their everyday (common sense) decisions.

POLITICAL EFFECTS OF COMMUNITY BOUNDARIES: THE DARK SIDE

Given the theoretical disagreements over the *definition* of community, it is perhaps not surprising that there is little consensus on what *effects* community boundaries can or should have. One could imagine instances where people who see themselves sharing a community come together to provide what individuals alone could not, like the barn-raisings of yore. The stories and myths of the frontier are filled with examples of people

---

[10] State leaders are also concerned about where their residents are choosing to spend their *non-tax* money; legislators in Maryland and Pennsylvania, for example, tried to legalize gambling in order to prevent trips across state borders to New Jersey, West Virginia, Delaware, and New York. Governor Robert Erlich of Maryland supported this legalization, arguing, "For too long, Marylanders have funded teachers and textbooks in West Virginia, Delaware and soon Pennsylvania at the expense of Maryland's children" (Dao 2004, A16).

literally or figuratively "circling the wagons" to form a united front to protect one another against threats, human or otherwise, where one man or family alone would have died. Songs of the 1960s were often filled with this type of hope of coming together to achieve ethical goals, as exemplified by James Taylor's song "Shed a Little Light":

> Oh, let us...recognize that there are ties between us
> All men and women, Living on the earth
> Ties of hope and love, Sister and brotherhood.

One could also imagine scenarios where notions of obligation that are limited to a particular community would conflict with, or be incompatible with, notions of equality and justice (Frohnen 1996; Karst 1989, 187; Niebuhr 1960). As Miller explains, "... to the universalist, particularism appears as the capitulation of reason before sentiment, prejudice, convention, and other such rationally dubious factors" (1995, 56). That so many of the atrocities committed against African Americans over the past century went unpunished is partially the result of such tight bonds and particularism among the local populations of whites (Williams and Bond 1992). These were not isolated events, as Tom Lehrer satirizes in his song "National Brotherhood Week":

> Oh, the poor folks hate the rich folks,
> And the rich folks hate the poor folks.
> All of my folks hate all of your folks,
> It's American as apple pie.

Therefore, as natural as moral parochialism may seem to some, arguments against it were made at least a millennium ago. In opposition to the parochial behavior of filial piety espoused by Confucius and his disciples, Mo Zi argued in the fifth century B.C. in favor of "universal love." In other words, there is no justice or morality in *denying* collective material and social goods to individuals depending simply on whether the individuals are excluded from community membership or not. This idea that one should treat everyone as one treats one's own family is carried on by current day cosmopolitan philosophers like Singer and Nussbaum.

While Singer agrees with Tamir (1993) that particularistic or parochial behavior is exhibited naturally between children and their parents, he argues that neither ubiquity nor evolutionary history can justify the behavior (2002). In arguing that there is no magic in the pronoun "my," he quotes both Sidgwick and Himmler to force a reader to acknowledge that "self-evident" special obligations are not always right. Parochial behavior by a mother that one might describe as natural becomes grotesque in the speech of a Nazi official. He argues that impartiality is the basis of ethical behavior, and favoring one's community is a problem to be solved. Moral parochialism is indefensible, and a neighbor's child is therefore the equal to that of a Bengali stranger ten thousand miles away.[11]

Nussbaum also argues that one does not have special obligations to one's immediate community that supersede the needs of strangers. For Nussbaum, the "community of human argument and aspiration…is, fundamentally, the source of our moral obligations" (1996, 7). The community of one's birth is accidental, and should not create boundaries that divide. Instead, she argues, "We should recognize humanity wherever it occurs, and give its fundamental ingredients, reason and moral capacity, our first allegiance and respect" (7).

This sentiment is echoed (to a certain extent) by political observers who argue that "community" is snake oil, touted as a cure for all the country's ills (Freie 1998), while really breaking apart the nation into restricted and isolated factions. One journalist wrote the following:

America has been cross-cut into so many communities [that] we're suffering an end of community. "Community" is now a charlatan's word of exclusion rather than inclusion, the us community versus the them community (Morse 1997, A2).

Being defined outside the boundaries of a community can lead to more than a denial of help. The same mechanism that leads someone to come to the aid of his community can also lead him to harm others. Work on moral exclusion focuses on linking attitudes across a wide range of social policies and perceptions of moral communities (Batson et al. 2002; Crosby and Lubin 1990), and exclusion "occurs when individuals or groups are perceived as outside the boundary in which moral values, rules, and considerations of fairness apply. Those who are morally excluded are perceived as nonentities, expendable, or undeserving" (Opotow 1990, 1). Questions of animal rights rest on whether they belong in the "scope of justice," and when people are stripped of their human qualities, they, too, may be excluded from moral considerations (Opotow 1993; Staub 1992).[12] Similarly, Kelman and Hamilton's theory about what leads to

[11] One could argue that Singer either recognizes no community boundaries, or that he envisions the entire world as one community (which is the title of one of the chapters in his 2002 book, *One World*); the outcome would be the same.
[12] Research on "scope of justice" (which is also sometimes called "moral community") defines the community as composed of those to whom "our moral values, beliefs, rules, and norms apply" (Opotow 2008, 28). In contrast, this book focuses first on how a community is defined, before testing whether values or beliefs apply.

crimes of obedience like the My Lai massacre emphasizes a stage of dehumanization: the victims are stripped of the human characteristics that would make their abuse or deaths morally problematic (Kelman and Hamilton 1990). It is more difficult to feel empathy for an animal or a "gook" than for a noncombatant villager, for example.[13]

Although the cases in this book do not concern war crimes or human rights violations, I mention such examples to emphasize that moral exclusion is another effect of community definition, where the impact of moral parochialism falls on those *outside* the boundaries of obligation. Bounded morality can lead to particularistic behavior that favors members of a community, as well as to moral exclusion that ignores the welfare of individuals who are not members.

IMAGINED COMMUNITIES OF GEOGRAPHY, NATION, AND RACE

How people imagine their communities and whether they decide to act on behalf of members of those communities are questions that can apply to numerous different types of communities. In this book, I examine whether people's perceptions of their own communities are based on three factors: race and ethnicity, geographical proximity, and immigrant status.[14] I chose these three broad factors because they provide examples of a community defined socially (race), another defined by place (locality), and a third that can be seen to straddle both relational and geographic boundaries (nation). In addition, race, locality, and nation each have boundaries that can be defined objectively or perceived subjectively; thus, I can compare the effects of both types of boundaries on people's attitudes about the allocation of personal and government resources to others. The three factors also clearly matter for politics, with people continuously fighting over the dividing lines of each. Nevertheless, while I focus on three types of imagined communities, the scope of my arguments applies broadly to other communities.[15]

---

[13] It is perhaps not surprising that some proponents of cosmopolitanism, like Nussbaum and Singer, are also theorizing and advocating about animal rights.

[14] Race and ethnicity are related concepts (Omi and Winant 1994), although the U.S. census defines them as distinct and mutually exclusive. Furthermore, research on race and ethnicity often sit on opposite sides of a subfield divide (Nobles 2004). Nevertheless, because the arguments I make apply to both racial and ethnic groups equally, I often refer to both at the same time, even if I only mention "race" or "ethnicity."

[15] For example, I replicated some of the analyses from Chapter 3 for communities imagined along lines of religion and found similar patterns. I believe I would find similar outcomes for other communities as well.

Furthermore, studying these three types of communities allows me to bring together three separate research traditions – in local politics, race relations, and nationalism – that rarely cross paths; although they use different terminology with different aims, I show that some of the concepts and phenomena studied are, in fact, similar at their core. Recent research on local politics has focused on issues of diversity and allocation of services and goods; underlying the research is the argument that living next to strangers leads people to distrust other political actors, withdraw from political engagement, and seek to withdraw their resources from the common pool (see, for examples, Habyarimana et al. 2007 and Putnam 2007). Simultaneously, research has shown the benefits of social capital on civic and political engagement, emphasizing the positive effects that social ties can have on political opinions and actions (Putnam 2000). These questions could be reframed as questions of how people imagine their local communities – e.g., who counts as a member and who is outside – and for whom am I willing to sacrifice and from whom should community benefits be withheld (i.e., who are nonmembers?).

Research in racial politics has tended to focus on the effects of black political identity (branching recently to Latino and Asian American identity) on political attitudes and behavior and on ethnocentrism (primarily on the part of whites). For both, there is an assumption of a community – "objectively" defined as black or white, respectively – and scholars examine the varying levels of parochialism shown: for example, are blacks motivated to help their (assumed) community by turning out to vote (Bobo and Gilliam 1990; Dawson 1994; Tate 1993), and are whites motivated to deny political benefits to and harm individuals outside the boundaries of their communities (again, assumed by researchers to fall along racial lines) (Bobo et al. 1997; Kinder and Sanders 1996)?

Finally, research on immigration politics in the United States focuses on the political effects of national chauvinism and nativism among the general population, and also examines the assimilation of immigrants into American society (Alba and Nee 2003; Citrin et al. 2001). National chauvinism and nativism are both examples of phenomena whereby individuals express varying levels of moral parochialism, paying attention to national boundaries that they believe form the limits of their communities; those individuals outside suffer the consequences of being Them and not Us. And assimilation is a redrawing of community boundaries, whereby immigrants may imagine new communities to which they belong, shedding old obligations and gaining new ones with regard to promoting the welfare of their fellow community members.

Despite the similarity in these questions – in terms of how communities are imagined and whether the location of community boundaries have political effects – these areas of research rarely corroborate their findings outside their own single case (i.e., locality, race, immigrant status). Not only does looking at these three types of community help emphasize the similarity in the phenomena under study, it also allows the hypotheses and theories to be free of the constraints, limits, and assumptions of any single case.

To illustrate the claim that an individual's determination of a relevant community may affect her feelings of obligation, I provide an example of the effects of people's imagined communities from a national survey. It provides a representative sample of Americans' views about why they got involved in politics, and more specifically, on whose behalf.

MEASURING THE EFFECTS OF COMMUNITY ON POLITICAL PARTICIPATION IN AMERICA

Do Americans think of their communities – explicitly or implicitly – when they make political decisions? The Citizen Participation Study, a national survey of Americans conducted in 1990 by Verba, Schlozman, and Brady, provides some answers to that question (Verba et al. 1990). The survey, which resulted in one of the most important studies of political participation, *Voice and Equality*, was designed to examine the extent of political participation in the United States and the factors motivating individuals to engage in various activities (Verba et al. 1995). Those respondents who had reported acting politically in some way – where the acts included working as a political volunteer, contributing money to a campaign, voting, contacting government officials, participating in protests, and getting involved in church and other organizations – were also asked the following question about the issues or problems that led to their behavior:

Thinking about the issue [that led you to become active in a candidate's campaign/other activity], which of these categories best describes who was affected by the problem?

The category options were:

1. only myself/family,
2. only other people,

TABLE 1.1. *For Whom Do You Act Politically?*

	Only myself/ family	Only other people	Myself/ family/ others	All the community	All the nation
Volunteer in a campaign	3%	1	10	56	30
Contribute money to a candidate	5%	1	9	52	33
Contribute money to an organization	0%	2	11	23	62
Vote	1%	1	7	46	45
Contact a public official	16%	4	15	41	24
Attend a protest or march	0%	3	11	27	59
Engage in church/ synagogue activities	10%	5	19	33	34
Engage in organizational activities	8%	2	19	31	40
Serve on a board or council	1%	2	12	79	6
Attend board or council meetings	6%	0	12	77	6
Work informally in community/ neighborhood	1%	2	19	68	10

Data: American Citizen Participation Study, 1990

    3. myself/family/others,
    4. all the community, and
    5. all the nation.

Table 1.1 shows that the most common response for who was affected by the issue or problem that led to the various acts of participation was "all the community."

    Social desirability most likely played a role in naming an interest greater than oneself or one's family, because few people like to admit that they are only out for themselves, even when they are guaranteed anonymity on a survey. Furthermore, there are laws against some self-interested behaviors, like giving money to a candidate explicitly in exchange for a job. However, it is not obvious that "all the community" should be chosen as the "best-sounding" motivating factor. "Myself/family/others" captures both self and group interests, and one might argue that the *most* socially desirable or admirable answer for why an individual acted are the altruistic answers, to benefit "all the nation" (which could include, of course, one's self and group interests) or "only other people" (which is the truly selfless answer). An "ideological" answer should probably result in choosing "myself/family/others" or "all the nation," since one would assume that choices based on ideologies or values should be applicable broadly.

Participating in a protest or demonstration seems to be driven more by issues that affect the entire nation than by issues that affect any subgroup. However, why does a majority of Americans volunteer to take part in campaigns, make political contributions to a candidate, or attend a board or council meeting? They report that they do so on behalf of their community (however they imagine it).

These survey results clearly indicate that the term "community" resonates with ordinary Americans when they are asked about the reasons for their political engagement. They do not tend to explain their activism in terms of self-interest, group interest, or selfless altruism; they are not acting on behalf of only themselves, their families, or other people. Instead, across a wide range of possible political acts, Americans choose to become engaged on behalf of their community. So, even if we do not yet know what the content of "community" is – i.e., who belongs within the boundaries and how varied are the images of communities in people's imaginations – and how its political effects may vary, we do know that community matters.

In addition to political participation, the analyses in this book will cover a range of behaviors that may result from imagined communities. Because an individual feels ties to other members of her community, she may choose to work for the community to improve it and want to have access to the governing of that community. This type of behavior coincides with Hirschman's (1970) notion of loyalty and voice (as opposed to exit),[16] where an individual chooses to make some type of investment in or express a commitment to the community, which sometimes might pertain to a ruling institution or not. In addition, she may work to help

---

[16] Exit is always an option, because membership is subjective. An individual may not be able to leave the vicinity physically, but she can define her community not to include her immediate surroundings. So, she is less likely to be alienated from other members of the community or from its decisionmaking bodies.

community members via supporting government policies that would benefit them, deciding indirectly what she is willing to do for her community. And, she may choose to police the borders of her community, deciding who and what belongs inside and outside of her community's boundaries. One outcome of this policing is keeping outsiders from gaining access to advantages and goods that should be reserved only for community members.

BOOK OVERVIEW

Ordinary Americans may be making choices of where to live based on their visions of community, and political theorists, social scientists, and politicians may be interested in the special obligations inspired by these imagined communities, but the discussion thus far resides largely in the domain of academics or political elites. I want to test empirically whether or not communities, as they exist in the minds of Americans, really have an effect on whom they want to help and to whom resources should be allocated.

My argument about the effects of community boundaries on political attitudes and actions is developed over the course of the next five chapters. I will not simply rely on Americans to use the word "community," but will use a number of different measures to tap the commonality that Americans perceive or feel in relation with others, where the others are connected geographically and/or socially. (See Table 1.2 for a quick summary of the datasets and measures that will be employed in the book.)

Chapter 2 explains the ways that I will measure the boundaries of imagined communities. I describe what constitutes a "good measure" of community, and draw support from previous research by political scientists, sociologists, and psychologists on "communities" and "groups." My discussion links research – in rural sociology, community psychology, reference groups, and social identity – that has heretofore remained segregated, and the "good measures" I choose emphasize the subjective nature of boundary drawing (Lamont and Molnar 2002). How scholars understand and measure "community," however, is only part of the larger picture; therefore, I also focus on how ordinary citizens think of their own communities, and how they use "community" in everyday language.

My analyses in this chapter involve different types of research methods, and this diversity, I believe, makes my discussion richer and bolsters the argument that the measures of community I choose are appropriate. I use survey questions that I designed for the 1997 National Election

TABLE 1.2. *Datasets and Measures Used in the Book*

Chapter	Dataset	Measure of Community	Dependent Variable
Chapter 1			
	American Citizen Participation Study 1990	"Thinking about the issue [that led you to become active in a candidate's campaign/ other activity], which of these categories best describes who was affected by the problem: only myself/family, only other people, myself/ family/others, all the community?"	
Chapter 2			
	Social Capital Benchmark Survey 2000	"What gives you a sense of community or a feeling of belonging?"	
	Indivisible: Stories of American Community 1999–2002	Any mention of the word "community"	
	National Election Studies 1997 Pilot Study	"Please read over the list [of groups] and tell me the number for those groups you feel particularly close to, people who are most like you in their ideas and interests and feelings about things."	
Chapter 3			
	General Social Survey 1996	"How close do you feel to...(a) your neighborhood (or village), (b) your town or city, (c) your state, (d) America, (e) North America?"	

(continued)

TABLE I.2. *(continued)*

Chapter	Dataset	Measure of Community	Dependent Variable
	Social Capital Benchmark Survey 2000	"What gives you a sense of community or a feeling of belonging? (a) the people in your neighborhood? (b) Living in [city]?"	Trust in local institutions, political alienation and efficacy, civic engagement, intolerance
	Public Policy Institute of California Survey 2003	"Would you say the neighborhood you live in has a sense of community, or not?"	Support for initiatives to provide local services and make voting for services easier, civic engagement
	Public Policy Institute of California Survey 2003	"In general, do you most identify with Southern California, your religion, the place where you were born, your racial or ethnic group, Los Angeles County, your city, or other?"	Support for initiatives to provide local services and make voting for services easier, civic engagement
Chapter 4	General Social Survey 1996	"Some people say the following things are important for being truly American. Others say they are not important. How important do you think each of the following is?"	Policy preferences concerning immigration, refugees, isolationism, spending on crime, capital punishment, government programs to help blacks, antimiscegenation laws, privacy concerning sexual orientation, tolerance
	General Social Survey 2004	"Some people say the following things are important for being truly American. Others say they are not important. How important do you think each of the following is?"	Policy preferences concerning immigration, isolationism, citizenship rights, spending on crime, gay marriage, political obligations, national pride, trust in government

Chapter	Dataset	Measure of Community	Dependent Variable
	General Social Survey 1996	"How close do you feel to America?"	Policy preferences concerning immigration, refugees, isolationism, citizenship rights, spending on crime, capital punishment, government programs to help blacks, antimiscegenation laws, gay marriage, privacy concerning sexual orientation, tolerance, political obligations, national pride, trust in government
Chapter 5			
	National Election Studies 1996	"Please read over the list and tell me the number for those groups you feel particularly close to – people who are most like you in their ideas and interests and feelings about things."	Support for government programs to help blacks
	General Social Survey 1996	"In general, how close do you feel to blacks? And in general, how close do you feel to whites?"	Support for government programs to help blacks, social distance between whites and blacks
	National Black Election Study 1984	"Please tell me if you feel very close, fairly close, not too close, or not close at all to the following groups. How close do you feel in your ideas and feelings about things to whites in this country? Black people in this country?"	Attitudes about equality in America, black nationalism, and government programs to help blacks

(continued)

TABLE 1.2. *(continued)*

Chapter	Dataset	Measure of Community	Dependent Variable
	National Politics Study 2004–2005	"How close do you feel to each of the following groups of people in your ideas, interests, and feelings about things? Very close, fairly close, not too close, or not close at all?"	Attitudes about interracial marriage, intergroup cooperation, intergroup competition, affirmative action, descriptive representation, racial profiling

Studies (NES) Pilot Study to discover which groups in society people include within the boundaries of their community (Rosenstone et al. 1997). I also use data from the 2000 Social Capital Community Benchmark Survey, which asks a national sample of Americans what gives them a sense of community or a feeling of belonging (Saguaro Seminar 2000). To complement the survey data, I draw on transcripts of interviews that were conducted as part of a national documentary project on civic engagement, *Indivisible: Stories of American Community* (Rankin 2000). The interviews capture how people talk about "community" and whether some sense of obligation or duty is implied by its usage. I use these transcripts to provide a "thicker" description that complements the analyses of survey responses. In the end, the analyses and discussion in this chapter provide the justification for the measures of community boundaries that I use in Chapters 3, 4, and 5.

Each of the three chapters addresses a different type of community, explaining the tensions between objective and subjective boundaries, while showing variations in the categorization of the self and others into the community. In each, I begin to address the question of how feelings of community originate, and the question of whether there is commonality across local, national, and racial communities. Each chapter then provides evidence that how people imagine their community affects who they are willing to help and who they think should benefit from government policies. These effects of imagined communities exist, above and beyond concerns of self- and group interests and ideology.[17] I study

---

[17] The models corresponding to most of the figures are in the appendix at the end of the book. Because of space limitations, however, all additional models I ran are posted on the book's Web Appendix: http://carawong.org/Boundaries-Appendix.pdf.

three separate communities that not only serve as examples of the range
from geographic to relational communities, but that also highlight many
important issues in the ongoing American debates about multiculturalism
and identity politics. Each provides a different example of how community boundaries can engender ethical particularism, bringing together a
number of theories concerning ethnocentrism, national chauvinism, and
NIMBY issues.

Chapter 3 focuses on the extent to which people feel a sense of community based on geography. Geography can be defined as one's neighborhood or even one's continent. Using data from two national surveys
(the General Social Survey (GSS) and the Social Capital Community
Benchmark Survey) and a survey of Californians, I show how people's
imagined geographic communities affect their civic and political orientations and actions (Baldassare 2003; Davis and Smith 2007). Individuals
who feel a sense of community where they live are more willing to trust
institutions in that locale, they are more likely to work and volunteer on
the community's behalf, and they are more willing to tax themselves to
provide more or better local services.

Chapter 4 describes how an individual may draw the boundaries
of her national community, focusing particularly on who belongs as a
member. Using data from the GSS, the chapter provides evidence that
the exclusion of those deemed not "truly American" affects not only attitudes about immigrants and foreigners, but also attitudes about policies
regarding other groups in the United States. I show that most Americans
are not willing to extend the boundaries of their national community
to encompass the legal definitions of citizenship. The significance of this
restrictive definition of who is "truly American" cannot be overstated,
for it drives attitudes about who can partake of the American Dream and
who should benefit from government services.

Chapter 5 focuses on the importance of people's perceptions of com-
munities based on racial and ethnic characteristics. Using data from the
NES, GSS, the National Black Election Study, and the National Politics
Study, I show that when white, black, Latino, and Asian Americans
choose to extend the boundaries of their perceived communities to cross
DuBois's "color line," this extension has strong effects on their racial atti-
tudes and policy preferences (Jackson et al. 1984; Jackson et al. 2004;
Rosenstone, Kinder, and Miller 1996).

Finally, Chapter 6 provides a conclusion, summarizing the main
arguments and findings. By analyzing three different types of communities and more than eight national surveys in the book, I find empirical

support for the theoretical argument that Walzer makes in *Spheres of Justice* (1983, 31):

The primary good that we distribute to one another is membership in some human community. And what we do with regard to membership structures all our other distributive choices: it determines with whom we make those choices, from whom we require obedience and collect taxes, to whom we allocate goods and services.

A deeper understanding of people's definitions of their communities and how they affect feelings of duties and obligations provides a new lens through which to look at diverse societies and the potential for both civic solidarity and humanitarian aid. Who is Us and who is Them is a dichotomy played upon by campaign consultants – with the idea that We, the good, the patriotic, the generous yet frugal, should vote for presidential candidate X – that often exaggerates Our redness or blueness. At the same time, the purple is what binds society together in a larger national community, and it is necessary for the health of the welfare state, so that *all* can benefit from *Our* public education, health care, unemployment insurance, and old-age pensions. And as political leaders remain ambivalent about issues such as intervention in Darfur, land disputes in the Middle East, or the acceptance of greater numbers of refugees, their decisions about who counts as a member of their communities are central to political calculations. Arguments about interests and values are driven (and restricted) by the boundaries of who counts as Us.

2

The Boundaries of Imagined Communities

Children often play games where they try to recognize "which one of these things is not like the other."[1] For example, they know triangles of various dimensions are similar to one another, while a square is something different. As adults, categorization occurs just as frequently. Stories about Wimbledon are in the sports section of the newspaper, apples and cucumbers can be found in the produce section of a store, and according to taxonomists, platypuses are mammals.

Of course, classification is not always so easy: wars have been fought over what constitutes "the good life," and "I know it when I see it" is one amusing, yet unhelpful, judicial standard for pornography. Sometimes vagaries in definition and measurement are acceptable; however, if one is interested in understanding what constitutes a community and in observing the political effects of what people perceive to be their community boundaries, then more clarity and precision are needed.[2]

---

[1] Children's magazines and workbooks have such exercises, and *Sesame Street* has a song about it, which begins, "One of these things is not like the others."

[2] Disney movies and songs are often also focused on the question of belonging to communities. For example, the following are lyrics from *The Little Mermaid*, *Tarzan*, and *Pocahontas*:

> Up where they walk, Up where they run
> Up where they stay all day in the sun
> Wanderin' free, Wish I could be, Part of that world.
>   Put your faith in what you most believe in
>   Two worlds, one family, Trust your heart,
>   Let fate decide, To guide these lives we see.
> You think the only people who are people,
> Are the people who look and think like you.

To examine how people imagine their communities and the extent to which the psychological boundaries that result from these images affect political attitudes, we need to know how to recognize a community when we see it; in other words, we need good measures of "community." Good measures ought to fit the conceptualization laid out in Chapter 1. They would first provide information about the commonality that people believe they share with others in their community – the quality or feature that connects these individuals, such as feelings of similarity, closeness, proximity, or sympathy. A good measure of community does not need to include the word itself, but it should assess whether an individual feels a sense of commonality or belonging with a number of other individuals. Second, good measures would allow for the boundaries of an individual's community to be perceived by that individual (and not simply assumed or fixed by the researcher).

Finally, good measures would be flexible enough to capture both the geographic as well as the relational communities to which individuals believe they belong. In other words, assessing one type of community with a thermometer and another with a ruler, metaphorically speaking, would make it difficult to compare the drawing of boundaries and their effects across different types of communities. Because I argue that moral particularism or parochialism can occur regardless of whether boundaries are defined locally or socially, I want to ensure that I am able to make comparisons across types.

In addition to explaining how my "good measures" will meet these requirements, there are three other goals of this chapter. I want to convince the skeptical reader that (1) "community" is not simply a concept used in the discourse of academics or politicians, like "anomie" or "social capital" – it has meaning to ordinary citizens, and it resonates in their decision-making processes; (2) the concept of community in empirical research is new, not simply old wine (e.g., "reference groups" or "social identity") in a new bottle; and (3) the concept of community is politically relevant, affecting opinions as well as actions, above and beyond the "usual suspects" of interests, ideology, and values.

MEASUREMENT OF COMMUNITY BOUNDARIES

How does one measure the boundaries of an imagined community? Its limits have to be based on something more tangible than sentiment alone, because otherwise the definition is tautological: a sense of community is derived from being a part of a community, and a community is defined by those who feel this sense of belonging.

In order to operationalize "community," I build on the work of researchers in sociology, psychology, and political science who have tried to study and gauge parochial attitudes and behavior. Although research on this topic remains rather segregated – with little systematic or sustained comparison of findings across fields – good measures of community can borrow from these seemingly disparate literatures to capture both local and relational types. As I will show in Chapter 3, rural sociologists and community psychologists offer a basis for assessing the commonality at the core of a person's community; later in this chapter, I will discuss how social psychologists and sociologists provide the foundation for measures to gauge the subjective nature of the boundaries of people's communities and their effects. Although all these scholars may not explicitly recognize their work as part of the study and measurement of communities and their boundaries, there is a common link between these fields of research. The key is to find measures that can be used broadly to assess the content and quality of communities.

Measuring Community Boundaries: Indivisible Interviews

First, I want to determine if ordinary Americans use the term "community" in the way in which it was conceptualized in the previous chapter. In order to determine the ordinary language meaning of "community" (Pitkin 1972), I look at qualitative interviews where the term was used.

In answering a survey, respondents are restricted by what they can mention, and they are also constrained by the language presented by the public opinion researcher. To assess the potential validity of survey questions measuring a sense of community, in this section I examine how those in a sample of ordinary Americans use the word "community" in normal conversation. Do the communities they talk about refer to neighbors or members of their racial group? Do they refer to other members of their nation when they talk about their sense of community? Finally, when people talk of their communities, do they also talk about duties and responsibilities that may result from membership? Preliminary answers to this final question would provide the first insight into what I might find in Chapters 3 through 5.

Indivisible: Stories of American Community is a national documentary project conducted from 1999 to 2002 by the Center for Documentary Studies at Duke University and the Center for Creative Photography at the University of Arizona. As part of the project, interviewers and photographers went to twelve towns around the nation to interview people with the broad goal of "explor[ing] how individual Americans are identifying local needs and working together to address them."[3] The interviews were conducted by radio producers, oral historians, and folklorists, and these interviewers were all given a fair amount of autonomy within the places they visited.[4] The locations themselves were chosen for geographic and demographic diversity, but not because they were any sort of model or ideal location. And, because of the general focus of the project on local civic engagement, it is obvious that the interviewees would often use the word "community."

The *Indivisible* sites are not meant to be representative of all American towns, nor are those individuals interviewed meant to be a representative cross-section of the American public. Nevertheless, the interviews do capture how a diverse set of ordinary people talk about "community" and what they mean when they use the term. The interviews also convey whether some sense of resultant obligation or duty is implied by people's usage and definition of "community"; this feeling of obligation may then lead to desires to help other members of the community. I use the transcripts from three sites to provide rich material for content analysis, which complements the analyses of survey responses.[5] A total of 83 interviews were gathered from the following three communities: Yaak Valley, Montana; Delray Beach, Florida; and Eau Claire–North Columbia, South Carolina. These three sites were chosen because residents' main concerns center on geography, nation, and race, and the locations could provide evidence of whether or not people indeed think of "community" in these particular geographic and relational terms.

Yaak Valley, located in the Kootenai National Forest in Montana, is a rural district of about 150 families that is reliant on the timber industry. Residents also include environmentalists who are concerned about endangered species, and local debates often focus on balancing forest management and economic viability. The individuals interviewed in the Yaak Valley Forest Community included people who work as tanners, landscape designers, writers, school principals, and tavern owners, among others. In other words, they are ordinary citizens, not political elites.

Delray Beach is a city in Florida with more than fifty thousand residents, a third of whom are Haitian immigrants. African Americans, whites,

---

[3] www.indivisible.org/faq.htm.

[4] In other words, they were not academics with an established battery of questions to be replicated at each site.

[5] The transcripts of all of the interviews are housed at the rare books library of Duke University. An overview of the entire project can be found at the website www.indivisible. org and in the book, *Local Heroes: Changing America*, edited by Tom Rankin.

and the Delray Beach police have had to learn to work with the various populations, with the help of the Haitian Citizens Police Academy and Roving Patrol and MAD DADS, an African American community anti-drug street patrol group. Interviewees in Delray Beach included a radio DJ, an immigration advocate, a parish priest, police officers, and community policing volunteers.

The need to negotiate and promote understanding between racial groups is also present in Eau Claire, a suburb north of Columbia, South Carolina. The Eau Claire Community Council is a biracial group whose leadership alternates each year between blacks and whites. The Eau Claire Community of Shalom, part of a national project of the United Methodist Church, has brought together a historically black church with one that is historically white. These two initiatives in Eau Claire have united more than 70 churches and more than 30 neighborhood associations with the goal of improving the city as a place to live. In addition to council and church members, interviewees included a policeman, neighborhood residents, and local educators and artists.

To determine if people talk about their "communities" in ways that resemble what survey questions ask – in terms of possible sources of feelings of commonality, and what the possible meanings entwined with community boundaries are – transcriptions of the interviews at the three sites were carefully read and coded. There were a total of 1,427 statements of "community" from 85 individuals in the three sets of interviews, and the statements were coded along a number of dimensions.[6] First, does the term refer to a geographic, racial, or national community? Second, does "community" refer to similarity among individuals or boundaries between people? Similarity can refer to similar ideas, interests, or feelings, common hopes and needs, and shared qualities or appearance; boundaries emphasize exclusion and inclusion, as well as segregation. Third, when individuals used the word "community," could one infer a sense of duty or obligation from the way they used it? This encompasses feelings of wanting to give back to the community or needing to be involved. Each statement could be coded in as many categories as appropriate.

Given the site-specific interviewing and the focus on local organizations at each site, about three-quarters of the total mentions of "community" are in reference to geography and the local area in all three sites. Among Yaak interviewees in particular, more than 90 percent of the

---

[6] If "community" was used more than once in a sentence, it was coded as a single statement. The coding of each mention was done by two different research assistants in order to prevent idiosyncratic coding decisions.

mentions are about geography. For example, a woman who worked for the U.S. Forest Service talked about "… the issue of community stability, trying to get work for the local residents." In Delray and Eau Claire, there was often an overlap in the usage of "community," such that it was difficult to discern if someone was speaking of the "local community" or "black community" in terms of only geography or race, or both.

There were few mentions of a "national community" among the residents in Yaak Valley and Eau Claire, areas of predominantly native-born Americans and where the prominent local issues pertain to the environment and race relations. However, in Delray, a city with a large number of immigrants, over half of the mentions of "community" refer to a national one, oftentimes "the Haitian community" and sometimes "the American community."[7] The salience of "national communities" varies by location, but in contexts where immigration and foreign policy are important concerns, it is one of the main ways that people use the word "community" in their conversations.

Across the three sites, 13 percent of the time that interviewees said the word "community," it was in reference to race, such as "the African American community" or "the white community." "Community" was predominantly used this way in Delray and Eau Claire, but not Yaak Valley, which is racially homogeneous. Again, the salience of race in people's references to "community" varies by context, but in areas that are racially diverse, "race" is often paired with "community" in people's discussions.

People also said "community" to emphasize the differences between Us and Them, either in terms of physical boundaries or in terms of similarity among community members (and implied difference from Them). References to similarity and boundaries were each mentioned about 10 percent of the time that the word "community" was used. For example, in emphasizing similarities, people would talk about the "logging community," or a "front-porch community," or a "community of renters"; in these mentions, community members shared characteristics, whether of interest or vocation. The boundaries dividing members of a community from outsiders mentioned in these interviews arose from many different factors. For example, in Delray, one African American resident noted the divide caused by ethnicity compounded by language differences:

And [the Latinos] started speaking in Spanish, and I didn't know what the hell was going on. When they laughed, I would laugh. And, you know, and I bet they felt that way plenty times in our community. (C. Ridley)

---

[7] If one averages the number of mentions of a national community over the three sites, this particular usage appears in a little over 20 percent of the statements.

And another Delray resident noted boundaries that were geographic borders defined by her neighborhood:

And I guess I've almost taken a perspective of defense for those people that have become my friends in the neighborhood, when outsiders, so-called do-gooders want to come in and they don't respect the community that they're entering. (J. Siccone)

Finally, ideas of obligation and duty were wrapped up in people's usage of the word "community" about 10 percent of the time. For example, here is how it is mentioned to explain civic engagement:

I have such an affection for this landscape and both the human and plant and animal communities up here that I just feel it would be selfish to not work on behalf of those values, to just continue to take the benefits from this landscape without working on its behalf. (R. Bass in Yaak Valley)

...I need to help the community and for my children [to] grow up safely. That is why I joined the patrol mostly. (J. Noreus in Delray)

[We moved] because we had heard that Eau Claire was one neighborhood in Columbia where people were really trying to work together to improve the neighborhood, and they had an actual cohesive communicating neighborhood association. And to us that was really important. We've lived in a lot of places in Columbia without having that feeling of neighboring concerns, neighbors being concerned about neighbors and about their community. (T. Ely in Eau Claire)

Obligations are often wrapped up with other motivations as well. Although the first speaker appears to be largely altruistic in his reasons for civic engagement, the second and third speakers express a sense of duty to their "community" at the same time that they believe their actions will help themselves. They volunteer their time and move to a particular locale at least partially because they want to benefit their own families; however, their willingness to become active exceeds strict self-interest.

The *Indivisible* interviews confirm that when people say the word "community," they often refer to geographic, national, and racial communities. In addition, their use of "community" implies that they perceive boundaries dividing people into Us and Them, what the bases for the boundaries are, and the potential effects of those communities, particularly with respect to duties and obligations. This provides some initial support for the overall hypothesis that community boundaries can affect the sense of obligation that individuals feel as they make judgments about public policies.

The qualitative data gathered from these *Indivisible* interviews with ordinary Americans also provide guidance for my choice of a survey measure for community. The presence of important political groups in people's perceptions of their communities – pertaining to race, nation, and geography – should be detectable. Furthermore, the relationship between the emotional significance of a group and the potential willingness to act on its behalf is clarified through the *Indivisible* interviews. However, while shared interests and feelings of obligation are clearly motivations for favoring members of one's community, parochial behavior can also arise simply because there are boundaries. And obligations do not automatically follow as a result of community membership. These findings all inform the choice of what I argue counts as a good measure of community: the "group closeness" question. Before moving to a discussion of this measurement, though, I want to discuss two conceptual cousins of community and how the study of reference groups and social identity provides some guidance for the empirical study of community.

Imagined Community Boundaries: Building on Reference Group Theory

The argument in Chapter 1 about community boundaries and the parochialism that results from these boundaries is related to sociological discussions of reference groups. Reference groups are "taken as a frame of reference for self-evaluation and attitude-formation" and the boundaries of groups can shift (Merton 1968, 287). There are three criteria for groups according to Merton's theory of reference group behavior: social interaction, self-definition as a member, and recognition by fellow members and nonmembers that an individual belongs to the group. In other words, if boundaries of groups shift, it is because the social interactions of members can vary over time, not because individuals perceive different boundaries for a group. Also, group members do not have to objectively belong to a certain social category, yet group membership must be a matter of both self-definition and acknowledgment by all others in the group. Merton does recognize that individuals do not always identify with their ingroup: "it is the problems centered about this fact of orientation to nonmembership groups that constitute the distinctive concern of reference group theory" (1968, 288). However, by "orient[ing] themselves to groups other than their own," he argues that individuals alienate themselves from their own group (288, 323).

My conceptualization of community reflects this work on reference groups; however, there are three important distinctions between what constitutes a reference group versus a community, in particular in regard to interaction, perceptions by others, and obligations. Merton makes a distinction between groups and collectivities, explaining that a nation is an example of the latter because a nationality group lacks interaction among members. Community, I argue, straddles both these categories, especially since it is not clear why the political effects on individuals should differ for groups and for nations, theoretically or empirically. A man may be willing to fight (literally or metaphorically) if his country is under siege, if policies benefiting his ethnic group are attacked, if his political party is in a close race, or if a nuclear waste site is proposed for the outskirts of his town. The level of adrenaline and willingness to act may vary from case to case, but they are not categorically different because of differing levels of interaction between community members.

Recognition by others of the membership of a particular individual is also not necessary if one is interested in that individual's attitudes and behavior; although a lack of recognition by others may affect her comfort with or strength of attachment to a particular self-definition, it does not preclude her from considering herself a part of the group or community and acting as such. For example, many blacks may describe the rapper Eminem as a white musician and not a part of their community, but that does not preclude him from thinking of African Americans as his community and acting on his beliefs.

Finally, reference group theory does not articulate a sense of obligation among group members. Merton and Rossi refer to the first criterion of a group as the "enduring and *morally* established forms of social interaction" (1968, 340, emphasis added), but this moral nature is not explained. In my conceptualization of "community," I explicitly state that duties and obligations may arise from membership, which would lead to the morally particularistic behavior discussed in the previous chapter. "Community" in this project plays an important causal role in driving individual outcomes that are politically consequential.

What is clear in reference group theory is that individuals use their groups to situate themselves; this is much like the purpose served by Dawson's black utility heuristic (1994; Walsh 2003). One's group interest can serve as a proxy for one's self-interest; this form of bounded rationality helps people determine their political attitudes and behaviors when they cannot expend the time or effort to gain full information before making a decision. As such, married men may feel they are suffering more than their single counterparts from induction in the military (a case cited by Merton from *The American Soldier*), or blacks may believe whites have too much influence in the political sphere. I argue that people's perceptions of community can act as proxies for interests, but that these frames of reference do not have to be restricted to interests alone or to homogeneous ingroups; a soldier's community can include both the married and single men in his unit, and he may share their interests in opposing involuntarily extended terms of service as well as their attitudes about patriotic duty and honor. These shared interests and values serve as the commonality defining the community.

My idea of a community that can contain overlapping group memberships also builds on Simmel's (1955) work on group affiliations. In a note on his English translation of Simmel's "The Web of Group Affiliations," Bendix writes that he translates "circle" as "group," using the translation "group formation" when Simmel refers to "social circle," and "group-affiliation" when Simmel says an individual "belongs to a social circle." Bendix justifies these changes by arguing that a literal translation of the phrase "intersection of social circles" is almost meaningless; because an individual belongs to many groups, Simmel refers to him as "standing at the intersection of social circles." I would argue that the advantage of "circle" is that it is not as freighted by numerous social science definitions as is "group," so one can think of a circle of friends, for example, with no distinguishing characteristic – to an outsider, at least – except that the individuals share a common bond of friendship. In this way, an intersection of social circles is a succinct way to describe a community, because its members can claim membership in a number of reference groups or ingroups – be they union members, blacks, or Catholics – and still feel a part of a larger supragroup formation or community. In addition, a circle emphasizes the fact that there are boundaries separating community members from everyone else. Therefore, an important consideration in the measurement of community is the necessity of asking people about their own sense of community instead of assuming membership based on their objective group status, regardless of whether that "objective" status is defined by the government or by the recognition of others.

Imagined Community Boundaries: Building on Social Identity Theory

This issue of who decides on an individual's membership in a group or community is in the forefront of social psychological research on social identity. In many ways, a discussion of community membership may seem remote from social psychology's "minimal group" paradigm (Brown 1986), which describes how randomized assignment of individuals into groups leads to ingroup favoritism and outgroup denigration, even in the absence of competition, past history, or future interactions. Nevertheless, social psychological work on group identity focuses on the creation of boundaries and subsequent behavioral consequences, much like the aforementioned sociological work on reference groups.[8]

Among social psychologists, social identity emphasizes not only its derivation from group membership (e.g., "I am a woman"), but also the personal meaning associated with that social categorization. Tajfel, for example, defines social identity as follows:

...that part of an individual's self-concept which derives from his knowledge of his membership in a social group (or groups) together with the value and emotional significance attached to that group membership. (1981, 255)

Building on Tajfel's work, Turner emphasizes contrasts when he defines social identity as "self-categories that define the individual in terms of his or her shared similarities with members of certain social categories in contrast to other social categories" (Turner et al. 1994, 454). These definitions emphasize boundaries (drawn because of some "shared similarities") and the "emotional significance" of membership, much like my argument about community boundaries and a sense of belonging in the community.[9] I will therefore be able to draw on the measurement of identity for my "good measures" of community.

Much of the early work on social identity was conducted using experiments – both in and out of the laboratory – that involved placing subjects in groups and observing the attitudinal and behavioral consequences of those placements. The power – but, I would argue, also a limitation – of much of this experimental work is that it often relied on group memberships with which subjects had no prior history, e.g., people who preferred the artist Klee and those who preferred Kandinsky (Wong 1999). The findings from this research about the power of identity are strengthened because there are no confounds with competing or reinforcing variables, like past history or group interests. The limitation, however, concerns the external validity of these experiments; if membership in a group is

---

[8] "Identity" itself has an interdisciplinary history, and Deaux calls it "an intellectually seductive concept, capable of drawing on a number of diverse literatures, from the structural concerns of sociology on the one hand to psychoanalytic probes of individual personality on the other" (1991, 77).

[9] In related work in social psychology, scholars studying collectivism measure it with similar questions about identity, attachment, and belonging, while treating it as a corollary to individualism. Collectivism involves "a focus on social roles and fulfilling duties," and "success in a collectivist context is represented as sensitive fulfillment of one's duties and obligations toward one's ingroup" (Oyserman et al. 1998, 1607).

important, no matter how trivial, are we to assume that all arbitrarily drawn group memberships are equally important as long as they are made salient? Is right-handedness as important as race, and is allegiance to the Horde in the World of Warcraft game as important as partisanship? Furthermore, there are subtle differences between "identity" as used by the experimentalists, whose subjects are assigned an identity (i.e., a group label); group membership, where individuals belonging to a group in the real world may or may not have a "collective perception of their own social unity" (Turner 1982) (e.g., right-handed people); and identification with a group, with an accompanying sense of attachment or value to that group membership. These differences rest on who ultimately decides on membership, the researcher or the individual subject.

Survey research on social and political identity has relied on the third definition of identity, and operationalized it as a combination of at least two measures: objective group membership and a psychological sense of attachment to that group (Conover 1984). Groups studied in surveys, it should be noted, are usually large, easily recognizable, and have "objective" boundaries that are difficult to cross. Some examples are blacks, whites, poor people, businessmen, women, and Jews (Miller et al. 1981). These are significantly different from Tajfel's groups, based on the toss of a coin or preference for a Klee over a Kandinsky, yet most of the theories concerning social identity were developed and applied broadly across methods and groups. In an article on the many parameters of identity, Deaux et al. explain that this phenomenon is acknowledged in past work, but never addressed:

Tajfel (1981) discussed possible differences between categories to which one is assigned and social groups to which one belongs. He suggested the two terms may simply represent "the beginning and the end of a long social psychological process" (1981, p. 311), but he never developed this analysis. (Deaux et al. 1995, 280)

I would argue that the measurement of group identification in surveys has led to a definitional shift in the meaning of group identity.[10] No one has explicitly conceptualized identity differently in experimental and public opinion work, but the standard for recognizing that an individual "identifies" with a group is set higher in survey work as a result of its

[10] Here I am only referring broadly to the literature on social identity. If one looked at the domain of racial identity specifically, for example, one would find a wide range of meanings behind the concept (Cross 1971; Deaux 1993; Ethier and Deaux 1994; Gurin, Hatchett, and Jackson 1989; Lewin 1948; McGuire et al. 1978; Reid and Deaux 1996; Robinson 1987; Shingles 1981; Tate 1993; Thompson and Carter 1997).

measurement, with objective group membership and the added emphasis on psychological attachment. In experiments, social identity is defined simply as the perception of membership in a group (i.e., recognition that a group label applies to oneself), and the extent of the emotional value of the identity is the outcome of interest. In surveys, the significance of membership is considered part of the measurement of identification: respondents look at a list of groups and are asked which of the groups they feel "close to – people who are most like [the respondent] in their ideas and interests and feelings about things."[11] If they are an objective member of a group they name, those respondents are then categorized as group identifiers.

As theorized by the experimental social psychologists, I would argue that "group identity" is the same as "belonging in a community"; a community is simply a group, and its potential effects are the same. However, because "group identity" becomes intertwined with objective group membership in survey research, my use of the survey measure for an individual's psychological attachment to a group – without requiring objective membership – to assess "community" is broader and allows for identification by someone who is not objectively a member of the ingroup. I therefore borrow from both research traditions – based on experiments and surveys – in developing good measures of "community."

Closeness to groups by nonmembers has been called "group sympathy" by some researchers (see, for example, Conover 1987). However, I would argue that the label "sympathy" is too broad, at least in terms of the ordinary language use of the term. Various dictionary definitions of "sympathy" mention the sharing of feelings of others or an affinity between individuals such that whatever affects one affects the other. Generations of viewers of *The Yearling* and *Bambi* have cried and felt sad, yet it would be hard to argue that these feelings of sympathy led them to feel close to or most like their fellow moviegoers (or, alternatively, to deer with tragic lives) in their "ideas and interests and feelings about things." Closeness is instead, I argue, an operationalization of the commonality underlying Toennies's community of spirit, representing the common core of a community.

A community may cut across group cleavages, and thus it is plausible, for instance, for a white man to consider his community to include blacks without considering himself black. There are a number of different reasons why someone would say that he feels close to a group, in spite of his

---

[11] This is the question wording used by many political science scholars to measure group identification (see, for example, Conover 1984, Miller et al. 1981).

objective status outside the group, and I would like to consider them as possible manifestations of a sense of community: one may be a potential group member (e.g., a childless woman who feels close to mothers), an aspiring member who views a group as his reference group (e.g., a poor person who feels close to the middle class), or an empathetic individual who may also be expressing solidarity with another group (e.g., a native-born American who feels close to immigrants in the United States). And one may also perceive a number of different groups overlapping with the circle of his community, some of which are groups to which he objectively belongs while others are not.

Furthermore, because the groups that are studied in surveys in American politics are usually demographic, ideological, or economic, we tend to have images of relatively clear borders between groups, and we believe we can easily place respondents inside or outside those boundaries based on their self-description. The work that led to social categorization and identity theories, however, stressed the powerful discriminatory effects that could follow even the most arbitrary assignment into groups. The perception of belonging to a group based on underestimating or overestimating the number of dots on a screen, for example, is enough to trigger some ingroup/outgroup bias (Tajfel 1970). It is not obvious that the equivalent of the "minimal group" perception in survey research would be a black individual who feels close to blacks. Studying the effects of psychological affiliations and their effects on political beliefs and behaviors will help us examine the well-known potential for politics to be more than strategies and machinations between objectively defined groups.

A GOOD MEASURE OF BOUNDARIES OF COMMUNITY: "GROUP CLOSENESS"

The qualitative interviews in the *Indivisible* project as well as previous research in sociology and social psychology provide the background and support for the measures of community boundaries that I will use. I recognize that no single measure of an individual's community is ideal, but the literature review supports my claims about what measures of community boundaries should capture. To the extent possible, I would like to use one common measure across all types of community in order to make comparisons of the similarities and differences between how people define the limits of their communities and their feelings of obligation. However, because a general measure may not properly capture all the nuances of a particular type of community, I will also use measures tailored to geographic, national, and racial communities to improve the validity of the measurement. Similarity of results across measures would give the reader greater confidence that the findings are robust.

In this section, I will argue that the "group closeness" question that I will use throughout this book meets the requirements for being a good, general measure: it gauges the value of membership (i.e., the quality or glue that connects community members), it allows for an individual's own definition of her community (i.e., imagined as opposed to objective membership), it can be used for both geographic and relational communities, and it has been included in many different surveys over time.

The "group closeness" question has been regularly used in the American National Election Studies (ANES), and has been included in other surveys as well. Objective group membership is not a prerequisite for being asked about various groups, and this question about closeness captures the "emotional significance" that Tajfel defined as an important part of social identity that triggers parochial behavior.

The wording for the "group closeness" item is almost unchanged from the way it was asked in 1972, when this question was first included in the National Election Study questionnaire to measure respondents' affinity with various groups in society. Respondents were shown a booklet that included a list of groups. When the survey interviewer reached the "group closeness" item, the respondent was directed to look at the list of groups in order to answer the question. Except for small grammatical changes over time (e.g., changing the format from a question to a statement), respondents have been asked the following:

Please read over the list [in the respondent booklet] and tell me the number for those groups you feel particularly close to – people who are most like you in their ideas and interests and feelings about things.

One question about the "group closeness" item is whether the groups presented to the respondent in the list are the "right" ones to be included in the survey. In other words, are they the most salient or important groups to individuals in American politics today?

As part of a proposal I made to the National Election Studies, the 1997 NES Pilot Study included an open-ended version of the "group closeness" item that was asked of everyone in the national sample – to test whether Americans really thought of themselves in terms of NES's list of groups – and respondents were also given one of two versions of the standard closed-ended question, where the versions differed in the list of groups included – to determine if *other* groups in society were more relevant politically. As a result, the NES, and the 1997 Pilot Study in particular, is the ideal survey for examining the "group closeness" question as a valid and reliable measure of community. I will begin by discussing and presenting results concerning the close-ended questions, which also serve as the basis of comparison for the open-ended responses.

Measuring Community with "Closeness": Validity Test 1

Half of the respondents in the 1997 Pilot Study received a standard "closeness" list, with 17 different groups that the NES had used in previous surveys, referring to race, gender, age, ideology, occupation, class, and region. The other random half of the respondents had a list with eight of the same groups plus five "new" groups, for a total of thirteen groups. This second list included groups such as "people at your place of worship" and "people in your neighborhood."[12]

The lists represent a variety of types of groups. Some categories are more visible than others; some are voluntarily chosen while others are based on ascribed characteristics; some are groups whose membership requires more effort to maintain than others; and some groups are seen as desirable or undesirable ones to which one may belong (Deaux 1991). The list from which NES respondents choose their affiliations presents groups that are different in type and kind, and they include both geographic and social groups. Closeness to an ideological group, such as "liberals," is an affiliation with individuals who hold a relatively established set of political beliefs and attitudes. This is significantly different from feeling close to young people, a demographic group that does not remain the same from year to year (unless one considers young people in 1997 as a generational cohort). Therefore, as I discuss feelings of closeness to the different groups, it is worth keeping in mind what type of group or community is being considered.

From Table 2.1, we can see that the new groups tested in ballot 2 were very popular. Between 45 and 50 percent of the respondents given ballot 2 chose "People at [their] place of worship," "People in [their] neighborhood," "People at work," and "Americans in general" as close groups.

---

[12] The Pilot Study was conducted over the phone, so booklets were sent to respondents ahead of time. If a respondent did not have a booklet – either because they did not receive one in the mail or because they could not locate it easily – the interviewer read them that second list, pausing after each group for a response. This is "ballot 3" in Table 2.1.

TABLE 2.1. *Group Closeness, 1997 NES Pilot*

Question Wording:
Looking at page 3 of the booklet, there is a list of groups. Please read over the list and tell me the number for those groups you feel particularly close to, people who are most like you in their ideas and interests and feelings about things.

	Ballot 1 (blue booklet)	Ballot 2 (yellow booklet)	Ballot 3 (no booklet)
Asian-American	4%	–	–
Blacks	11	15	14
Hispanic-Americans	11	14	11
Whites	42	47	34[b]
Women	47	43	32
Men	27	–	–
Older People	39	–	–
Young People	35	23[a]	24
Liberals	20	–	–
Conservatives	32	–	–
Feminists	13	–	–
Business People	30	–	–
Labor Unions	18	–	–
Middle-class People	69	65	52[b]
Working-class People	60	58	46
Poor People	20	18	16
Southerners	13	–	–
Christian Fundamentalists	–	15	11
People at Your Place of Worship	–	45	30[b]
People in Your Neighborhood	–	45	26[b]
People at Work	–	46	37
Americans in General	–	50	46
N	224	228	97

Note: Ballot 3 refers to respondents who did not have a respondent booklet and were therefore read the list of groups contained in ballot 2 by the interviewer.
– Group was not included on this ballot.
[a] The percent mentioning this group on Ballot 1 is significantly different from the percent mentioning it on Ballot 2 at p<.05.
[b] The percent mentioning this group on Ballot 2 is significantly different from the percent mentioning it on Ballot 3 at p<.05.

Not only did people choose these groups that emphasize interaction as a "close group," they were often singled out as the "closest group" in a follow-up question (see Wong 1998). Given the nature of these groups – based on contact and interaction between individuals – we are not seeing something unexpected about American group identity. The availability of these groups just reminds us that churches are important centers of membership and community in this country, and that the traditional loci of political organization (geography and workplace) still enjoy substantial allegiance from Americans (Fischer 1982). Overall, almost all of the groups included in the two versions of the question appear to be salient in people's minds as they think of individuals with whom they share "ideas, interests, and feelings about things."[13]

Measuring Community with "Closeness": Validity Test 2

It is, of course, possible that the groups listed in both ballots of the closed-ended group closeness question are irrelevant when it comes to Americans' politics and their perceptions of their communities; respondents may simply be reacting to whatever groups are provided by the interviewer. There may be an entirely different set of groups that are more politically important to ordinary Americans than the groups about which the survey asks. To ensure that this scenario is, in fact, not true, the 1997 NES Pilot also included an open-ended version of the question for comparison.

The open-ended question did not use "close" in its wording. All respondents in the survey were asked the following:

We are interested in finding out what kinds of people you think are most like you – in their ideas and interests and feelings about things. Thinking about the different groups in society, which ones would you say are most like you?

People could name as many or as few groups as they liked. If more than one group was chosen, respondents were asked, "Of the groups you just mentioned, which one do you feel closest to?" Comparing the responses to the open-ended question with responses to the closed-ended question can help us determine if the groups listed in the closed-ended question are what come to mind when Americans think of groups in society "like them" and who might belong in their communities.

Most of the groups included in the closed-ended "group closeness" items were mentioned in responses to the open-ended item, confirming

[13] The popularity of groups on Ballot 1 is relatively constant over time (see Wong 1998).

that the list of groups in the closed-ended versions are salient political ones (see Wong 1998 for more on the validity and reliability of the group closeness item). Despite the slight difference in question wording, there is still a great deal of overlap in the types of groups mentioned across question formats; groups pertaining to ideology, race, gender, age, and class or income were all mentioned as ones that people said shared their interests and ideas. The four "new" groups from ballot 2 that focused on "Americans" and people with whom a respondent might come into contact were all cited in the open-ended question. These results provide additional support for the findings from the *Indivisible* interviews that race, nation, and geography can serve as determinants of people's communities. Table 2.2 lists some of the broad, overarching categories, which include both local and social groups.

The open-ended question also allowed people to give more detailed descriptions of their "close groups." Joint groups were very common; for example, respondents gave answers such as "conservative Republicans," "Christian women," "white elderly population," "single mothers," "professional technical people," and "angry white males." The prevalence of these joint groups highlight the very complexity of the relationships between groups, identity, and communities. We get a clear picture of Simmel's overlapping circles, or of people's perceptions of their communities, which do not always follow along objective group boundaries.

Measuring Overlapping Circles

Joint groups are closely related to the idea of multiple affiliations. It is commonly accepted among psychologists, sociologists, and political scientists that individuals have multiple identities or reference groups. In fact, this is one of the crucial underlying assumptions of theorists of pluralism in American politics (Truman 1951). More generally, cross-cutting ties are necessary for creating communities of interest (Blau and Schwartz 1984; Briggs 2007; Varshney 2002). However, it is primarily psychologists who study this multiplicity (Deaux 1993; Deaux et al. 1995; Rosenberg and Gara 1985), and they are more interested in the structure and dimensionality of identities than in their attitudinal or behavioral outcomes. Within political science, much of the work on the role of groups has focused on single group identities and interests.[14] Examining multiple affiliations

---

[14] However, there has been some interesting work on the combined effects of racial and gender identities for black women by Gay and Tate (1998) and Robinson (1987). And, there is a growing body of research on intersectionality more generally.

TABLE 2.2. *Open-ended Responses to Group Closeness, 1997 NES Pilot*

% of all Responses for Overarching Categories*

Question Wording:

We are interested in finding out what kinds of people you think are most like you in their ideas and interests and feelings about things. Thinking about the different groups in society, which ones would you say are most like you?

21%	POLITICAL IDEOLOGY / PARTISANSHIP
	Party Identification
	Ideological Identification
	Other Political Identifications
20	CLASS / INCOME
	Middle Class
	Working Class / Working People
	Poor People
12	RELIGION
	Conservative Christians
	"Christians" (no further specification)
	Other Christians (denominations given)
	Other Religious Groups
	Other references to religion or church
10	OCCUPATION
10	AGE
5	FAMILY
	Marital Status
	Parental Status
	Other references to family
5	GEOGRAPHY
	Neighbors
	Americans
4	EDUCATION
4	RACE / ETHNICITY
4	GENDER / SEXUAL ORIENTATION
3	HOBBIES / ACTIVITIES / SPORTS
3	PERSONAL ATTRIBUTES
3	PEOPLE R HAS CONTACT WITH
3	AVERAGE, COMMON PERSON

* *For a full list of categories and more details on the coding, see Wong (1998).*

emphasizes the importance of the variety of groups from which an individual can choose concerning his affiliations and how his perceptions matter in making those choices.

How many groups are included in people's perceptions of their communities? The mean number of "close" groups chosen by respondents in the closed-ended versions was about four.[15] What does it mean when a respondent mentions multiple groups? Are earlier mentions more important in her perception of who composes her community? Although the format of the closed-ended closeness item does not allow one to compare *when* a group is mentioned (i.e., in order of importance), an issue raised by these multiple responses is whether a group is mentioned *only* when more than one group is named. For example, of the respondents who mentioned one or two close groups for ballot 1, none of them mentioned "whites" as a close group; only among people who gave three or more mentions were "whites" chosen as a close group.[16] One possible interpretation is that whites are not the defining characters of people's communities, and that respondents only mention closeness to whites after they have listed other affiliations first. This phenomenon is reflected when one compares the percentage of respondents who feel close to whites with that of respondents who feel *closest* to whites: more than 40 percent feel close, but less than 10 percent name whites as their closest group. I will come back to this issue in Chapter 5.

The number of multiple affiliations does also confirm that individuals can feel close to several groups simultaneously. One could picture these various groups as Simmel's overlapping circles, clustered under a larger umbrella of "community." And, of course, the choices that people make, among their many potential communities, can change over time, depending on particular policy discussions, environmental changes, and personal circumstances (see Wong 1998 for more discussion of the stability and

---

[15] I created a count of the number of groups mentioned, and tried to predict what led respondents to choose more than one affiliation or "close" group. Ninety-two percent of the respondents given ballot 1 named more than one close group (range from 0 to 16), as did 83 percent of those administered ballots 2 and 3 (range from 0 to 13). Clearly, Americans do have multiple affiliations. Regression results show that the only significant predictors of multiple mentions are the dummy variables for race: for ballot 1, blacks and Hispanics were more likely than whites to name multiple close groups, and for ballots 2 and 3, blacks were more likely to name groups than whites. Demographic characteristics like age, sex, income, and education had no impact on the number of groups mentioned as close.

[16] Among respondents given ballot 2 who named only one close group, "whites" was named by two individuals. In the 1996 NES, however, none of the respondents who mentioned only one close group chose whites as that group.

reliability of the closeness measures within persons and in the population in general over time).

Measuring Who Feels a Sense of Community

In addition to the question of who people say are "most like them" is the issue of why people choose particular groups and not others. I argue that how an individual perceives her community cannot be assumed in advance, based only on her objective group status. For example, in studying parental identity, Dion found that approximately 80 percent of women who have children list "parent" as one of their salient psychological identities, compared with only 50 percent of men who have children (cited in Deaux 1991).

Group Salience by Objective Members. Public opinion scholars often want to know when and how an identity gets activated in politics, and therefore are interested in the salience of a group identity. Table 2.3 shows that group identification is most salient for racial minorities (blacks and Hispanics, though not Asian Americans), women, young people, and the elderly; they are most likely to include their objective group in their communities.[17] However, feelings of closeness are not limited to objective group members.

Group Salience by Non-Objective Members. In discussions of politics in the United States, it is important to know how an individual imagines her community, regardless of whether she is an objective member of a group to which she feels close. For example, a white woman who feels close to blacks may have different policy opinions from a white woman who feels close only to whites, affecting not only the bottom line of opinion polls but also the possibility of pluralism and political coalitions. The main point to be taken from Table 2.4 is that when respondents are forced to name groups "like themselves" without the benefit of a list, they are more likely to name groups of which they are objective members. With a booklet in front of them, however, respondents are more likely to expand the boundaries of their community, listing groups to which

---

[17] Feelings of group closeness by objective members in general is much more common for respondents of the closed-ended question, although this would be expected, given the way the question was asked; since respondents mentioned many more groups in the closed-ended version, they are more likely to include groups of which they are objective members. Noticeably, however, salience as evaluated using the open-ended question is much higher for the ideological and age-related groups than for racial minorities and women, in contrast to what is found using the closed-ended question.

TABLE 2.3. *Salience of a Group for Objective Members, 1997 NES Pilot*

Among respondents who are "objective" members of a group, the % who mention being close to that group.[a]

	Closed-Ended[b]		Open-Ended	
Asian Americans	0%	(3)	0%	(2)
Blacks	73	(30)	9	(22)
Hispanics	64	(45)	9	(32)
Whites	47	(370)	6	(322)
Women	63	(277)	8	(227)
Men	48	(94)	3	(155)
Elderly (65 years +)	73	(55)	18	(87)
Young People (18 to 31 years old)	67	(55)	16	(58)
Liberals	51	(75)	20	(130)
Conservatives	51	(124)	18	(226)
Labor Unions	53	(40)	3	(69)
Poor People (<$20k family income)	35	(104)	10	(97)
Southerner	29	(80)	no mention	
Christian Fundamentalists (measured as Evangelical Protestants)	30	(77)	4	(7)[c]

[a] The numbers in the parentheses represent the number of individuals who mentioned the group for each question format. DK responses were excluded for both the closed and open-ended columns.
[b] This includes only ballots 1 and 2 of the split sample. Asian Americans, Men, Elderly, Liberals, Conservatives, Labor Unions, Southerners, and Christian Fundamentalists were only asked on one ballot.
[c] Respondents who answered anything under the category of "Conservative Christian" for the open-ended question were considered identifiers for this case.

they feel some psychological attachment, but to which they do not objectively belong. For example, among respondents who said they felt close to blacks for the closed-ended question, only 38 percent were themselves African Americans. The same pattern of feelings of community by non-objective members holds true for closeness to young people, the elderly, and poor people.

One question that may arise in examining closeness choices by objective outgroup members is that of social desirability. Are individuals claiming

TABLE 2.4. *The Relationship Between Membership and Salience of a Group, 1997 NES Pilot*

Among respondents who mentioned being close to a group, the % who *also* are "objective" members of that group.[a]

	Closed-Ended[b]		Open-Ended	
Asian Americans	0%	(8)	0%	(1)
Blacks	38	(58)	67	(3)
Hispanics	52	(57)	75	(4)
Whites	86	(201)	90	(20)
Women	86	(204)	100	(19)
Men	74	(61)	100	(5)
Elderly (65 years +)	46	(87)	62	(26)
Young People (18–31 years)	28	(131)	75	(12)
Liberals	86	(44)	93	(28)
Conservatives	90	(71)	93	(43)
Labor Unions	51	(41)	40	(5)
Poor People (<$20k family income)	46	(87)	72	(14)
Southerner	77	(30)	no mention	
Christian Fundamentalists (measured as Evangelical Protestants)	68	(34)	71	(7)[c]

[a] The numbers in the parentheses represent the number of individuals who mentioned the group for each question format. DK responses were excluded for both the closed and open-ended columns.

[b] This includes only ballots 1 and 2 of the split sample. Asian Americans, Men, Elderly, Liberals, Conservatives, Labor Unions, Southerners, and Christian Fundamentalists were only asked on one ballot.

[c] Respondents who answered anything under the category of "Conservative Christian" for the open-ended question were considered identifiers for this case.

closeness to outgroups in order to appear tolerant or unprejudiced, given that current societal norms would dictate this type of attitude is desirable? Although individuals may choose to say they are close to outgroups because of social pressures – rather than because they actually feel a sense of closeness – it is worth noting that there is little fluctuation in closeness responses over time. For example, closeness to blacks has not increased drastically from 1972 to 1996, despite marked changes in racial attitudes over those two decades (Schuman et al. 1997). In 1972, *not* expressing closeness could have been the socially preferred choice, whereas by 1996, explicit racial prejudice was largely frowned upon. If social desirability were driving responses to the closeness items, one should observe a steady increase in affirmative responses over the 24-year time span.

The results in Table 2.3 and 2.4 indicate that objective membership in a group does not lead automatically to feelings of closeness with that group, nor is it a requirement for feeling close to that group. The bottom line is that people's perceptions of their communities include both objective ingroup members as well as outgroup members, and that objective membership in a group is neither a necessary nor sufficient condition for feeling a sense of community with other group members.

Measuring the Effects of Community on Participation and Obligation: Convergent Validity

Even if the "group closeness" question captures a variety of ways that people can feel they have something in common, covers salient and important groups in American politics, measures communities perceived by both ingroup and outgroup members, and allows for both geographic and relational communities, it is possible that communities bear no relation to morally parochial behavior. I now turn to examine one effect of this measure of community: whether perceived community boundaries – closeness to a group – can affect political behavior. I will examine this question in more detail in later chapters, but one question of a measure's validity is whether it predicts what one believes it should predict; the following provides a small test.

Political scientists often try to understand when and why people get politically motivated and involved, and past research has found that racial identity and consciousness have an effect on political participation (Gamson 1971; Gurin and Epps 1975; Guterbock and London 1983; Junn and Jenkins 1997; Shingles 1981). I hypothesize that individuals' perceptions of their community, regardless of their own objective status, play a role in political engagement; restricting the researcher's gaze to ingroup identifiers alone forces one to miss the larger picture.

Because the 1997 Pilot Study sample was part of a panel study, all of the respondents were also interviewed in 1996. The 1996 NES contains a battery of questions about what types of organizations in which respondents are involved. Table 2.5 provides some comparisons between the participation rates of respondents who feel close to a group and those who do not. Respondents who felt close to a group in the 1997 Pilot Study are more likely to have participated in an organization, group, or

TABLE 2.5. *Group Participation, 1997 NES Pilot*

Question Wording (1996 NES):
There are many types of organizations, groups, and charities that people might be involved with. We're interested in what kinds of groups you might be involved with. I'm going to read you a list of different types of organizations. For each type, could you tell me the name or names of the organizations you are involved with.

	Participation in an organization, group, or charity that pertains to the group mentioned in the closed-ended "closeness" item		Participation in an organization, group, or charity that pertains to the group mentioned in the open-ended "closeness" item	
Close to Labor Unions	49%	(41)	60%	(5)
Not close to Labor Unions	9	(183)	15	(377)
Close to Business People	29	(68)	30	(10)
Not close to Business People	15	(156)	17	(372)
Close to Older People	26	(87)	35	(26)
Not close to Older People	6	(137)	14	(356)
Close to Racial / Ethnic Minorities*	13	(39)	0	(7)
Not close to Minorities	2	(185)	5	(375)
Close to Women	4	(204)	11	(19)
Not close to Women	1	(248)	2	(363)
Close to "People in Your Neighborhood"	28	(102)	33	(6)
Not close to "People in Your Neighborhood"	17	(126)	20	(376)
Close to Ideological group**	17	(115)	25	(69)
Not close to Ideological group	8	(109)	11	(313)

	Participation in an organization, group, or charity that pertains to the group mentioned in the closed-ended "closeness" item		Participation in an organization, group, or charity that pertains to the group mentioned in the open-ended "closeness" item	
Close to "People at Your Place of Worship"	87	(103)	93	(15)
Not close to "People at Your Place of Worship"	54	(125)	68	(367)

[a] Closeness to Racial / Ethnic Minorities combines closeness to Blacks, to Hispanics, and to Asians.

[b] Closeness to Ideological Group combines closeness to Liberals and to Conservatives.

Note: The numbers in the parentheses represent the number of individuals who chose the groups as "close" ones. I did not control for objective membership.

charity that pertained to the group mentioned.[18] For example, among the respondents who felt close to labor unions in the closed-ended question, 49 percent participated in labor groups; in contrast, among those respondents who did not feel close to unions, only 9 percent participated. Furthermore, this finding holds across a variety of groups and whether or not the close group was chosen in the open- or closed-ended item. It appears community sentiment – measured by closeness to groups – is related to political behavior.

Caveats to Using the "Group Closeness" Question

Thus far, I have used previous research to explain why the "group closeness" question constitutes a "good measure" of community, and provided a number of validity tests of the measure using the 1997 NES Pilot Study. Of course, the group closeness questions are not without flaws. For example, Conover (1987) criticizes these items on a variety of grounds. One problem she cites is that "close" can connote psychological attachment, or empathy, sympathy, or "simply just proximity."[19] Scholars have tried to address this concern in a number of different ways. It is difficult to differentiate empirically between empathy, sympathy, and attachment from a single survey question, but scholars are able to differentiate between

---

[18] The closeness measures are reliable over time, such that one would not expect large differences in closeness responses from 1996 to 1997 (Wong 1998).

[19] In fact, closeness was originally used to measure objective interaction patterns, not cognitive closeness (Aron et al. 1991; Berscheid et al. 1989).

emotional attachment and judgments of proximity by asking respondents follow-up questions about the level of contact that they have with these "close" groups.[20] While interaction is clearly related to feelings of closeness, "group closeness" is not simply a measure of contact. Also, although Lau agrees with Conover that the question wording of the "closeness" items blends concepts, he explains that "the more generic 'feel close to' operationalization was used in the NES surveys rather than the more theoretically precise 'identify with' because the former wording was understood more widely by the general public" (Lau 1989, 223). And, the results from the open and closed-ended questions in the 1997 Pilot Study were similar, despite the word "close" only being used in the latter version.

Another of Conover's criticisms is that the phrasing of the question "rests implicitly on the assumption that group identification and influence stem from a sense of shared self-interests" (1987, 7). It is possible for individuals with common interests to develop into a group, although shared self-interests alone do not define an identity. Furthermore, the question wording also allows for "ideas" and "feelings" to be alternative sources of "closeness," so while shared interests may be sufficient, they are not necessary prerequisites for group identification. Tajfel defined identity partly as the "value and emotional significance" of group membership; this "emotional significance" can include ideas, interests, "feelings about things," or any combination of them (1981, 255). Ideas, interests, and feelings can all serve as the common glue that binds together a perceived community.

An additional concern mentioned by Conover is that the closeness questions seem to conflate "psychological attachment" and "subjective membership," which are two different aspects of group identification. This, however, is only a problem if a researcher is interested in group identification, focused on objective ingroup members. For a community, "subjective membership" is based on "psychological attachment" to other community members.

Overall, I would argue that Conover's criticisms of the "group closeness" items used as measures of "community" are not fatal. As previous research on communities makes clear, people's sense of community can be based on proximity, belonging, attachment, or shared values and interests. Both membership and the reasons for membership in a community are subjective, and if a measure were specifically tailored to capture only geographic proximity, for example, many communities perceived by

[20] For example, in 1997, 60 percent of respondents said that they talked to members of their closest group seven days a week, and all respondents (given ballot 1 or 2) reported speaking to members of their closest group *at least* four times a week.

individuals would be missed. It is instead fortuitous that the many interpretations of the "closeness" question overlap with the many possible
interpretations of how people imagine their communities.

For similar reasons, the language of closeness is as applicable to the
concept of community as it is to identity. It is also important to develop a
measure of community that is valid and reliable in researchers' minds, yet
straightforward and plain for the general public. The question of whether
and how the more precise language of "sense of community" is understood by the general public is what I turn to next.

Measuring What Creates a Sense of Community

Social scientists of various stripes understand what a community is, even if
they disagree among themselves about a precise operational definition. But
this may be irrelevant in "the real world" of (primarily) non-academics.
The *Indivisible* interviews provided some evidence that Americans do, in
fact, see "community" much as researchers define it. This section provides
additional support, looking at some of the possible bases of community
membership in the minds of Americans in addressing these questions.

The data I use in this analysis are from the 2000 Social Capital
Community Benchmark Survey, which had a nationally representative
sample of 3,003 Americans (along with forty-two additional community
samples). The survey was conducted from July 2000 to November 2000,
and was sponsored by the Saguaro Seminar at the Kennedy School at
Harvard University.

The 2000 Social Capital Survey asked respondents whether different
groups gave them a sense of community. The question read as follows:

This study is about community, so we'd like to start by asking what gives you a
sense of community or a feeling of belonging. I'm going to read a list: For each
one, say YES if it gives you a sense of community or feeling of belonging, and
NO if it does not.

1. Your old or new friends,
2. The people in your neighborhood,
3. Living in [R's city],
4. Your place of worship,
5. The people you work with or go to school with,
6. People who share your ethnic background,
7. The people you have met online on the computer.

The groups resemble the groups listed in the NES "closeness" question.
These groups also provide a reasonable range to define Americans'

TABLE 2.6. *Sources of Community*

What gives you a sense of community or a feeling of belonging?

	Percentage Responding that the Group gives R a Sense of Community
Your old or new friends	89%
The people in your neighborhood	80%
Living in [city]	79%
Your place of worship	82%
The people you work with or go to school with	80%
People who share your ethnic background	71%
The people you have met online on the computer	17%

Data: Social Capital Community Benchmark Survey, 2000

underlying sense of community, from people they live and work with, to people met online whom they have not met face-to-face. As Leach explains, emphasizing geography and social ties again,

[Community] always has a provincial character. It takes shape first as connections to families and friends, then to neighborhoods, towns, and regions, and finally, to the nation and the world. It is through the formation of this *sense of place*, beginning with the home and parents, that people develop their *loyalty to place*, but it is only after the earliest concrete ties are formed that the bigger connections can be forged; the process cannot begin the other way around. (1999, 180)

As Table 2.6 shows, almost all of the groups listed provide respondents with a sense of community.[21] More than three-quarters of the sample feel a sense of community with individuals with whom they interact, such as their neighbors, friends, coworkers or classmates, and members of their place of worship. These are the same individuals who make up people's social networks (Fischer 1982; Huckfeldt 1986). Furthermore, it is possible for others who live in the same city or who share the same ethnicity to come into regular contact with respondents, but regardless of the nature of these relationships – face-to-face or not – fellow city-dwellers and co-ethnics also prompt a sense of community or feeling of belonging

---

[21] No more than 1 percent of the sample chose the "don't know" response or refused to answer for any of the seven groups listed in the battery.

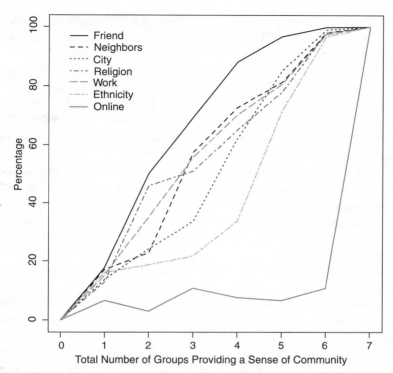

FIGURE 2.1. "Difficulty" of Choosing Groups in One's Community.
Data: Social Capital Community Benchmark Survey 2000.

for most Americans. The only group that does not provide this sense of community for a majority of respondents is people met online.[22]

The vast majority of Americans say that they feel a sense of community with six of the seven groups listed.[23] When one compares who mentions which groups, a distinct picture of what inspires feelings of community appears (see Figure 2.1). Among respondents who say that only one of the groups gives them a sense of community – emphasizing the relative importance of that group in creating a sense of community – the likelihood

[22] Given the relative novelty of the Internet in 2000, this lack of a sense of community with people met online is not surprising. However, many theorists argue that the online community, in fact, is the ideal public sphere for deliberation in a community to take place (see, for example, Connery 1997 and Healy 1997).

[23] The mean and median number of groups from the provided list that give respondents a sense of community is 5. Furthermore, less than 1 percent of the sample does not feel a sense of community from at least one of the groups.

of that group being any from the list is the same, except for the people met online. No one group always comes to mind when people think of their community. In other words, among respondents who felt a sense of community from only one group, 18 percent said it came from friends, 17 percent from neighbors, 16 percent from co-ethnics, 15 percent from co-workers or classmates, 14 percent from fellow city dwellers, and 13 percent from other members of their place of worship.[24] Communities, in other words, are seen as relational and geographic, with no predominant vision of what a community must entail.

Respondents' friends were the "easiest" or most common choice of groups that inspire a sense of community. When one examines those respondents who name more than one group that inspires a community feeling, friends are always named more often than any other group. The other groups vary in their prominence; for example, among respondents who felt a sense of community with two groups, co-workers were chosen more frequently than neighbors, but among respondents who named four groups, neighbors were named more often than co-workers. However, to say that friends make up one's community does not provide much explanatory power – unless one is interested in social networks and therefore gathers information about the friends' attitudes as well – and seems circular, especially since "friends" make up the only group for which it is the case that people explicitly choose to feel close to all its members. Instead of directing my attention to social networks and friends, in Chapter 3 I will focus on whether geographic communities – not all of whose residents are personally known by respondents – have an effect on political attitudes and behavior, using this particular measure. Here, I want to focus just momentarily on one other group listed in the survey: co-ethnics.

People of the same ethnic background as respondents are the second least-mentioned community group after people met online. However, as can be seen in Figure 2.1, it follows a trajectory more similar to that of fellow city-dwellers than to that of online acquaintances, and as was shown in Table 2.6, almost two-thirds of Americans state that people of the same ethnic background give them a sense of community. Although one can picture one's friends, neighbors, co-workers or classmates, and people at

---

[24] Only 7 percent of those who chose one group that inspired community sentiments selected people met online, and for half of all the respondents who extended community boundaries to online acquaintances, this option was chosen only when all other groups had also been described as providing a sense of community. Clearly, the virtual community is still a low priority for many Americans.

one's church or temple or mosque, and it is relatively straightforward to imagine the approximate boundaries of one's city if not its inhabitants, it is more difficult (if not impossible) to draw physical boundaries around one's co-ethnics, given the demographic diversity spread geographically across America. I will return to the question of the political importance of co-ethnics in Chapter 5 to examine the effects of racial and ethnic communities.[25]

In addition to the *Indivisible* interviews and the NES surveys, the Social Capital Community Benchmark Survey provides another look at what constitutes the basis of people's communities. These data show that people feel a sense of community from a variety of factors – including ones covered by the "group closeness" measure – and that contemporary Americans are quite different from the Americans Tocqueville described in *Democracy in America* as islands unto themselves:

Each one of [a multitude of men], withdrawn into himself, is almost unaware of the fate of the rest. Mankind, for him, consists in his children and his personal friends. As for the rest of his fellow citizens, they are near enough, but he does not notice them. He touches them but feels nothing. (1969, 691–2)

As I explained at the beginning of this chapter, good measures of "community" should capture both geographic and relational communities; be appropriate measures for communities based on locality, nationality, and race; allow for individuals' perceptions of their own communities; capture the quality that holds members of a community together, such as proximity or similarity; and be valid and reliable measures that can be tested in models of attitudes and behaviors. Although I will also use other measures in the following chapters, depending on the type of community being examined, the "group closeness" question fulfills these requirements and is one that will be common throughout the analyses in Chapters 3, 4, and 5.

CONCLUSION

In this chapter, I have discussed a couple of different measures of community, focusing most directly on "group closeness" survey questions. Their validity as measures of a sense of community is confirmed by survey data asking respondents about this directly (i.e., what gives you a sense of community, using the Social Capital Community Benchmark Survey),

[25] I will not use this survey question, however, because its wording only allows for community boundaries being drawn around a respondent's ethnic ingroup.

and with the open-ended versions of the question in the 1997 NES Pilot Study, and by qualitative data from the *Indivisible* project that explains what people mean when they use the term "community." In Chapter 1, I laid out a definition of the concept of community, based on Anderson's notion of the "imagined community." In moving to measure community, I am aware of Hillery's (1959) conclusion that "[Redefining community] has been attempted enough now to demonstrate its futility" (1959, 241). His advice was to remember that conclusions derived from one kind of defined "community" might not be applicable to another. My conclusions about how people imagine their community and the effects of these boundaries are therefore restricted to a conceptualization of community that emphasizes a sentiment of commonality while being applicable to both geographic and relational communities. The "closeness" measure also allows me to examine where community boundaries are imagined for both objective and subjective members of a group.

The analyses that follow concentrate on how communities are perceived and the consequences that result from the definition of their borders: how, in fact, do people define their compatriots who take priority? This drawing of boundaries can both be self-focused – placing oneself within the community or Simmel's circle – or other-focused – determining who else belongs in the "circle of We" (Hollinger 1995).

Mertz writes, "...how people think and feel and perceive their world is important in how they act: that out of the myriad of possible avenues for action only a small subset is usually considered to be available..." (1994, 975). This narrowing of possibilities is the focus of my analysis. I show how individuals imagine their geographic, national, and racial communities, what subset of people they believe fall into these communities, and what effects the boundaries of communities have on their political decisions.

3

Imagined Gates and Neighbors

The narrator in Thornton Wilder's *Our Town* begins his monologue by setting the stage so that his audience can picture the small town of Grover's Corners.

Well, I'd better show you how our town lies. Up here – is Main Street. Way back there is the railway station; tracks go that way. Polish Town's across the tracks, and some Canuck families. Over there is the Congregational Church; across the street's the Presbyterian. Methodist and Unitarian are over there. Baptist is down in the holla' by the river. Catholic Church is over beyond the tracks. Here's the Town Hall and Post Office combined; jail's in the basement. (Wilder 1965, 4)

It has ethnic and religious diversity, a railway linking the town to the wider world, and a political center. However, Grover's Corners is more than simply a backdrop; its residents feel a sense of commonality with one another because of a long history living in close proximity and the web of social relationships that have developed as a result. The sense of community or "glue" that holds people together is what ties the story of George Gibbs and Emily Webb with that of their friends and neighbors. Living in this town affects its inhabitants' attitudes toward one another, toward the local paper and their constable, and toward serving and dying for their country. Defining Grover's Corners as their community affects how they think of their own roles, identities, and obligations, and how they view their relationships with other members of the town.

While these fictional characters live most vividly in the minds of high school drama students, the residents of *Our Town* fit the picture conveyed in the previous chapters by surveys of ordinary Americans. How people imagine their communities is determined by both geographic and relational ties, and this perception leads people to act on behalf of other

individuals who are believed to be members of their community by virtue
of a shared locality or social ties.

The study of mass political behavior began with such localized work
by Berelson, Lazarsfeld, and their colleagues at Columbia (1944; 1954).
This tradition continues with the work of Huckfeldt and his colleagues,
in which they study the political effects of social networks and how information is gained and transferred between friends and relatives, focusing
their studies on localities such as South Bend, Indiana (1991; 1993; 1995).
More generally, for both studies of voting behavior and information dis-
persion, a growing number of researchers are interested in the places in
which individuals live and interact. Scholars have studied the mediating
effects of local contexts on people's racial and political attitudes, ranging from the level of country to region to county to zip code (for a few
examples, see Gay 2006; Oliver and Mendelberg 2000; Quillian 1995;
and Taylor 1998).

In this book, I pursue four operationalizations of how people may
see their local contexts as forming the basis of imagined geographic
communities:

1. Feelings of closeness to people in a particular geographic entity,
2. A sense of community inspired by individuals in one's neighborhood and town,
3. Identification with a particular geographic entity, and
4. Recognition of who belongs within one's geographic community's
   borders.

These ways of thinking about community emphasize both who
belongs "inside" as a member and what an individual will do to assist
other members, and who is "outside" and what an individual will with-
hold from them. I use the case of the national community to examine
the fourth operationalization in more detail in Chapter 4; in this chapter,
I concentrate on addressing the first three. I focus on people's perceptions of their local context – their imagined geographic communities –
because these are often what first come to mind when people think of
the word "community." I show how perceptions of commonality on the
basis of geography and place can play a leading role in political decisionmaking. The sense of community Americans may feel from living in
a particular locale is the variable of interest: I hypothesize that a sense
of community predicts special obligations or parochial moral behavior,
whereby individuals privilege the needs of their neighbors over others,
and it promotes civic engagement on behalf of those neighbors. It also

affects an individual's attitudes about local political institutions and policies that serve the area, as well as their intolerance of outsiders. This may seem intuitive, but as I will show in this chapter, how people imagine their community is not simply reducible to self- or group-interested behavior – such as NIMBY activities – nor is it a proxy for one's general values or ideology.

Including one's neighbors in one's definition of community has clear implications for both political opinions as well as actions. After a brief discussion of how one can think of communities with geographic boundaries, subsequent sections of this chapter will address the following questions:

(1) How ubiquitous is including one's neighbors in one's community?
(2) What leads to feelings of closeness or community with people living in various geographic locales?
(3) What are the effects of these feelings of geographic community on attitudes about one's belonging and role in the governing of that community, particularly one's trust in political institutions, tolerance of dissent, and political participation?
(4) What is the effect of feelings of community on decisions about reallocating resources to other members of the community?

The analyses help explain the extent to which imagined communities affect for whom individuals act, who is trusted to represent their interests, if individuals feel they can make a difference to help their community, and for whom they will tax themselves.

HISTORICAL AND INSTITUTIONALIZED BOUNDARIES OF GEOGRAPHIC COMMUNITIES

American history seems to tell the endless saga of men and women on the move, whether one reads of American Indians or of the various immigrants arriving over the past half millennium. Even as villages and cities were built and families set down roots, the common American story is one of men and women moving to the frontier for loamier fields, more elbow room, or riches of gold, oil, and endless dreams (Fischer 2002; Herting et al. 1997; Tobey et al. 1990). In *Democracy in America*, Tocqueville commented on this particular roaming nature of Americans, which has endured over time:

An American will build a house in which to pass his old age and sell it before the roof is on; he will plant a garden and rent it just as the trees are coming into bearing; he will clear a field and leave others to reap the harvest; he will take up a profession and leave it, settle in one place and soon go off elsewhere with his changing desires. ([1834] 1969, 536)

The exercising of one's rights to "life, liberty, and the pursuit of happiness" often entailed geographic mobility en route to social mobility. Armed with the notion of Manifest Destiny, with homesteader laws, and with new transportation pathways, Americans marched across the continental United States, seeking personal fortune and even new identities while supposedly spreading democratic values. Along the way, Americans have moved to many different types of places, urban and rural, large and small, and more recently, suburban and exurban; they are willing to travel across considerable distances, not restricting their moves to neighboring towns. Values, economics, and political institutions all play a role in the fluidity of Americans' movements.

Nevertheless, Americans are not literally nomads. The moves are not seasonal, but are often directed at finding better homes and better communities. For example, the large-scale migration of African Americans in the early decades of the twentieth century from the South to the North was prompted by agricultural disasters in the South and labor shortages in the North as a result of World War I (Lemann 1992). In addition, a constant theme in American history is "the Lockean notion that citizens should have a property stake in society" (Tobey et al. 1990, 1395). By the time of the New Deal, home ownership was seen as a crucial part of the social contract, and according to President Roosevelt, to be an American citizen in a healthy democracy entailed having the fundamental right to a stable home (Tobey et al. 1990). The federal government decreased mobility by creating and insuring long-term home mortgages. In addition, with boom times (including a good economy and high marriage and birth rates) and the G.I. Bill, more Americans were having families that needed and could afford places to live, often in the suburbs (Jackson 1995; Tobey et al. 1990). After World War II, suburbia – and suburban home ownership – became a mass phenomenon. As Duany et al. (2000, 8) explain,

Intentionally or not, the [Federal Housing Administration] and [Veterans Administration] programs discouraged the renovation of existing housing stock... Simultaneously, a 41,000-mile interstate highway program, coupled with federal and local subsidies for road improvement and the neglect of mass transit, helped make automotive commuting affordable and convenient for the average citizen. Within the new economic framework, young families made the finally rational choice: Levittown.

Migration to the United States from Europe and Asia also slowed over time – partly as a result of legislated immigration restrictions and wars – and moves to the frontier and cities from farms declined as the land became populated and families were better able to overcome shocks such as natural disasters or the death of the main breadwinner. This increasing resilience was partly caused by the growing benefits of social safety nets, both institutionalized and informal (Fischer 2002; Herting et al. 1997). As a result, residential mobility – the rates for which had already declined between the nineteenth and twentieth centuries – continued to decline from 1950 through the turn of the twenty-first century (Fischer 2002).

As Americans decide to move or stay put, they consider economic, political, and social factors when deciding where to settle. There is often a psychological component as well: in order to protect Us – who are united in our shared ideas of the collective good – from Them, who could thwart progress via free-riding, neglect, or outright opposition, people often seek idealized communities that can institute barriers to keep out unwanted individuals. The reasons for these exclusions have ranged from age to lifestyle to race.

For example, in the past decade there has been a rise in the number of "active adult communities" that bar families with children from living there. Children are not exactly excluded from these residents' self-defined *social* communities, but as one resident explained, "... when you get to be a certain age, you want to be in a community where people around you are the same age you are" (Caldwell 2006, 14). Residents of these housing developments may not feel any animus toward parenthood or children in general, but the exclusion of families implies the presence of a barrier around the community, regardless of whether the motivation is benign.

The boundaries of a community can be largely invisible, yet people inside and outside can still sense the walls that demarcate membership. Orthodox Jews cannot work outside the home from sundown on Friday until sundown on Saturday, and the creation of a symbolic wall to extend the area considered to be private or "home" allows greater movement. In Los Angeles, Orthodox Jews began in 2002 to lobby to hang several miles of fishing line around parts of Santa Monica, Venice, and Marina del Rey; without this largely invisible symbolic wall or eruv, they argued, young families would leave and the Orthodox community would suffer.[1]

---

[1] They ran into opposition by environmentalists, who worried about the lines killing endangered terns, and beachfront residents, who worried about their views and

In this instance, the almost invisible borders were necessary for keeping members in the community, not to keep nonmembers out.

Using this language, the mayor of Mount Laurel, New Jersey, Joe Alvarez, explained why he sought to keep out people seeking affordable housing in his town: "It's like grafting a good healthy skin so you can graft in cancer skin and blend it in. Here you have a healthy area. Bringing these people in here, you don't know who they are ..." (Kirp 2000, 88). The poor, in other words, are not part of Us, and trying to include them in the community would only be to the detriment of the current community members. For a similar reason, incorporation rates in rural southern towns are also significantly related to the size of the black populations in surrounding areas (Lichter et al. 2007, 47–48): "Annexation – or the lack of annexation – can therefore be a political tool used by municipal leaders to exclude disadvantaged or low-income populations, including minorities, from voting in local elections and from receiving access to public utilities and other community services." Gainsborough (2001) argues that to the extent that cities and suburbs within the same metropolitan area are composed of very different populations, suburban residents are likely to withdraw support for federal spending, increase support for devolving power to local levels, and oppose the formation of city–suburb coalitions. One interpretation is that white or wealthier residents choose to institutionalize imagined community boundaries drawn along the lines of race and class.

One incentive for having boundaries drawn officially around one's community is the financial concern about Us paying for Them. The official lines, ranging from gates to zones to state lines, all provide the rationale – legally, if not ethically – for keeping resources within the imagined community.

The number of neighborhoods with visible walls – "gated communities" – has risen rapidly over the past three decades (Blakely and Snyder 1997). Although only a fraction of the American population actually lives in these planned developments, these neighborhoods, defined by physical and legal boundaries, emphasize the potential range of effects that geographic places can have on their members and on those individuals who are on the "outside." Homeowners' associations in these walled

---

property values. Emotions ran high at times, and although environmental and homeowner concerns were clear motivations for the opposition, values and self-interest were often entwined with people's perceptions of Us and Them. Tolerance of other communities was not always a paramount consideration, with one local resident suggesting that the fishing line be strung using Christian crosses and Muslim crescents (AP 2006).

neighborhoods provide and maintain roadways, sanitation, police protection, sidewalks, streetlights, and parks and recreation (swimming pool, clubhouse, tennis, playground, park, basketball), and libraries (Blakely and Snyder 1997, 24–5). They also lobby to receive tax adjustments because they provide these services for themselves, and have been successful in a number of states already in restricting their local tax burdens so that they do not have to pay to fix *other* people's problems. In other words, in the extreme, people living in these places are willing to help one another and few others, at least through taxes that support public services.[2]

This pattern holds true at larger geographic units as well. Sandy Springs, a largely white and wealthy community in Georgia, for example, chose to incorporate as a city so its residents would be free from the rest of Fulton County (which contains Atlanta) (Dewan 2006). Feeling that they subsidized police and fire services in poorer parts of the county, they chose to leave with their $70 million in tax revenues and privatize their own municipal services.

Even when outsiders are not so sharply defined by class, there can be resentment about paying taxes to benefit people who fall outside the imagined community. Residents in New York chose to incorporate into villages in order to prevent Kiryas Joel – a nearby village populated by ultra-Orthodox Jews, many of whom rely on public assistance because of their large families – from expanding into their communities (Santos 2006).

Although financial choices often drive these boundary-drawing decisions, sometimes there is conflict over who in the community should benefit from these choices; if outsiders bring in revenue, should they be allowed to join? For example, because of the increasing costs of college, a number of state schools are admitting out-of-state students (with their higher tuition payments, required of nonresidents) more quickly and with more perks than in-state applicants. The colleges argue that these nonresidents often choose to stay in the state after graduation, helping the state's economy. However, this is not always a convincing argument; as one state representative said, "It was anathema to me that this university is funded by taxpayers who are being denied acceptance while out-of-state [students] are allowed to come in" (Marklein 2006, 2A). The purpose of the state's college system is in conflict: should it serve the state's residents,

[2] This pattern of interest-driven behavior coincides with that studied by scholars of tax revolts (Sears and Citrin 1985).

who subsidize its operation, or should its desire for greater revenue (and possibly more widespread renown and prestige) favor out-of-state students? Who is Us, and which path gives Us the greater benefit?

THE IMAGINED NATURE OF GEOGRAPHIC COMMUNITIES

As people move across the country, it is reasonable to expect that their sense of geographic community may change. Some may shed their old communities and adopt new ones as part of remaking themselves and starting new lives; others may leave their hearts and communities "back home," while they feel compelled to move in search of better economic opportunities. However, a person's sense of geographic community does not depend on where she lives; she may be born, live, and die in the same town and yet never really feel a sense of belonging with her fellow townspeople. In other words, one's perceptions of community can be affected by both physical movement across boundaries and psychological placement within or outside imagined community boundaries.

In their work on identification with dwelling, community, and region, Cuba and Hummon (1993) define what they call "place identity" and its functions in the following manner:

...place identity can be defined as an interpretation of self that uses environmental meaning to symbolize or situate identity. Like other forms of identity, place identity answers the question – Who am I? – by countering – Where am I? Or Where do I belong? From a social psychological perspective, place identities are thought to arise because places, as bounded locales imbued with personal, social, and cultural meanings, provide a significant framework in which identity is constructed, maintained, and transformed. (112)

This definition is helpful in situating the discussion of geographic communities or place identities in the framework of social psychology and social identity theory discussed in Chapter 2. However, a discussion of geographic *community* shifts the focus from ties to a place to ties to the people living in that place. In other words, I am interested in whether people feel a sense of community living in California with other Californians, for example, and not whether they commune with the land and its mountains and beaches.[3]

---

[3] Higher place attachment (to the environment and the landscape), however, can lead to actions intended to maintain qualities of a place or setting (Clayton and Opotow 2003; Stedman 2002). Scholars have also found that people's sense of identity is affected by moving, that people can refuse to move despite the possible recurrence of a major

What do people believe holds the members of their community together? There are a number of ways to operationalize this "glue" in one's measures of community: contact and interaction caused by proximity, and similar function, interests, values, norms, and feelings. A sense of similarity also may arise from shared addresses or shared experiences. Rural sociologists, for example, often define "community" as the town, city, or "place" in or near where one resides, shops, and receives services, and the rural area around it (see, for example, Allensworth and Rochin 1998; Fernandez and Dillman 1979).[4] Respondents in these studies are asked to identify their communities based on this definition. The implicit assumption is that geographic proximity determines the people with whom one interacts on a daily basis, and that proximity and interaction determine one's community.

However, some problems arise from simply assuming that town limits or census districts define communities, whether individual members share contact, function, or interests in common. It is doubtful that average citizens often know or "see" the exact official boundaries of their town or place. Also, these "objective" lines all begin as subjective creations by human minds, creations that can shift over time. Perceptions of "pictures in our heads" precede the drawing of any lines on a physical map (Lippmann 1965; Scherzer 1992), so one could argue that imagined boundaries are at root the important ones. Pioneering work by Galpin (1915) and de Vasconcelos Barros (1957) captured this perception of the social boundaries of rural communities. They identified these boundaries by locating the major services and agencies of a place and then locating the main and neighborhood roads leading from the center into the rural areas; asking local merchants to locate their most distant customers on a map; and interviewing residents about who they believed lived on the outermost limits of the area and their level of engagement and contact with other individuals. Boundaries of community were *then* drawn, based on these interpersonal interactions.[5] Thus, people's imagined community

disaster, and that people still express positive ties to places even when the living conditions are strained (Feldman 1990). The aftermath of Hurricane Katrina has provided a vivid example (Nossiter 2006).

[4] The census geographical unit of "place" is defined as a "community," and "places" are densely settled concentrations of people that are identifiable by name but are not legally incorporated.

[5] For a replication and extension, see, for example, Haga and Folse 1971. However, even if the boundaries of a community are subjective, the researcher still needs to know which community the respondent is picturing in her mind. Communities defined by function and interaction can be impossible to study if there is no clear and unambiguous referent,

boundaries form the basis for the outlines of locales that later may become institutionalized.[6]

Even the exact location of regional borders may differ from person to person. Ayers et al. explain that as Americans have become more disillusioned by "big structures and transhistorical dreams," they have turned their focus (and hearts) away from the nation-state to regions (1996, 2).[7] Even if the focus moves from the more immediate to a larger scale, regional communities are also imagined. If the boundaries of a man's community surround the people living in "the South," this definition still relies on his knowledge of approximately where the Mason-Dixon line was drawn. Even that line, however, is perceived differently in the minds of residents of border states than it is in elementary school textbooks; Kentuckians would be quick to disagree, for example, that Southern hospitality and culture stop at the Tennessee border.[8]

Kirp emphasizes the point that borders can be both objective and subjective in his book *Almost Home* (2000). On the one hand, he refers to the figurative walls of zoning laws designed to keep out the "wrong" type of people, and the literal walls of some planned developments.[9] On the other hand, the zones and gated community walls are often based on the attitudes that people in the areas hold about who is part of Us versus

---

consistent across all subjects studied, for the entity being evaluated (Molnar et al. 1979; Seilers and Summers 1974). For example, researchers have developed models of "community satisfaction" that incorporate satisfaction with services such as water, sewage, garbage, telephone, fire protection, health care, public schools, and recreation – all without much justification for their particular unit of analysis. As such, the functional nature of a community is captured without knowing to which particular community a respondent is referring.

[6] Blake points out that although borders may seem "morally arbitrary" because they result from what appear to be historical accidents, "they acquire moral significance on account of what takes place within them" (2001, cited by Macedo 2008, 25). Posner (2004) provides evidence that geographic boundaries can trump ethnic ones.

[7] As I will show in this chapter, it is not at all obvious that Americans are, in fact, turning away from the nation to smaller geographic units.

[8] The same subjectivity of borders exists at all levels, even ones with which individuals have the most direct, personal interaction (Guest and Lee 1984). MacDonald (1998) finds that even among members of neighborhood groups, no one drew their neighborhoods to include the same blocks. Even long-term residence and interest in local politics do not guarantee agreement about how to draw maps of one's neighborhood.

[9] These walls also affect questions of rights and responsibilities. For example, should Greenwich, Connecticut, be allowed to have a residents-only beach (Herszenhorn 2001)? Should a "retirement community" be free from fees that help pay for school construction (*New York Times* 2000)? And should a city neighborhood, regardless of its liberal reputation, be able to keep out a nursing facility for AIDS patients (Balin 1999)?

Them. These walls – both invisible and visible, objective and subjective – are built to create exclusivity, clearly demarcating who belongs and who does not, just as sharply as the moats of yore were crossed only by the privileged.[10]

At the same time that these new developments often make clear where the physical boundaries of the neighborhood are drawn with gates and fences, the planners are also trying to break down the walls *within* the planned development that surround people's dwellings. One developer described his work to Blakely and Snyder as an attempt to broaden a resident's feeling of community:

> When you drive home, you would feel that you were home at one of two places: when you turn onto your street or when you turn into your driveway. When I put a gate on an entrance, I can extend that feeling of home, which is so strong in you, it feels unbelievable. I can extend it from as far away as your house is from the gate. (1997, 19)

In other words, a "sense of community" can range from one's dwelling to one's neighborhood and beyond.

Citizens' definitions of their communities can also focus on similarity of attitudes and a common feeling of belonging – different measures again of *subjective* perceptions of a community, not its actual physical boundaries. A person's community can be seen as sharing its own set of values and common norms of social behavior, and this solidarity can be measured as consensus about behavior, community spirit, interpersonal relations, and family responsibility toward others (Fessler 1952). The rural sociologists Haga and Folse (1971), for example, found that belonging to or identification with a community is primarily a symbolic relationship based on sentiment, not on economics.[11]

Community psychologists have also found that a "sense of community" may affect the health of an area's residents and the social capital of a place.[12] In their seminal article on a "Psychological Sense of Community" (PSC), McMillan and Chavis (1986) define a sense of community as a feeling that members have of belonging, a feeling that members matter to one another and to the group, and a shared faith that members' needs

---

[10] Obviously, one's subjective and objective communities may, in fact, be identical.

[11] They also found that distance is the most reliable predictor of community identity patterns, bringing the focus back to geographic proximity.

[12] Community psychologists also discuss a number of concepts that are related to a "sense of community," including community attachment, community identification, neighborhood cohesion, neighboring, community satisfaction, neighborhood attachment, and community involvement (Bolan 1997; Fernandez and Dillman 1979).

will be met through this commitment to be together. In other words, PSC is a way of measuring what holds people together in a community, capturing identity, shared needs, and emotional connections.

Measurement of PSC has varied from Glynn's (1981) scale of 120 Likert-style items – half of which measure perceptions of one's own community, and half of which refer to one's ideal community – to Davidson and Cotter's (1993) scale, which asked respondents to agree or disagree with the following five statements:

1. I feel like I belong here.
2. When I travel I am proud to tell others where I live.
3. It would take a lot for me to move away from this city.
4. I like the neighborhood in which I live.
5. This city gives me an opportunity to do a lot of different things.

Readers of this work may find it difficult to distinguish between indicators of a "sense of community" and variables cast as measured outcomes of that sense. For example, in some research more civic participation and more contact with neighbors are considered indicators of a greater sense of community (Foley 1952; Hunter 1975). In other studies, participation and contact are measured outcomes of a sense of community (Davidson and Cotter 1986, 1993; Pretty 1990).[13] This confusion in measurement is something to avoid: an individual's imagined community may have political effects, but it is not automatic. In my analyses, political attitudes and behavior are something to be explained by a sense of community, not elements of the measurement of this concept.

Even though the conceptualization of a "psychological sense of community" always includes a number of possibilities for types of "community," almost all articles in both rural sociology and community psychology pertain to geographic communities. Towns and villages – the subject of rural sociologists – with barn-raisings, quilting bees, tavern discussions, and first-name interactions between merchants and consumers, have long provided the images of the proper breeding ground for a psychological sense of community (Glynn 1981, 791).

---

[13] Along a similar vein, scholars argue that social capital could be strengthened by greater interaction between neighbors or residents in a city (Fischer 1982; Frug 1996; Putnam 2000).

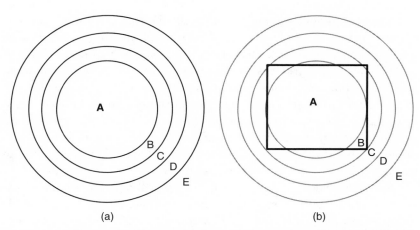

(a)   (b)

FIGURE 3.1. Geographic Community from the Perspective of Person A. The concentric circles in (a) represent A's neighborhood, city, state, and nation. In (b), the bold box represents A's imagined community, extending beyond her neighbors to include B, a fellow resident of her city.

MEASURING THE BOUNDARIES OF GEOGRAPHIC COMMUNITIES

Surveys show that Americans feel close to their neighbors (Table 2.1) and feel a sense of community with people in their neighborhood and city (Table 2.6). But if a "feeling of home" can extend to a neighborhood gate, it may be possible to push that sentiment even farther afield. Do Americans feel close to larger geographic areas in the same way that they feel close to their neighborhoods? As one moves further and further away from one's dwelling, what is the extent or limit of communities defined geographically?

Figure 3.1(a) provides a simple schematic representation of how individual A can be situated within geographic concentric circles that represent A's neighborhood, city, state, and nation, for example.[14] B is

---

[14] Nussbaum writes that the Stoics perceived individuals to be at the center of concentric circles, with the innermost circle around the self and the outermost reserved for "humanity as a whole" (1996, 9). This image of concentric circles is also used by Brewer to represent social identity theory, with personal identity at the center, surrounded by rings of social identities (1991, 476). Shue (1988) also uses the image of the concentric circles formed when a pebble is thrown into water, but assumes that adjacent circles represent *physical* proximity; this assumption is not necessary, and it limits the applicability of the circle metaphor.

a neighbor, C is another resident of A's city, D lives in A's state, and E is another American. Some rural sociologists and community psychologists would simply assume that a variety of these geographic locales mattered to A; Figure 3.1(b) provides another way of thinking about A's outlook. The box in bold represents the community that A imagines; the boundaries of her community include her neighborhood, and she considers B to be part of her community. Of course, A could also have "drawn" a larger box in her mind, extending her community to the limits of her state, or drawn no box in the diagram, choosing to imagine her community in ways that do not coincide with where she lives.

I now turn to determining how this theoretical representation matches with empirical reality: I examine what geographic locales inspire people to feel a sense of closeness and of community. Using "closeness" measures similar to those described in the previous chapter, I examine and compare the perceptions of community boundaries based on one's neighborhood, city, state, country, and continent.

Do people feel close to multiple, different areas? And if so, which ones are more popular as sources of a sense of community? The data I use to answer these questions are from the 1996 General Social Survey (GSS), which is a national survey of 2,904 Americans, conducted by the National Opinion Research Center (NORC) as a part of its biannual survey series. The 1996 GSS asks respondents the following set of questions:

To begin, we have some questions about *where* you live: your neighborhood or village, your town or city, your county, and so on. (By "neighborhood" we mean the part of the town/city you live in. If you live in a village, we take this as your "neighborhood.") How close do you feel to…

A. Your neighborhood (or village)
B. Your town or city
C. Your state
D. America
E. North America

The options ranged from "very close" to "not close at all." The question does not clarify what is meant by "close," although given the list of geographic places that form, in essence, circles centered on the respondent's home, physical distance alone cannot be the focus; after all, it is difficult to explain how *close* one feels to something that one is *in*. Instead, the most likely interpretation is that "closeness" to a place is seen as "closeness" to the people who make up that place, with the concomitant ambiguity about what "closeness to people" means, mentioned in the last chapter. The emphasis is on subjective definitions of community,

TABLE 3.1. *Closeness to Geographic Area*

How close do you feel to...

	Very Close	Close	Not Very Close	Not Close at All
Your Neighborhood	15%	42	31	13
Your Town or City	13%	47	31	8
Your State	14%	48	28	10
America	35%	46	15	4
North America	18%	41	30	12

Data: 1996 General Social Survey. (Row percentages are reported.)

since how people imagine their neighborhoods, and nation, for example, affects whether they will feel close or not.

People may, of course, have multiple geographic communities. As Cuba and Hummon argue, people can "locate a sense of self in more than one place and that some configurations of place loci are more likely to arise than others" (1993, 122). However, while they may live in a particular town, county, state, and nation – and recognize themselves as residents – it does not automatically follow that they will feel a sense of community with others of any of these locales. In situations where an individual is not able to live with others like herself – however she imagines such similarity – then it follows that she may be less likely to imagine her community as including any of her neighbors.

Table 3.1 shows it is clear that Americans feel close to the different areas in which they live, and a majority feels close to all of the geographic units listed. There is, however, clearly variance in opinions, such that we cannot assume residents feel their community consists of all the areas in which they live. Only 7 percent of the sample do not feel close to any of the locales presented as options. In Chapter 2, I explained that "closeness" measures can be used to measure group identification and one's imagined community, so one could argue that about six out of ten Americans identify with their neighborhoods or that they consider their neighborhood to constitute a geographic community.[15] If we compare these results with the "sense of community" questions from the Social Capital Benchmark

[15] The addition of objective group membership is moot given the question wording; you cannot be asked about feelings of closeness to *your* neighborhood if you do not also live in that neighborhood.

Survey and the closeness battery in the 1997 NES Pilot Study, there is strong corroboration that Americans feel close to their neighbors and draw the boundaries of their community to include their neighborhood.[16] However, it is far from a universal response, despite the popular usage equating "community" with the neighborhood in which one lives.

Comparing the responses in Table 3.1, we can also see that the different geographic locales are not viewed identically: although 57 percent of respondents said they feel "very close" or "close" to their neighborhood, 81 percent feel "very close" or "close" to America. A respondent's neighborhood, city, state, country, and continent are concentric circles forming larger and larger geographic units in which individuals live, but it is clear that the size of the circle does not always determine an individual's sense of belonging within it. Physical proximity and interaction with other residents are not the only determinants of where boundaries of community are drawn. The aftermath of Hurricane Katrina provided a vivid example that proximity does not define one's community. The residents of Baton Rouge did not welcome displaced residents of New Orleans with open arms; instead, gun sales increased.

Nevertheless, as Table 3.2 shows, the correlations between these items indicate that units that are closer in distance (theoretically) are more strongly related. For example, the correlation between closeness to one's neighborhood and one's city is stronger than that between closeness to one's neighborhood and one's state. Furthermore, factor analyses of the "closeness" items show that respondents' neighborhoods, cities, and states load on one factor, while America and North America load on a separate factor.

What is also clear from Table 3.1 is that America occupies a unique position in the minds of Americans, which is why the next chapter focuses solely on the national community. America stands out, with respondents clearly feeling closer to America or imagining their nation as an important community, more than with any other locale. If respondents only feel

---

[16] In the 1997 NES Pilot Study, 45 percent said that they felt close to their neighbors. I believe the difference between the NES and GSS responses are largely results of different question wording – "neighbors" in the NES and "neighborhood" in the GSS, and "closeness" is not explained as sharing "ideas and interests and feelings about things" in the GSS – as well as the different question formats. In the GSS, respondents are asked about each locale separately, whereas in the NES, respondents looked at a long list and stated to which groups on the list they felt close. The NES response options were also dichotomous, while the GSS had four categories. The importance of neighborhood to people's senses of community is confirmed in the continuing importance of social ties at the neighborhood level (see Guest and Wierzbicki 1999 for an analysis of social ties using the 1974–1996 GSS.)

TABLE 3.2. *Correlations between Geographic Closeness*

	Neighborhood	City	State	America	North America
Neighborhood	1.00				
City	.58	1.00			
State	.37	.56	1.00		
America	.20	.32	.51	1.00	
North America	.17	.22	.38	.56	1.00

N = 1,197
Data: 1996 General Social Survey.

close to one geographic area, America and then their neighborhood are the "easiest" or most common choices: 47 percent of those respondents who felt close to only one geographic community chose America and 32 percent chose their neighborhood. For other respondents, closeness to one's city or town, state, or North America comes only *in addition to* identification with one's neighborhood or as an American.[17]

POTENTIAL PREDICTORS OF IMAGINED GEOGRAPHIC COMMUNITIES

Who feels they are a part of a geographic community, at whatever level? And, are there different explanations for closeness to one's city than to one's nation, for example?

One major factor that scholars have found affects people's willingness to put down roots is their level of *investment*. For example, do they own their own home? Some scholars have argued that home ownership alone is the major factor in explaining the dropping rates of residential mobility in the United States.

Owners are more likely than renters to have a stake in the quality of life in the location of their home and therefore act as "homevoters" (Fischel

[17] These findings are largely consistent with those from the World Values Survey. Furia (2001) finds that when respondents are asked, "Which of these geographical groups would you say you belong to first of all?" Locality or "town where you live" is chosen most frequently, then "your country as a whole." This was true whether he analyzed surveys ranging from fifty-four countries from 1981 to 1997, or with a panel of ten countries over the entire time period. Although the percentages fluctuated, the order remained the same in terms of importance of identity: town, nation, province, world, and finally, continent.

2001; Highton 1997). And home ownership would probably have an effect on feelings of closeness to one's place of residence. The causal story may run in the opposite direction, though; feelings of community and closeness to a particular geographic area may also lead an individual to decide to settle or buy in that locale. I will apply the research on moving to my research on imagined communities.

Between March 1999 and March 2000, for example, 43.4 million Americans moved (Schachter 2001). More than half these moves (56 percent) were local (within the same county), 20 percent were between counties in the same state, 19 percent were moves to a different state, and 4 percent of movers came from abroad. These figures are not unique: about 16 to 17 percent of Americans have moved each year from 1990 to 2000.

Several factors may play a role in whether people choose to move or stay in an area, which may also affect their sense of community. In 1998, the Current Population Survey showed that among the reasons movers gave for their actions, 20 percent mentioned their careers, 26 percent mentioned family, and 45 percent mentioned housing (Fischer 2002, 185). Career opportunities are one of the reasons the college-educated tend to make more moves across county lines relative to those with less education (Fischer 2002, 184). Researchers have found that employees are reluctant to accept moves between dissimilar communities (i.e., rural vs. urban) (Noe and Barber 1993). Family status also plays a role in mobility choices, as the presence of children at various stages in life affects judgments about housing needs (Lee et al. 1994). It is hypothesized that being married and having children may create a sense of "settling down" that results in a greater feeling of attachment to one's place of residence, much like home ownership. It is often through friends of spouses and children that individuals' local social networks expand and they set down roots. In addition, the presence of children could lead to a greater concern about the services provided in the local area, such as schools and recreation parks. Older individuals and married ones are less likely to move, and the presence of young children also deters moves from cities to suburbs (South and Crowder 1997); however, the younger the children, the greater the probability of moving, relative to those families with children in schools (Long 1972). And resources matter; those who are economically marginal – such as elderly renters and service workers – experience high rates of mobility (Fischer 2002). Therefore, in applying the research on moving to imagined communities, I will look at the effects of education, income, parenthood, marital status, and home ownership.

Length of residence is also related to choices to move. As Highton (1997, 573) writes, "...mobility indicates lack of community integration and connectedness." Does an individual have a network of friends in the area? Is she satisfied with her local neighborhood as a place to live? With each affirmative answer, an American's sense of belonging in a locale may grow, and the desire to leave may diminish. Residential satisfaction, for example, is related both to the desire to move and to actual mobility in the following year (Speare 1974). Satisfaction decreases with rising levels of crime and congestion in people's surroundings (Lee et al. 1994, 249). Overall, when people are satisfied with their neighborhood, they feel a stronger sense of attachment to it and expect any future changes in it to be positive, and ultimately are less likely to think about leaving (Lee et al. 1994, 261).

Social scientists believed that the greater the "rootedness" in a location, the stronger the social ties and sense of home that individuals could draw from in their daily lives (Fischer 2002). Just as research conducted before purchasing a house gives buyers more information about their potential new home, simply living in an area for a longer period of time allows an individual to become familiar with his neighborhood and city and develop a greater sense of attachment and identification with the area (Gerson et al. 1977; Sampson 1988). The longer he lives in the same place, life-cycle and socioeconomic considerations play a smaller and smaller role in influencing the building and maintenance of social networks (Tobey et al. 1990, 1412). The neighborhoods in which these stable residents live are also more orderly and have less crime; social links and structures have solidified over time, as neighbors spend time with each other, control the children and others in these surroundings, and have a stake in the well-being of the area in which they live (Fischer 2002, 180). As Herting and his colleagues explain, "...high rates of persistence not only signal the operation of spatial boundaries, but further strengthen those boundaries by providing the demographic continuity needed to reproduce region-specific cultures and behaviors" (1997, 268).[18]

---

[18] Of course, rootedness alone cannot maintain a community. The occasional news story appears, for example, about an American town that is dying, often in more rural areas (Egan 2003). The young people move away to the cities in search of better educational or job opportunities and no newcomers replace them. Regardless of how long the "old-timers" remain, mortality is inevitable, and the population size trickles down until the institutional structures of a town cannot be sustained. In the extreme, there may come a time for a town to die, as in Ogama, Japan, where the remaining eight elderly

Age may have an effect on one's closeness to one's geographic communities like that of length of residence: older respondents may have more free time and therefore engage in more activities where they live, but they may also have lived longer in a geographic area than their younger counterparts (Goudy 1982; Sampson 1988). And, because the nation is also a potential source of feelings of community, tenure in the country, that is, being born in or immigrating to the United States, may also lead to greater identification with America, if not also other geographic areas. Therefore, in addition to tenure, I will also examine the effects of age and birthplace.

In addition to individual-level characteristics, the environment in which a person lives may also affect her perceptions of where her community boundaries are drawn. Researchers have identified a number of variables related to residential environments that may affect an individual's perception of community boundaries; heterogeneity along a number of different dimensions can lead to redrawing community boundaries to include only those individuals with whom one feels one belongs. For example, the effects of racial homogeneity or heterogeneity on whites have been a focus of research with a long and noted history, resulting in a number of different theories (Glaser 1994; Key 1949; Lichter et al. 2007; Oliver and Mendelberg 2000; Wong 2007). Contact theory, for example, predicts that interaction will lead to more positive intergroup relations – if certain conditions hold – while the power threat hypothesis poses the idea that the larger the outgroup, the more intense the feelings of intergroup competition and outgroup hostility. The theories do not predict how racial diversity will affect attitudes about an individual's community specifically, although one could assume that intergroup hostility within a contained locale will diminish an individual's sense of geographic community; at the very least, intergroup amicability will not make her more estranged from her neighborhood. One may even imagine situations where intergroup harmony increases feelings of community within a locale.

Racial and economic heterogeneity in an area can also lead to less trust, more discomfort interacting with others, and less social capital, if people's perceptions of community are based on racial or economic homogeneity (Alesina and Ferrera 2000; Glaeser et al. 2000; Stolle et al. 2008). Nevertheless, Oliver (2001) has found that heterogeneity in a suburb can

residents decided to move from their ancestral land and sell it to a waste management company for a landfill (Onishi 2006).

lead to more political participation. Context and the environment in which people live may affect their feelings of community and their subsequent political attitudes and actions in a number of different ways.[19]

MEASURING THE PREDICTORS OF IMAGINED GEOGRAPHIC COMMUNITIES

To test these ideas, I regressed closeness to the different locales on these predictors for tenure, immigrant generation, age, parenthood, marital status, and home ownership, controlling for other sociodemographic characteristics (including race, education, income, gender, and region). Previous research indicates that women are more likely to use their home as a spatial reference point for their community than men (Krupat 1985); individuals of different races have very different perceptions of both an "integrated" neighborhood and an "ideal" community (Krysan and Farley 2002); and region is a very blunt instrument for capturing some of the racial differences and politics between the South and non-South in the United States. Measures of socioeconomic status can determine if people feel close to the people living around them; some prefer homogeneity in their surroundings while others do not, but in either situation, a certain level of income is often needed for people to live where they would like to live. As one of the individuals interviewed in Wolfe's Middle Class Morality Project explained, "... coming from an environment where I lived in upper-middle-class neighborhoods all my life, I was not ready to settle for anything less. That's the bottom line. I was not going to settle for anything less than being in an upper-middle-class community" (Wolfe 1998, 185). This desire to feel comfortable (which is probably related to feeling close to one's neighbors) may be more than some people can afford, and if they cannot live where they want, they may not develop close feelings to their neighborhood.

As Figure 3.2 shows, the one variable that is consistently related to identification with all geographic communities is age: the older a respondent, the more likely he is to feel close to his neighborhood, town, state, country, and continent. Given the data, one cannot discern if older respondents are more likely to feel close to their local areas because of an aging effect, compared with a cohort effect. Despite intuitions about

[19] Because the focus of this body of research primarily has been on whites and blacks, and my measure of racial context from the GSS is descriptions by respondents of whether they have black neighbors, I limit the use of this predictor in the GSS analyses to white and black respondents asked about their neighborhood.

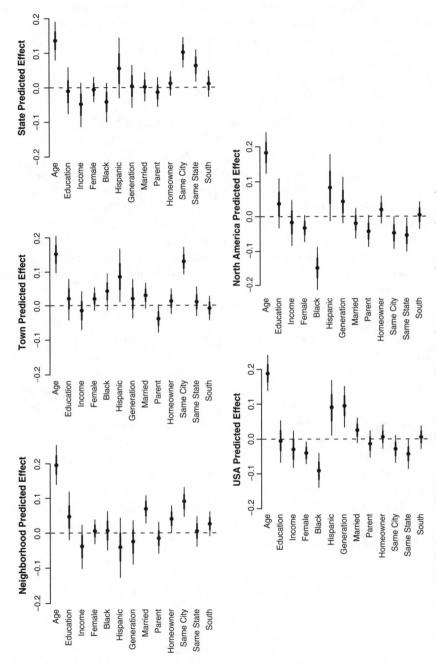

FIGURE 3.2. The Relationships Between Closeness to Geographic Areas and Personal Attributes.
Data: 1996 General Social Survey.

84

interests and investments to the contrary, socioeconomic status has little or no effect on where community boundaries are drawn. In other words, wealthier individuals who can afford to live in neighborhoods (or cities, counties, and so on) of their choosing are no more likely to feel close to their neighbors than are poorer individuals whose housing choices (and choice of neighbors and neighborhood amenities) are much more limited. Home ownership does have an effect in the hypothesized direction for identification with one's neighborhood, with owners more likely than renters to feel attached to their local community. This could be caused by self-interest and investment in one's property, or it could be a result of self-selection: those who feel a sense of community with a neighborhood and its residents may be more likely to buy rather than rent. However, home ownership has no effect beyond the neighborhood. Married respondents were also more likely to feel close to their neighborhood (and town, given a one-tailed test of significance), although parenthood has no effect on closeness to neighborhood and it has a negative relationship to closeness to one's town or city. Also as predicted, immigrant status has an effect on identification with America, with immigrants less likely than second and subsequent generations to feel that the United States defines the bounds of their community. Hispanics are more likely to feel close to the United States than are non-Hispanic whites.[20]

Tenure is operationalized by two dummy variables, one of which asks whether the respondent is living in the same city as when she was 16 years old, and another that asks if she is living in the same state but a different city than when she was 16. (The comparison is with respondents who live in different states than when they were teenagers.) For feelings of closeness to one's neighborhood, city, and state, living in the same city since one's adolescence has a significant effect: those who live in the same city as when they were 16 are more likely to imagine these as forming their geographic communities. Living in the same state since childhood also leads to feelings of closeness to one's state. On the other hand, tenure in the same city and state throughout one's adult life leads one to feel less close to both the United States and to North America. One reason for the change in direction of the effect of tenure, depending on the geographic community specified, may be that individuals who have lived in the same city or state for their entire adult lives are more

---

[20] Hispanics are also more likely than whites to feel close to their city and to North America (p<.10). However, caution must be applied to interpreting all of these results, given that there were fewer than 120 Hispanics in the entire 1996 GSS sample, and the closeness items were only asked of half the sample.

parochial in outlook. By not living in different areas in their country and continent, they may be less cosmopolitan and draw the boundaries of their communities closer to where they have always lived. In contrast, respondents who have lived in multiple states (if not also countries) in their adulthood may have a sense of belonging to multiple areas across the country or continent, and therefore their sense of closeness or community more appropriately ranges across a broader geographic swath.[21] From the data, we cannot determine if the moves (or choices to remain) are voluntary or not.

Across the geographic regions, it appears that advanced age is the one consistent factor related to a greater sense of geographic community. Long-term residence in one's city or state is also related to attitudes about all five areas, but while they predict greater closeness to one's neighborhood, town, and state, they are negatively related to closeness to the United States and North America. One could posit that the experience that comes with moving is related to a greater appreciation and closeness with the nation and continent as a whole. Experience may also explain why African Americans are less likely than whites to feel close to the United States and North America, although there is no difference in their attitudes about the smaller geographies. Neighborhoods, towns, and states implemented a variety of practices and laws – ranging from egalitarian to racist –whereas only in the past half century could one argue that the U.S. government (and other countries in North America, perhaps) has tried to embrace blacks fully in the national community.

In analyses to look at the effect of racial context, white and black respondents were analyzed separately. (Results from these analyses are in the Web Appendix: http://carawong.org/Boundaries-Appendix.pdf.) Among white respondents, reporting black neighbors is negatively related to imagining one's neighborhood as one's community: those reporting having any blacks or African Americans living in their neighborhoods are less likely to feel close to their neighborhood. This may be support for the threat hypothesis, and evidence that even if the contact theory were working at the individual level to diminish prejudice and ethnocentrism, racial diversity alone does not walk hand in hand with greater attachment with one's neighborhood. However, the same negative effect

---

[21] Of course, one can be a cosmopolitan in spirit, if not in fact, given the availability of media sources. In addition, the GSS does not provide a measure by which the frequency of travel (domestic and foreign) could be captured.

can be found among black respondents (although it does not reach statistical significance). African Americans who report that they have black neighbors are also less likely to feel close to their neighborhood. This finding – while counterintuitive if one thinks only in terms of threat and contact theories – fits with Harris's research supporting the racial proxy hypothesis: both whites and blacks are averse to neighborhoods with many black residents because they are seen to suffer from poverty, crime, and other social problems (2001). However, it should be noted that white and black respondents' fear of crime near their home has no effect on feelings of closeness to their neighborhood.[22] Furthermore, this effect of racial context is localized: having black neighbors has no effect on white respondents' closeness to their cities or towns.

These results show that Americans feel a sense of community at multiple geographic levels, and their feelings of closeness are related to length of time in an area and the ties they develop as a result. The latter finding provides additional evidence that the closeness question is a good measure of a feeling of community: according to Glynn (1981), length of residency is consistently one of the strongest predictors of a "Psychological Sense of Community." However, the results from Figure 3.2 also indicate that feelings of community are not reducible to any of these objective characteristics. In other words, feelings of community are not simply proxies, for example, for length of residence in one's home.

MEASURING THE WILLINGNESS TO MOVE

One could imagine that a lack of closeness or attachment to a geographic location can be measured by the willingness to move away from the area (Gustafson 2001). The 1996 GSS asked respondents about their attitudes about mobility, in a battery similar to that for measuring geographic closeness:

If you could improve your work or living conditions, how willing or unwilling would you be to...

    A. Move to another neighborhood (or village)
    B. Move to another town or city within this state
    C. Move to another state
    D. Move outside America
    E. Move outside North America

---

[22] Respondents were asked, "Is there any area right around here – that is, within a mile – where you would be afraid to walk alone at night?"

TABLE 3.3. *Willingness to Move*

If you could improve your work or living conditions, how willing or unwilling would you be to move to...

	Very Willing	Fairly Willing	Neither Willing nor Unwilling	Fairly Unwilling	Very Unwilling
Another Neighborhood	35%	36	10	10	10
Another Town or City within this State	24%	34	12	13	16
Another State	21%	23	15	17	25
Outside America	6%	10	12	16	57
Outside North America	6%	9	11	14	60

Data: 1996 General Social Survey.

As Table 3.3 shows, Americans' willingness to move diminishes with distance.[23] At the same time, however, they are largely willing to move at least a little distance to improve their work or living situation. Over half are willing to leave their neighborhoods or towns, and almost half are willing to leave their state for better work or living situations. However, fewer than one in six respondents are willing to move outside the United States or North America.

So, while a majority of respondents said they feel "very close" or "close" to their neighborhood, 71 percent of Americans are also "very willing" or "fairly willing" to move to another neighborhood. And even among those who said that they felt "very close" or "close" to their neighborhood, 66 percent are still "very" or "fairly willing" to move for better work or living conditions. Similarly, among those who feel close to their town, 54 percent are willing to move from their town; among those who feel close to their state, 39 percent are willing to move from their state. In other words, even if people imagine the boundaries of their community to coincide with their neighborhood, for example, they

[23] When one compares the "difficulty" of moving, the results follow in a logical pattern: for example, if a respondent is willing to move from North America, she is also likely to be willing to move from her neighborhood, her town, her state, and her country.

are willing to leave the community for self-interested reasons (where "interest" includes considerations of both economic and living situation concerns).

In contrast, 73 percent of Americans are "very" or "fairly unwilling" to move outside America. And, among those who feel close to America, only 14 percent are willing to leave the country to improve their working or living conditions. Identification with North America is similar: for those who feel close to the continent, only 16 percent are willing to move to another continent.

While almost a quarter of Americans (22 percent) are willing to move to any geographical location in order to improve their lives, 16 percent are unwilling to move at all. Nonetheless, Americans do move frequently. I return to this issue of mobility and Americans' communities in the conclusion of the chapter. One question that arises from the evidence that Americans are quite willing to move, regardless of their feelings of closeness to the area, is whether a sense of community actually means anything. If it is easy to move, then does "community" mean anything beyond a cursory feeling of comfort? Does it have any role in people's decision making and in politics?

MEASURING A "SENSE OF COMMUNITY" WHERE ONE LIVES

Having described some of the different geographic boundaries of people's communities and what predicts feelings of closeness to the various levels, I replicate some of these analyses using different datasets with slightly different question wordings. People's subjective boundaries will be measured by asking them about what gives them a "sense of community," and I will use both a national survey and one conducted in California, each with slightly different question wordings, but both mentioning a "sense of community." If similar results are obtained from a different measure of community across a number of surveys, then we can have greater faith in the robustness of the findings. I then turn to examining what might be the political effects of these feelings of community.

In the 2000 Social Capital Community Benchmark Survey, 80 percent of respondents said that people in their neighborhood gave them "a sense of community or a feeling of belonging"; 79 percent said that living in their city gave them the same feeling. Although there is no explicit reference to "closeness" with this measure, the similarity in responses between the GSS and Social Capital items (given very different question formats)

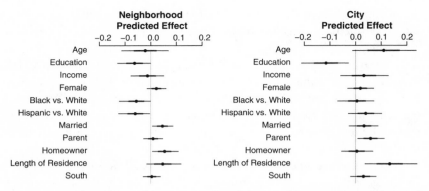

FIGURE 3.3. The Relationships Between Local Senses of Community and Personal Attributes.
Data: Social Capital Community Benchmark Survey 2000.

provides support for the results presented so far.[24] A majority imagines their neighborhood or city as communities, but these responses are not universal despite ordinary language usage equating "community" with one's neighborhood.

Who feels a sense of community in a geographic locale? The hypotheses are similar to those that predicted feelings of closeness to one's neighborhood, city, state, nation, or continent, since the latter are also measures of how people imagine their communities. Therefore, to the extent possible, I replicate the models presented in Figure 3.2. Because birthplace in America is not as relevant to feelings of community in geographic areas other than the nation, tenure in the country is not included in these models.

Figure 3.3 shows the results of logit models predicting whether one's neighbors are seen as a source of community feeling, based on sociodemographic characteristics, marital status, having children at home, region, tenure in the area, and home ownership. The hypotheses are confirmed only partially by the analyses. Similar to the GSS results, respondents who are married are more likely to feel a sense of community with their neighbors than are unmarried individuals. The more educated are less likely than respondents with less education to feel a sense of community, as are blacks and Hispanics (compared with white respondents), which are effects that did not appear in Figure 3.2 with the GSS data. Also in

---

[24] In the models that follow, I restrict the analyses to whites, blacks, and Hispanics in the national sample. There are fewer than 50 Asians in that sample, and diagnostics of the models showed them to be outliers.

contrast with those models predicting feelings of geographic closeness, the effect of age on respondents' "sense of community" with their neighborhood is indistinguishable from zero. The strong effect of home ownership, however, is replicated in these analyses: respondents who own their homes are more likely to feel that their neighbors give them a sense of community than renters. One possible explanation for the differences between the results of the GSS and Social Capital data analyses are the differences in question wording, response options, and year in which the surveys were conducted.[25]

Figure 3.3 also shows the comparable results for whether living in her *city* gives a respondent a sense of community or a feeling of belonging. The predictors of feelings of belonging to neighborhoods and cities differ slightly in statistical, though not substantive, significance. Parenthood is clearly related to how people imagine their communities: parents are more likely to feel a sense of community from living in their city than are non-parents.[26] Those respondents whose tenure in a community is greater are more likely to feel like they belong in their city, but home ownership – as was the case with the GSS data – has no effect on city-level feelings of community. Confirming the GSS results, older respondents are more likely to feel a sense of community with their city than younger respondents. Education again has a significant effect on a respondent's feeling of belonging: the better educated are *less* likely to feel a sense of community living in their city, compared to those individuals with less education. It is difficult to interpret these education relationships with both neighborhood and city community feelings, particularly since education had no effect on feelings of closeness to one's neighborhood or city (Figure 3.2).[27]

---

[25] One difference in the effect for age can be explained by the different relationships with age and home ownership across surveys. The GSS sample is, on average, 12 years older than the Social Capital sample, and the mean age of homeowners in the GSS is 55 compared to 39 for the Social Capital Survey.

[26] Although the variable in both the Social Capital and GSS models is labeled "parenthood," in the latter it refers to having any children, and in the former, respondents are asked about any children 17 or younger in the household. So, one reason for the difference in the relationship between parenthood and community feelings is this distinction: the average ages for non-parents and parents in the GSS are 36 and 49, respectively. In contrast, the average ages are 51 and 37 for the Social Capital survey. Clearly, parents with school-age children (or younger) feel a greater sense of community with their city.

[27] At the bivariate level, there appears to be a weak and largely linear relationship between education and feelings about one's city – with 82% of those with less than a high school degree compared with 75% of those with a graduate degree feeling a

I also reran these models, looking at the effect of racial context on feelings of community (see Web Appendix for the results). For these analyses, I merged 2000 Census tract-level data with the Social Capital Benchmark Survey; the median household income, the percentage of foreign-born residents, and the percentage represented by a respondent's ingroup are the measures of context.[28] The hypotheses are that the smaller one's ingroup in the area, the poorer the tract, and the more foreign-born residents, the less likely one is to feel a sense of community with one's neighborhood or city.[29] Feeling isolated, removed from more affluent surroundings, and not understanding the customs and languages of one's neighbors may diminish one's attachment. The results show that the economic context of one's immediate surroundings had no effect on neighborhood feelings of community, but had strong effects at the city level: for residents of all races, the wealthier one's neighbors, on average, the less likely one was to feel close to one's city. The presence of foreign born in the tract had little effect when they were a small minority; when the percentage of foreign born rose above 40 percent, it had a negative effect on feelings of community at both neighborhood and city levels for whites and blacks (which, admittedly, is not the demographic reality for a large part of the sample). This seems consistent with Coffe and Geys's (2006) findings that there is a significant negative relationship between social capital and the number of nationalities in a municipality.

For white, black, and Hispanic respondents, the more whites, blacks, and Hispanics, respectively, that lived in their city, the more they felt a sense of community with their city. At the neighborhood level, racial context had an effect on feelings of community for black and Hispanic respondents: the greater the percentage of blacks and Hispanics, respectively, that lived in their area, the less likely it was that they would feel a sense of community with their neighborhood; this coincides with the results from the GSS data. However, once their ingroup is less than a quarter of the population in the tract, the percentage of outgroups has a strongly negative effect on community sentiment.

---

    sense of community with their city – but there is little relationship with neighborhood attachment. (The comparable numbers are 73% vs. 76% feeling a sense of community with their neighborhood.)

[28] The survey did not ask respondents if they lived near individuals of different races or ethnicities.

[29] The assumption is that most respondents are not foreign born. There is no question in the survey asking about birthplace, but because less than 7% are noncitizens, one could assume the percentage of foreign born is somewhat greater than that.

Overall, analyses of the Social Capital Survey confirm some of the findings from the General Social Survey about what leads to feelings of closeness or community with one's neighbors and city. Clearly, home ownership and marriage are related to greater neighborhood but not city-level feelings of attachment. Income appears to have no relationship with how one defines one's geographic communities. The greater one's length of residence in an area, the greater one's attachments to one's city or town. And, as might be expected, the effects of context are complicated and nonlinear.

MEASURING THE EFFECTS OF IMAGINED COMMUNITIES ON POLITICAL ATTITUDES AND BEHAVIOR

While living within different geographic units prompts a sense of community among many Americans, it is still an unanswered question whether a sense of belonging has an effect on political decision making. As Calhoun explains, "To know how much a class formed a group, we would need to know more about how influential this category was in determining patterns of association and action and how closely it overlapped with other categories of differentiation" (1991, 60). In order to answer this question about how much geographic communities form politically relevant entities, I examine a number of measures concerning people's locales and the institutions designed to serve them: (1) trust of various groups and institutions, feelings of political efficacy, and feelings of political alienation, (2) civic engagement on behalf of one's community, and (3) tolerance. A sense of community may have an impact on an individual's policy preferences and also affect other political attitudes – such as belief in "voice" and "loyalty" over "exit" (Hirschman 1970) – expressed via one's willingness to engage with the institutions and leaders in the community.[30] For example, are local institutions trusted, and do people feel they have a voice that can and should be heard? A sense of community may also affect one's willingness to work on behalf of Us, while limiting one's tolerance of the Other in society; as I discussed in Chapter 1, feelings of community may have a "dark side" of exclusion that complements the benevolent images of barn-raisings.

---

[30] Exit and voice are the options that Hirschman proposes as options for members when their organization is in decline. Applied to a political body, members can choose to leave (i.e., move) or stay and protest; loyalty to the body or organization can minimize the extent of both exit and voice.

The general hypothesis is that the more an individual derives a sense of community from his neighbors, the more he cares about members of that community and about politics that affect his neighbors, as in *Our Town*. Furthermore, according to Putnam's arguments in *Bowling Alone* (2000), the closer the ties that exist between individuals – the greater the aggregate-level social capital – the greater the sense of trust in others. Here I am interested not in generalized trust, but trust in the institutions that provide the machinery by which community members can assist one another.

Respondents were asked the following question:

...we'd like to know how much you trust different groups of people. First, think about (GROUP). Generally speaking, would you say that you can trust them a lot, some, only a little, or not at all.

Although they were asked about many different groups in society, I focus on the two groups that may have more political consequences: the local news media and the police in the local community. Respondents also were asked how much of the time they could trust the local government to "do what is right." I created an additive index of local trust from these three questions. The hypothesis is that a sense of community with one's neighborhood or city will lead to a stake in the local institutions and government.

It is possible that some individuals are simply more trusting across the board, so I added to this local trust model a control that measures how much the respondent thinks that "generally speaking...most people can be trusted." The other predictors in the model are the measures for "sense of community" with one's neighbors and one's city, the set of independent variables used to predict feelings of community in Figure 3.3 – age, education, income, gender, race, marital status, parenthood, tenure, home ownership, and region – and ideology (see the Appendix in this book for the full model).

The political effects of these "sense of community" measures can extend more broadly beyond questions of political trust. Feelings of belonging in a community may also be related to beliefs in one's ability to influence what happens to its members. Therefore, I also look at the relationships between "sense of community" measures and political alienation and efficacy. The expectation is that the greater one's sense of ties to one's community, the more one may believe that ordinary citizens have a role in the governance of their community. The governance, after all, is responsible for delivering assistance and benefits to community members.

Figure 3.4 also shows models predicting attitudes about political alienation and efficacy, with the same controls as were used in the local

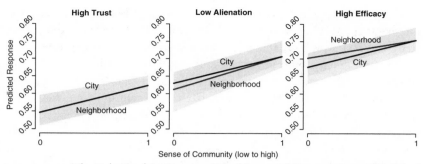

FIGURE 3.4. The Relationships Between Local Senses of Community and Political Trust, Alienation, and Efficacy. Americans who imagine their city and neighbors as their community are more likely to trust local institutions and feel they have a voice in local politics.
Data: Social Capital Community Benchmark Survey 2000.

trust model, minus the general trust measure. Respondents were asked how much they agreed or disagreed with the following statement: "The people running my community don't really care much what happens to me." They were also asked the following: "Overall, how much impact do you think people like you can have in making your community a better place to live?"[31]

Figure 3.4 shows the results of these regression models. Both the city and neighborhood senses of community have a strong impact on trust of local institutions and government. The more that a respondent feels a sense of community from her neighbors or from living in her city, the more she trusts the local media, the local police, and her local government. The effects of the two community measures are almost identical. Furthermore, the inclusion of the generalized trust measure did not change the results: controlling for a belief in the general trustworthiness of people, a sense of community arising from one's neighbors or one's city is still related to greater trust in the political institutions. Only social trust and age had larger effects than community feelings in their relationships with trust in local institutions. Socioeconomic status, ideology, and home ownership had no effect, and respondents' length of residence in their current home had a *negative* relationship with feelings of political trust, so investment in one's locale does not seem to increase one's faith in the local media, police, or government. Regardless of whether

---

[31] These question wordings treat "community" more as a synonym for neighborhood or city (or some fixed geographic unit). A sense of community, on the other hand, is what makes people living in close proximity feel as though they are tied to other members living in their area.

community boundaries are smaller (at the level of the neighborhood) or larger (at the level of the city), feelings of belonging to those communities correspond with greater faith in the communities' institutions.[32]

Are respondents who feel a sense of community with their neighbors or their city also more likely to believe local political leaders care about their constituents and that average citizens can help improve their communities? From the models presented in Figure 3.4, it is clear that the more a respondent feels that her neighbors or city give her a sense of community, the less likely she is to feel politically alienated and the more likely she is to feel politically efficacious. For political alienation, the effects of these localized imagined communities are larger than those of the more typical predictors, education and income; for political efficacy, the strength of their relationships are comparable. The coefficients for ideology and length of residence are indistinguishable from zero for both alienation and efficacy; home ownership only has a small, significant relationship with efficacy, despite the notion that owning property in the area would lead a resident to feel the rootedness and stake necessary for feeling efficacious. Instead, it is by imagining her neighborhood and city as her community that allows her to feel that she can have an impact on her community and is part of a collective enterprise.[33]

A sense of geographic community is also strongly related to political behavior. Lelieveldt (2004), for example, found that neighborliness and a sense of duty to the neighborhood were related to a willingness to engage in both informal and formal activities to improve the neighborhood. Of course, there are both potentially positive and negative attitudes and actions one can take on behalf of one's community: one may work on behalf of the community, and one may also work to exclude or purge the Other from one's community. Figure 3.5 explores both the light and dark sides of community. Respondents were asked the following three questions about their civic engagement:

In the past two years, have you worked with others to get people in your immediate neighborhood to work together to fix or improve something?[34]

---

[32] Along a similar vein, Tyler and Lind (1992) found that people are more likely to defer to authorities when they share a common membership, and they are also more likely to focus on procedural justice rather than on the receipt of favorable outcomes.

[33] These cross-sectional data cannot tell a causal story. However, it seems unlikely that trust in the local police, for example, will lead someone to feel a sense of community with his neighbors.

[34] This question was asked of only half the sample.

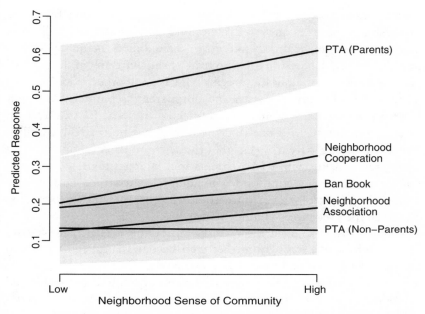

FIGURE 3.5. The Light and Dark Side of Neighborhood Sense of Community. Americans who consider their neighbors part of their community are more likely to engage civically and are more likely to support banning offensive books in the local library.
Data: Social Capital Community Benchmark Survey 2000.

Now I'd like to ask about other kinds of groups and organizations. I'm going to read a list; just answer YES if you have been involved in the past 12 months with this kind of group.

A neighborhood association, like a block association, a homeowners' or tenants' association, or a crime watch group.

A parents' association, like the PTA or PTO, or other school support or service groups.

One could hypothesize that NIMBY concerns will drive homeowners' actions. As Fischel explains, they do not free-ride when it comes to attending zoning hearings and school board meetings, for example; self-interest might limit concerns to one's own home, but public services and local amenities affect the value of the largest single asset that people own. Figure 3.5 shows that a respondent who has a feeling of belonging with her neighbors is more likely to work and meet on behalf of the neighborhood, both formally and informally, than were respondents who did not feel this sense of neighborhood community.[35] This relationship is present even controlling for home ownership, tenure in one's residence, and parenthood, all indicators of greater investment or self-interest in maintaining the quality of the neighborhood. Ideology also has no relationship with any of the types of participation. For the question regarding PTA and other school-related participation, I analyze parents and non-parents separately. As might be expected, very few nonparents are active in local PTAs, and feelings of community with one's neighborhood has no predictive ability. However, among parents, a neighborhood sense of community has a strong relationship with PTA participation. Interests matter, obviously, but imagining a neighborhood community has a strong relationship with action, controlling for interests, socioeconomic status (including NIMBY-type predictors), and ideology.

Not surprisingly, given the research on political participation, education and income strongly predict who becomes engaged in political activity (Rosenstone and Hansen 2003; Verba et al. 1995). However, a neighborhood sense of community has an effect, above and beyond respondents' socioeconomic status. And, it has a greater effect than education even, for explaining working with others to fix a problem.

Of course, the direction of causality could point in the other direction, such that civic engagement leads to a sense of community. By spending time working on behalf of a locale, an individual may become more attached to the place and feel a sense of community with those living in the area. And one could argue that self-interest may prompt the participation rather than feelings of community; I will come back to this possibility in the next section. However, from Figure 3.5, one cannot argue that the models simply provide evidence of social capital; definitions of community boundaries constrain the limits of such capital – engagement and participation occur on behalf of those one considers within one's community.

Replicating what Cuba and Hummon (1993) show in a local study of Cape Cod, analyses of this national sample indicate that social participation is strongly related to community identities. In contrast, a sense of community with one's city has no statistically significant effect on participation on behalf of the neighborhood (analyses not shown here); in other words, there is a match between the feelings of community drawn

---

[35] Because the participation questions refer explicitly to neighborhood and school-level activities, I do not include the city community measure in these models. All other independent variables are the same as in Figure 3.4.

around specific geographical boundaries – the neighborhood – and political participation on behalf of that particular locale.

As I mentioned earlier, there is an expectation that the greater one's sense of ties to one's community, the more one may believe that one's voice can and should be heard. Strong feelings of community may also lead to the belief that numerous, dissenting voices in that community should not be allowed to be aired. Intolerance in the Social Capital Community Benchmark Survey was measured by agreement to the following statement:

A book that most people disapprove of should be kept out of my local public library.

As Figure 3.5 shows, a sense of community with one's neighbors leads to more intolerance: the stronger one's sense of belonging, the greater one's willingness to ban an offensive book, and this is true, controlling for ideology, education, income, and age (see Appendix for the full model). As might be expected, respondents with higher socioeconomic status, liberals, and younger respondents were all more likely to be tolerant than their poorer, less educated, older, and more conservative counterparts. Again, home ownership and length of residence in an area have no impact.

Although the negative relationships at the individual level between a sense of community and alienation in Figure 3.4 coincide with Putnam's aggregate-level findings about social capital, the result about intolerance runs counter to his conclusions, although this difference may be a result of different levels of analyses. In *Bowling Alone*, Putnam argues that "social capital and tolerance go together" (2000, 356). The analyses here show that the more someone feels socially tied or connected with her neighbors, the more intolerant she is of a book that may affect the balance of civility or comfort of her community. It is possible that a sense of community and intolerance are related via neighborhood-level homogeneity, where the homogeneity refers to the similarity or fraternity that leads to feelings of community, not simply racial heterogeneity, for example. There are two possible interpretations of this finding that are related to local context. Intolerance may be a result of the fact that individuals living in a homogeneous area do not welcome the intrusion of Others; the residents all agree on a set of values and the "offensive book" is not consistent with those beliefs. Or an area could be diverse, and its residents may have to police carefully the language used in public to minimize misunderstandings and potential conflict; people may choose to avoid feelings of discomfort at all costs. Both are plausible explanations for why a greater sense of community would lead to greater intolerance.[36] Putnam has found that racial/ethnic homogeneity can lead to greater trust; one can also imagine greater homogeneity leading to greater intolerance. However, when I reran the model for the intolerance dependent variable, adding measures of racial, economic, and immigrant context, none of the environmental measures had an effect on the desire to ban a book, either directly or indirectly via neighborhood feelings of community (see the Web Appendix).

Because one might argue that feelings of community are simply proxies for affect or likeability, I also reran the models in Figures 3.4 and 3.5, with a control for how much individuals liked where they lived. There was no question directly asking respondents how much they liked their neighbors or neighborhood, but the Social Capital Community Benchmark Survey does ask, "Overall, how would you rate your community as a place to live – excellent, good, only fair, or poor?" It is possible that respondents only thought of the physical characteristics of their home or neighborhood, although it is difficult to imagine the cases where someone loves the trees, parks, and shops in her neighborhood; feels no sense of affinity with her neighbors; and *still* would rate her community as an excellent place to live. I assume rating a community as a place to live captures to some extent how much an individual likes where she lives. When the models are rerun with this control for likeability, the substantive results are similar, with only small changes in coefficient sizes and levels of statistical significance: above and beyond how someone rates her community as a place to live, if she feels a sense of community with her neighbors or city, she is more likely to feel a commitment to get involved – whether via feeling trust in local institutions, feeling like she has a voice that will and should be heard, or volunteering on behalf of her neighborhood – and more likely to want to exclude potentially disruptive voices (i.e., books) in her community (results in Web Appendix). Nevertheless, I would argue that feeling positively about one's community as a place to live can be part of why one draws community boundaries where they are drawn, so to focus on changes in coefficient sizes in these additional tests – which do provide evidence that how one imagines one's community is not simply a measure of how much one likes an area or one's neighbors – would be misleading.

---

[36] Although there are many possible dimensions of heterogeneity, using the community samples of the Social Capital Survey, I looked at the effect of racial context on responses to this tolerance question. As with the national sample, the effect of the size of one's racial ingroup in the community has no effect on whether a respondent believes a book should be banned or not.

From the results of these analyses of the 2000 Social Capital Benchmark Survey, it is clear that a sense of community originating from one's neighbors or from living in one's city of residence affects people's political attitudes and behavior. However, in order to get a better understanding of the relationship between feelings of community and attitudes about the redistribution of resources specifically, I turn next to a local survey of the most populous county in the United States. Does having a geographic sense of community mean that individuals are only willing to tax themselves for other members of their community? And is a sense of community different from NIMBY sentiments?

MEASURING THE EFFECTS OF COMMUNITY
VS. INTERESTS ON TAXES

The Public Policy Institute of California (PPIC) regularly conducts surveys to gauge the social, political, and economic attitudes of Californians. In March 2003, PPIC conducted a special survey of Los Angeles County, as part of a new set of surveys focusing on the county (in collaboration with the University of Southern California). Two thousand residents of the county were interviewed in English and Spanish, and they were asked a series of questions about social, political, and economic conditions of the area. A random half of the sample was asked the following:

Would you say the neighborhood you live in has a sense of community, or not?[37]

Sixty-seven percent of the respondents answered "yes," and I use this item as a measure of a sense of community. The other half was asked,

Five years from now, do you see yourself living in the neighborhood you now live in?

If the respondents answered "no," they were then asked, "Do you think that you are likely to move within Los Angeles County, or is it more likely

---

[37] This question wording is slightly different from that used in the Social Capital Benchmark Study. It is not obvious that a neighborhood as a physical entity can *have* a sense of community; this wording is more likely a shorthand for asking whether the residents in a neighborhood feel a sense of community. It is possible that a respondent does not personally feel a sense of community with his neighborhood, even if the neighborhood itself has a sense of community. However, this situation is not common: among the PPIC respondents who believed their neighborhood has a sense of community, 95 percent felt "very" or "somewhat satisfied" with the neighborhood in which they lived. I will come back to this satisfaction question later in the analyses of the PPIC data.

that you'll move outside the county?" Fifty-one percent answered that they thought they would still be living in their current neighborhood, 22 percent thought they would be living elsewhere in Los Angeles County, and 17 percent believed they would be living outside of Los Angeles County in five years. (Ten percent said they did not know.) I use this question as a measure of investment in an area; respondents who believe they would be living in a particular area over the long term may be more invested in its prosperity, both to protect home values and to receive benefits as residents of the area. By assigning a random half of the same to receive either a question about community or investment, the PPIC survey experiment allows me to tease apart the intertwined factors of interests and community definitions. The contrast is whether people's attitudes and actions are guided in similar ways by feelings of community and by NIMBY-like concerns.[38] Fischel argues that mercenary concerns with property values can motivate citizens to organize and make personal sacrifices for such things as public schools. In other words, he believes that positive outcomes are likely when "the motive to do good is lined up with the motive to do well" (2001, 18).

Respondents were also asked a number of questions about taxation for local services:[39]

At this time, would you favor or oppose raising the local sales tax by one cent to fund city-level police, parks, roads, libraries, and other services? (Parks Tax)

At this time, would you favor or oppose new taxes on alcoholic beverages and cigarettes in order to fund county-level public health and medical emergency services? (Sin Tax)

State law requires a two-thirds majority vote to pass any new local special tax. What if there was a state measure that would change the two-thirds requirement to a 55 percent majority vote for passing a local sales tax for transportation projects. Would you vote yes or no? (Easier Tax Vote)

What if there was a measure on the county ballot to increase the local sales tax for transportation projects by one-half cent? Would you vote yes or no? (Transportation Tax)

---

[38] The predictors of attitudes about community and investment are different (see Web Appendix). Older respondents, the less educated, whites, homeowners, and those who have resided in their home longer are more likely to anticipate living in the same place for the next five years. Having children under the age of 18 and being a homeowner are related to feeling a sense of community. Although I was unable to examine the relationship between racial context and community perceptions, the survey did include questions asking about whether respondents feared becoming victims of crime and whether they feared the effects of gangs and graffiti in their neighborhood. A sense of community in the neighborhood was not related to either environmental concern.

[39] Because of the split sample, no one received all the questions.

The respondents were pretty evenly split on the first and third questions, and a majority answered in the affirmative on the second and fourth questions, 64 percent and 59 percent, respectively. All respondents in the sample were asked about their local civic engagement:

On another issue, have you volunteered in your community during the past 12 months? (if yes: on average, about how many hours per week do you spend volunteering – 0 to 2 hours; 3 to 5 hours; 6 to 10 hours; or more?) (Volunteer)

Have you attended a meeting on local or school affairs (in the past 12 months)? (Attend Meeting)

If how people draw the boundaries of their community has an effect on whom they are willing to help, then one should find that those individuals who feel their neighborhood has a sense of community are more willing to pay taxes and spend time working to benefit that community. Ethical particularism would mean that perceived community boundaries limit people's feelings of obligation and responsibility. Arguments about NIMBY-ism would predict similar outcomes: participation and support for taxes as investments in one's real estate property. To test these hypotheses, all of the tax questions and the participation items were regressed on respondents' length of residence at their current addresses, age, education, income, gender, ideology, and either their sense of community or their "long-term" plan to reside in their current home.[40] All variables have been recoded to run from 0 to 1. The comparison is to models that included investment (i.e., intended length of residence) instead of community as a predictor.

Figure 3.6 shows the results, which support the argument that having a geographic sense of community affects individuals' willingness to work and sacrifice. The greater an individual's sense of community in her neighborhood, the more she is willing (1) to support raising the local sales tax for a variety of city-level services including parks, (2) to back a possible measure to make it easier to pass new local special taxes (p<.10), and (3) to increase the local sales tax for transportation projects.[41] Community feelings also led to more hours spent volunteering in the area and meeting

---

[40] Although it would be ideal to include all of the same controls used in the previous models of the GSS and Social Capital datasets, the PPIC survey did not include all of these questions.

[41] I also reran the models with controls for home ownership, race of the respondent, and children under the age of 18, but the addition of these variables did not change the overall pattern of effects (or lack thereof) of community sentiment or investment. I therefore present the more parsimonious models.

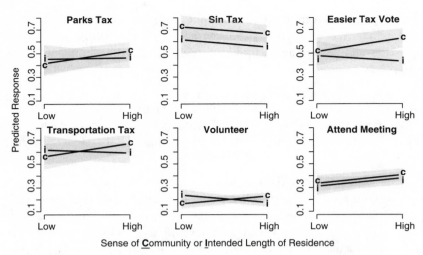

FIGURE 3.6. Neighborhood Sense of Community vs. Investment: Tax Votes and Civic Engagement. While imagining one's community to include one's neighborhood increases support for tax initiatives and participation locally, planning to live in the same area long term does not affect these attitudes or actions.
Data: Public Policy Institute of California 2003.

attendance on behalf of local or school affairs. Only for the sin tax question did a sense of community have no effect.

In contrast, anticipation of living in the neighborhood for the long term had no effect on any of the tax questions and had a negative relationship to volunteering in the neighborhood. In other words, potential worries about one's residential or real estate investment are not related to the types of attitudes and actions that are linked to feelings of community. While the common explanation for decisions in local politics often points to self-interest, at least in the case of these tax initiatives and acts of civic engagement, feelings of community are much more strongly related to decisions to increase taxes for community services, for example, than NIMBY attitudes.

When it comes to issues of taxation, income is another clear indicator of self-interest. Controlling for feelings of community, however, income level is only related to less support for one of the tax items – regarding taxes on alcohol and smoking – included in the survey. Another possible measure of self-interest is tenure, since the longer one's residence in an area, the longer one has a chance to benefit from local services and improved transportation. Controlling for community sentiment, the effect of tenure is only discernible from zero for the transportation item, and it is in the opposite direction from that predicted by self-interest. Instead, the more time one has lived in one's home, the less one wants sales taxes to be spent on improving transportation services.[42]

Of course, ideology is strongly related to attitudes about taxation. Conservatives are more likely to want a smaller role for the state, with private initiatives and organizations being the main source of aid to the needy; liberals are more supportive of the government providing a greater number and array of services for its citizens. Nevertheless, even with respondents' ideological self-identification as a control in the models, a sense of community still has an impact across four of the initiatives concerning taxes. Furthermore, when the same analyses are restricted only to those respondents who identified as conservatives – who arguably should be those individuals *most* opposed to the idea of raising taxes on principle – the results show that a sense of community significantly (statistically and substantively) predicts greater support for raising the local sales tax to fund city-level police, parks, roads, libraries, and other services (see Web Appendix). The investment concerns captured by respondents' intended length of residence, however, have no such effect. The PPIC survey results indicate that even among political conservatives, a sense of community leads to a greater willingness to pay for a variety of local services that can benefit community members. Ideology, of course, matters in predicting support for tax policies, but feelings of community affect political judgments above and beyond these broad values.

To try to separate the effects of a sense of neighborhood community from affect toward the neighborhood, I also reran the models with an additional independent variable in the models: neighborhood satisfaction.[43] Regardless of whether respondents felt a high or low level of satisfaction with their neighborhood, a sense of neighborhood community was still significantly related to support for sales taxes for city-level services, sales taxes for transportation projects, volunteering in the community, and attending meetings on local or school affairs. (See Web Appendix.) I consider neighborhood satisfaction to be strongly tied to whether an individual believes her neighborhood has a sense of community, but even

---

[42] It is possible that long-term residents have already worked out a mode of transportation that minimizes costs for themselves and do not foresee that improvements will affect them significantly or in the near future.

[43] Respondents were asked, "Overall, how satisfied are you with the neighborhood you live in? Are you very satisfied, somewhat satisfied, somewhat dissatisfied, or very dissatisfied?"

controlling for the former, the latter still predicts whether one will support policies to benefit members of the community.

Where people draw the boundaries of their community affects their attitudes about local institutions, efficacy, and tolerance. These boundaries also create a sense of obligation, such that individuals will participate politically on behalf of their community, and tax themselves to increase the welfare of fellow members.

Nevertheless, one could argue that there is a spatial mismatch between the "community" measure – concerning a neighborhood sense of community – and the various tax policy outcomes – largely concerning county-level services.[44] So, although the strength of the community measure in the PPIC survey is that it, too, mentions a "sense of community," one weakness is that the policy measures target benefits to individuals outside those small neighborhood boundaries. Fortuitously, the PPIC survey also includes a question that allows a closer geographic match, asking, "In general, do you most identify with...Southern California, your religion, the place where you were born, your racial or ethnic group, Los Angeles County, your city, or other?"[45] I recoded this item as a dummy variable to focus on respondents who identified most with their county, and reran the models of the tax items and participation questions, adding this measure of county-level identification. As Figure 3.7 shows, considering one's county to be part of one's imagined community predicts support for all four tax items (and does so better than the neighborhood sense of community measure). Individuals who identified most with Los Angeles County, as opposed to their religion or ethnic group or region, for example, were more likely to support tax policies that would benefit other members of their county-level community, controlling for ideological self-identification. *County*-level identification, however, was not consistently related to *neighborhood*-level civic engagement.[46]

So, although an imagined community encompassing a smaller circle may lead to support for policies that benefit some individuals outside that

[44] In California, sales taxes can be both city- and county-wide. The Metro is a subway for Los Angeles County as a whole.
[45] The order of the options was rotated so that the respondents were not always presented with certain choices first.
[46] I also looked at the effect of identification with Southern California, which was the most popular choice (25% of respondents selected this response). This identification with a larger geographic area, however, was not related to support for or opposition to taxes that would be spent to benefit Los Angeles County.

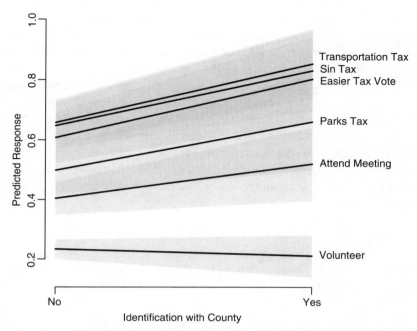

FIGURE 3.7. Identification with Los Angeles County: Tax Votes and Civic Engagement. Imagining one's county as one's community increases support for tax initiatives and participation locally.
Data: Public Policy Institute of California 2003.

circle (e.g., borders drawn at the neighborhood may still lead to support for policies that benefit neighbors *and others beyond those neighborhood lines*), it appears from analyses of both the Social Capital Benchmark Survey and this PPIC survey that community feelings at more expansive levels do not necessarily translate into support for assistance at a more localized level. In some ways, these results are not surprising. Residents may care about the environment in neighboring areas because of reciprocal relationships between locales and because the prosperity of one's community may depend on that of the larger surrounding area. And, if one thinks about the work of the U.S. Congress, legislation is, in fact, often the result of collective parochialisms. Members of Congress are elected to represent local interests – be they at the level of the district or of the state – yet policies that affect (and benefit) the nation are the outcome.

In order to test whether identification with county was more than simply affect or likeability, I also reran the models from Figure 3.7 with a measure asking about the quality of life in the county.[47] The substantive meaning of the results does not change. Whether individuals thought the quality of life was good or poor, identifying with the county led to greater support for taxes for a variety of services for other community members. (See Web Appendix for results.) The experiment asking respondents either about whether their neighborhood had a sense of community or about their intentions to stay in the area provides leverage to understand the effect of community separate from NIMBY or interest concerns. Adding measures for satisfaction or quality of life in one's locales to the models provides evidence that community identification is more than simply affect (even if it will often encompass positive affect).

CONCLUSION

A majority of Americans define their communities to include their neighbors, and they report that living in their cities also gives them a feeling of belonging. Furthermore, they feel close to their states, their country, and their continent. People's sense of community tends to grow with age and with ties in an area, either through home ownership or length of residence. And, overall, these feelings of community are related to greater political trust, efficacy, the willingness to tax oneself, and civic participation.[48] Feelings of community also lead to support for keeping out voices of Them that could offend community members.

Boundaries for community can be drawn in a number of different places, and it is clear from the surveys analyzed in this chapter that a

---

[47] The question wording reads, "Thinking about the quality of life in LA County, how do you think things are going – very well, somewhat well, somewhat badly, or very badly." I also reran the models with controls for respondents' perceptions of "the economy in LA today." I do not think the latter measure is as good of a measure of likeability or affect as is an assessment of the quality of life in the county. Nevertheless, in this additional test, the effect for identification with one's county on tax policy support was similar.

[48] Closeness to different geographic communities – as measured by the 1996 GSS items – also predicts greater vote turnout than among those respondents who did not feel a sense of closeness to their neighborhood, city, state, nation, or continent. Respondents were asked the following question: "In 1992, you remember that Clinton ran for President on the Democratic ticket against Bush for the Republicans and Perot as an Independent. Do you remember for sure whether or not you voted in that election?" Huddy and Khatib (2007) also find that national identity (measured with questions about closeness to America and the importance of being American) has a positive effect on voting.

majority of Americans feel a sense of community along several geographic borders. However, it should be noted that the effects of these feelings vary by community boundary, and not everyone feels a geographic sense of community. The effects of feeling a sense of community with one's neighbors differ from the impact of city-wide feelings of belonging. Each is associated with trust in political institutions and feelings of political efficacy. However, only the smaller community boundaries lead to intolerance of an offensive book and to a variety of acts of political engagement on behalf of one's neighborhood. One imagines, though, that feelings of community at varying geographic levels could have "light" and "dark" sides, promoting greater civic engagement on the one hand and buttressing greater intolerance of dissenting voices on the other.

These results do not in any way discount the effects of interests, affect, and values, which are all potential alternative explanations for the attitudes and behaviors studied. One could imagine scenarios where "community" is used as a tool of a NIMBY movement, and values are defended on behalf of one's beloved community. However, in this chapter, I provide evidence that a sense of geographic community is distinct from, and has effects beyond, homevoter interests or simply liking one's neighborhood or political conservatism, which are the much more common predictors in research on local politics.

There are two caveats to the findings. First, Americans imagine their geographic communities in noncontiguous ways. The 1996 GSS provides the potential for a picture of geographic communities as concentric circles. However, the results of the survey show that Americans do not think in such neat and tidy frameworks: if a respondent feels close to his neighborhood and his country, there is no guarantee that he will feel close to the intermediate groups of his city and his state. Therefore, while social scientists often study the effects of location, taken as objective fact, average citizens do not see, and may believe they are unaffected by, certain official boundaries.

The second caveat to concluding that a perceived geographic community has an enduring effect on politics is that this locale-based feeling of belonging may not be static over the lives of individuals. One in six Americans moves every year, and more are willing to move if given the opportunity to improve their lives, according to the GSS. This seems consistent with the mobility associated with the American Dream. At the same time, a vast majority of Americans feel a sense of community with their neighbors, and these sentiments have political consequences. How do we reconcile these findings?

One answer is that Americans quickly develop a sense of community wherever they live. As Ayers compares place identity with other identities, he notes the ease with which individuals can assimilate geographically:

...people seem able to "become" Southerners or Westerners in a way they cannot become black or white, Italian or Puerto Rican. Cowboy hats and blue jeans are worn by both Mexican-Americans and Anglos; hunting and fishing appeal to both black and white Southerners; professional sports enable white-collar and working-class people across New England to identify with one another and with their region. (1996, 4)

Respondents in the Social Capital Community Benchmark Survey confirm this American story of adaptability: among people who had lived in their community for less than one year, 75 percent felt a sense of community with their neighbors and 76 percent from living in their city. Even among those respondents who said that they did not expect to be living in their community five years down the road, a majority still felt that their neighbors and living in their city gave them a feeling of belonging. Furthermore, Americans who move a great deal may also seek a "continuity of residential experiences" (Feldman 1990, 186), so that their new homes resemble their old ones, and their sense of attachment and emotional bonds can be transferred easily.

I mentioned earlier in this chapter Hirschman's tripartite distinction of exit, voice, and loyalty. The latter two served as possible outcomes of a sense of community with one's geographic surroundings, and to a certain extent, survey questions about trust, alienation, and efficacy capture the expression of voice and loyalty when the "firm" is one's neighborhood or city. I would argue, however, that we should not apply Hirschman's model to all exits; according to this idea, people would move because of deterioration in the quality of their perceived community or because they felt no sense of community where they lived. This is likely true, although it would not explain the majority of Americans who imagine their communities to include their neighbors and still are willing to move. For the many Americans who do feel tied to their neighbors, for example, the pain of moving entails, in part, weakening those ties with distance rather than storming away in disgust or disappointment. This optimism may lead to greater desire to seek community among one's new neighbors. This argument, however, extends well beyond the cross-sectional data I have available.

Americans quickly develop geographic communities where they find themselves located, and these community ties affect their political attitudes and actions. Nevertheless, they are able to pull up roots and resettle relatively easily and frequently, repeating the process of developing new, meaningful feelings of belonging in their new homes. These feelings then help individuals decide who are their new compatriots, who will take priority when it comes to political attitudes and actions.

4

Restricting National Boundaries

> This land is my land, this land ain't your land...
> (Schoolyard version of the Woody Guthrie song, "This Land is Your
> Land")

During his 1996 presidential campaign, Pat Buchanan proposed the idea
of building a physical barrier along the entire southern border of the
United States to rival the Great Wall of China (Ogden 1996). The goal of
this 3,200-kilometer wall was to stop the flow of undocumented immigrants from Mexico into the United States; these illegal immigrants were
not Americans, and in Buchanan's mind, they clearly did not belong to
what Hollinger called the "circle of We" (1995).[1]

Buchanan's proposal remains unrealized for a number of reasons.[2]
Employers do not want to stop the flow of immigrants, documented
or undocumented. Libertarians see immigrants as a good source of
cheap labor; leaders in both the Democratic and Republican parties see
Latinos – who now make up a large proportion of immigrants – as a
growing constituency to be courted; and liberals perceive the building of
a wall as nativist and racist. There are also the costs of building a wall, as
well as the funds needed to pay federal agents to patrol it regularly.

---

[1] In fact, he compares the "invasion" of immigrants in the United States with the cause
of the downfall of the Roman empire and the beginning of the Dark Ages (Buchanan
2006).

[2] Although it will not run the span of the entire border, in October 2006, Congress
passed and the president signed legislation to build a 700-mile fence along part of the
border with Mexico (Stout 2006). Its construction has run into a number of hurdles,
but the Secretary of Homeland Security has been given unprecedented power to ensure
its completion (Liptak 2008).

In the debates over immigration arising after the terrorist attacks of September 11, 2001, there is one fact on which both pro- and anti-immigration advocates agree: the United States cannot currently control and follow all who come into the country. The patrolling of national boundaries, both physical and rhetorical, is what I want to examine in this chapter. How does membership in the national community affect who people are willing to help? In other words, do perceptions of who belongs in the American community affect public policy preferences?

In Chapter 3, I focused on the question of to which geographic community people believe they themselves belong. I now turn from self-placement in a community to the question of who else belongs in that community: who constitutes the "we" along with "me"?[3] In this chapter and the next, I am particularly interested in communities as a "circle of We" that may extend beyond the confines of objective group membership, or shrink within those boundaries. Huntington (2004), for example, is not only thinking of "objective" boundaries – geographic or legal – when he asks the following:

"We Americans" face a substantive problem of national identity epitomized by the subject of this sentence – Are we a "we," one people or several? If we are a "we," what distinguishes us from the "them" who are not us? (9)

The nation's borders are an example of geographic boundaries that can influence the drawing of community boundaries; as such, it is logical, based on the arguments in Chapter 3, to assume that those groups of people individuals consider part of an "American community" may influence policy preferences – both foreign and domestic – and whom people are willing to help with their taxes and political support. The consequences of how people imagine the American community are likely to be significant, given the large percentage of people who say they feel "very close" to America.

On the one hand, the boundaries of the American community may coincide with the nation's territorial boundaries. American schoolchildren commonly see maps of the continental United States, with two inset pictures of Alaska and Hawaii, hanging in their classrooms. They learn American history beginning with the thirteen colonies and following the

---

[3] Yack (1996) points out that the Alfred Dreyfus affair at the turn of the nineteenth century was a particularly poignant example where self-defined community and identity shrank in importance relative to the perceptions of others. Dreyfus expressed loyalty – to what might seem an irrational extent, serving in WWI despite unjust convictions of treason – to France because membership in that national community was so important to his personal identity.

growing nation as it spreads westward across the continent. On the other hand, perceived boundaries do not necessarily map onto such objective boundaries; one may live close to individuals without feeling close to them. In other words, "community" is relational; physical distance is not.

Even such objective boundaries as appear on maps can still be permeable and fail to distinguish between groups of people. Buchanan's model border, the Great Wall of China, did not stop the crossing and intermingling of invading forces in the end. Today, China is a multiethnic nation with a "national minorities policy" that considers these ethnic minorities separately from the Han Chinese majority.[4] Although the United States does not explicitly recognize such subdivisions in granting rights and responsibilities of citizenship, more than a tenth of the population in the country is foreign-born (Lollock 2001), elites debate the meaning and proper emphasis of *e pluribus unum* (Schlesinger 1992), and public opinion may not reflect constitutional practice. In other words, every American may not view all his fellow citizens (much less all U.S. residents) as members of his national community.

Thus far, while I have tried to rely on individuals' perceptions of their communities, they tend to imagine them in terms of subgroups such as neighbors and people in one's state. Although individuals use these categorically, the subgroups are themselves only approximations. For example, a man may feel that his neighbors are part of his community and that he is willing to fulfill obligations and duties to these other community members. But, by "neighbors," he is not referring to the curmudgeonly woman living on the end of his street who kicks small animals; he may only mean to include "good neighbors" in his community. Similarly, individuals' conceptions of the American community often encompass fewer people than legal norms would dictate – excluding legal immigrants or even some native-born Americans. This narrowing of their definitions of community (and Us) limits the extent to which these individuals are willing to support policies that are beneficial to Them.

Individuals living in the United States illegally are often considered to be outside the American community. During the debate over a $6.6 billion earthquake relief bill in 1994, Congressman Dana Rohrabacher argued that relief should be withheld from undocumented immigrants. He argued, "We have to lay down the principle that illegal aliens will

---

[4] "Han" may also be a nationalist invention that dates back only a couple of centuries (Smith 2003).

not receive the same benefits as American citizens and legal residents, whether it's emergency aid or anything else" (Sandalow 1994). In a similar vein, the fact that immigration status is not a consideration in organ donation is a source of anger: one American citizen on a transplant waiting list asks, "Why do we have to get in line behind immigrants, foreigners, when we have enough people here to fill the hospitals? It just seems obvious to me that we shouldn't be taking a back seat" (Gorman 2008). Some Americans consider assisting illegal immigrants to be fundamentally wrong, even in a private capacity. For example, 44 percent of the sample in a statewide poll conducted in Arizona in 2006 favored making it a felony to help illegal immigrants (Archibold 2006, A1).

Even legal permanent residents are often seen as outside the bounds of community, by the state as well as by the public. As Katz writes, "Through citizenship a community defines who does and who does not belong. As such, it serves as a criterion for denying people the benefits of the welfare state as much as it does for awarding them" (2001, 345). For example, as a result of the Deficit Reduction Act of 2006, children born in the United States to illegal immigrants, although they are American citizens, are no longer automatically eligible for Medicaid; their parents have to apply, providing a birth certificate proving their baby's citizenship (Pear 2006). And the Military Commissions Act of 2006 removed the right of habeas corpus from green-card holders in the United States (Zakaria 2006).

Nevertheless, I hypothesize that this "dark" side of community may be complemented by a "light" side. Individuals who have a clear sense of who belongs – who is part of the national community – may have a greater commitment to that community than those who do not. A clear vision of where the boundaries are drawn may lead to a greater love of the country and a greater willingness to participate or sacrifice on behalf of the imagined We. This is a hypothesis I will test.

Figure 4.1 provides a diagram for the case of extending or shrinking community boundaries, where individual A is situated within the circle of the United States. B is another person living in the nation, and C is a foreigner. The circle could represent the geographic borders of the United States or the legal bounds of citizenship. However, these "objective" boundaries may not matter to A. Figure 4.1(b) shows a situation where A's community (the bold box) falls well within the legal and physical limits of what it means to be an American. C is still a foreigner, perhaps a Canadian or Mexican citizen. B could be a permanent resident in the United States who does not yet have citizenship, but B could also be a native-born citizen who is not part of what A sees as her national

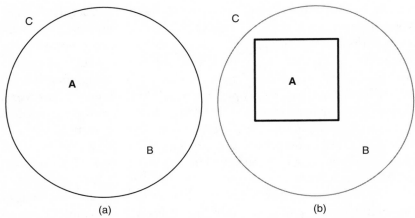

FIGURE 4.1. National Community from the Perspective of Person A. The circle represents the "objective" borders of the United States, either defined physically or legally. The box represents A's imagined American community, which does not include B, who may be a legal resident, a naturalized immigrant, or a native-born citizen.

community, perhaps because she perceives B's attitudes or behavior as deviant or un-American. It is how A perceives her national community – not the "objective" boundaries of her country – that affects her political attitudes and behaviors. A may work to exclude B from national benefits, while working extra hard to benefit anyone who is considered a member of her imagined American community.

HISTORICAL AND INSTITUTIONALIZED BOUNDARIES OF THE AMERICAN COMMUNITY

American traditions have restricted American citizenship throughout the nation's history (Kettner 1979), and even the more inclusive liberal vein expects a level of assimilation before an individual becomes a "true American" (Yoshino 2006). However, there are also citizenship laws that are relatively clear about who is or is not an American.[5] One could argue that the "national political community" is "the group of people officially entitled to the rights and responsibilities of citizenship" (Lieberman 2003, 3). But do Americans think that naturalized citizens

---

[5] The status of adult illegitimate children of American fathers born abroad is still at issue (see *Nguyen v. INS*), but laws concerning birthright citizenship and naturalization are relatively straightforward in general (Schuck and Smith 1985).

are as American as baseball and apple pie, and if not, does being "less American" place one outside community boundaries? The Constitution, for example, mandates that only a "natural born citizen" may become president of the United States. While this clause was intended to exclude the British and other Europeans and is today largely irrelevant, it has not been amended over the last two centuries.[6] Are naturalized citizens, much less legal residents, considered equal members of the American community, deserving of the full benefits of membership?

The history of legal immigration and naturalization in the United States is fraught with expansions and constrictions of the boundaries of the "circle of We." National citizenship laws were not even formalized until the latter half of the nineteenth century, and until then, states decided who could become an American indirectly and implicitly via their own state citizenship laws (Kettner 1978).

Of course, the vast majority of Americans are so because they were born in this country. The idea of birthright citizenship was inherited from Britain, and the notion was included in the Constitution, at least for free white persons.[7] There were many residents who did not fall into this category. Blacks did not gain citizenship until the Civil War era with the passage of the Fourteenth Amendment. American Indians were excluded even after that point; in 1884, the Supreme Court ruled in *Elks v. Wilkins* that Indians born under the jurisdiction of a tribe – regardless of their current affiliation and place of residence – did not fall under U.S. jurisdiction and therefore were not granted citizenship by the Fourteenth Amendment (Aleinikoff 2002, 20). As, Aleinikoff argues, residents of the Philippines and Puerto Rico (when they were American possessions) were in similar situations: "... the indigenous peoples were neither aliens nor nonresidents, yet despite their birth and residence on U.S. soil, the Supreme Court was not prepared to include them within the circle of full membership" (18). It was not until 1917 that Congress made Puerto Ricans U.S. citizens, and in 1924, Indians finally entered the U.S. political community when they were made citizens by statute.[8]

---

[6] It is not irrelevant, of course, to a handful of prominent foreign-born politicians such as governors Arnold Schwarzenegger and Jennifer Granholm, who might otherwise consider running for higher office.

[7] The Naturalization Act of 1790 established this restriction of citizenship for "free, white persons." In 1870, naturalization laws were changed to allow persons of African descent to become citizens.

[8] Nevertheless, citizenship did not guarantee full membership in the national community with equal rights and privileges. Even today, residents of Puerto Rico and Guam do not have access to the full panoply of citizenship rights.

There were also situations in which one could lose one's birthright citizenship. The Expatriation Act of 1907 made it possible for American women to lose their citizenship if they married an alien man, even if they continued to live in the United States and their lives remained largely the same. This policy, which was upheld by the Supreme Court in *Mackenzie v. Hare*, stated that these women's status was contingent on that of their husband's regardless of their own birthplace (Tichenor 2002, 329). At various points in American history, serving as an officer in a foreign army could signal an individual's choice to renounce his citizenship, as could voting or holding political office in a foreign country. Generally, though, moving citizens from inside to outside the boundaries of the American community is not something that the federal government can do easily.[9]

Where the government has more discretion is in the area of immigration – who is allowed to set foot on American soil – and naturalization – who is allowed to enter the official political community. Before the Constitution, states had discretion to decide their own restrictions. For example, Maryland required a declaration of "belief in the Christian religion" in its Act of 1779 (Kettner 1978, 215). These religious concerns continued over the next century into the national arena, as nativist groups lobbied to exclude Jews and Catholics from immigrating to the United States (Gerstle 2001, 47). America was seen as "God's country," and being a Protestant was part of being an American (Gerstle 2001, 362). In a number of cases, the Supreme Court affirmed the power of the federal government to create "an American nation-state in which Christian institutions and benevolence would suppress, reform, or replace uncivilized peoples not deemed capable of proper self-government or participation in the American polity" (Aleinikoff 2002, 31).

When the federal government took more control over immigration, it barred a variety of groups from entry into the United States: prostitutes, criminals and convicts, lunatics and idiots, Chinese, Asians more generally, homosexuals, polygamists, anarchists, Communists, and anyone who seemed likely to become a public charge (Tichenor 2002, 3–5). These "types" – including those seen to be antithetical to U.S. laws and institutions – did not fit the prevailing vision of the American community.

Even when individuals were allowed to enter and reside in the United States, they were not guaranteed the right to become full members of the

---

[9] Johnson (2005) argues that *Ng Fung Ho v. White* (259 U.S. 276, 284 (1922)) makes clear that U.S. citizens cannot be deported or removed from this country. Nevertheless, several hundred thousand American citizens (by birth or naturalization) of Mexican ancestry were "repatriated" by the United States to Mexico in the 1920s and 1930s.

community. In 1798, the Federalists, for example, passed the Sedition Act, which allowed for the prosecution and deportation of critics of the government, and the Naturalization Act extended the residency requirement for naturalization from five to fourteen years (Pickus 2005, 35). The Federalists also wanted to deport aliens who were under suspicion for some wrongdoing without a trial by jury or finding of guilt; such an alien who returned or refused to leave could be sentenced to hard labor for life. Nonetheless, these noncitizens had the right to vote in some locales up through the beginning of the twentieth century, and all men, regardless of citizenship, were expected to register with the Selective Service once that was established.[10]

In the 1790s, which legal residents would be permitted to become citizens was an open question. During the debates over the Alien and Sedition Acts, Robert Goodloe Harper, a representative from South Carolina, argued that "nothing but birth should entitle a man to citizenship in this country" (Sanderson 1856, 131). He was not successful in persuading the other members of the House, but it shows the extremes to which some legislators wanted to restrict citizenship. Immigrants had to prove they had basic knowledge of U.S. civics and history; a connection had been made between knowledge of the nation and "feeling American." James J. Davis (who was secretary of labor in 1922) argued that "Citizenship can come only from the heart... If we compel the alien to know America, I have no fear that there will come that change of heart necessary to produce an American citizen" (Pickus 2005, 117). He believed that the United States would always come out ahead in any comparison, and to know the country was to feel American. The importance of English was also stressed. In the mid-twentieth century, Congress raised the naturalization requirement from speaking and understanding English to also reading and writing in the language.

Of course, even when the law was on the side of the immigrants, it was not always observed. Local officials in Texas often stopped Mexican immigrants from becoming naturalized citizens at the turn of the twentieth century because the latter were seen as nonwhite and unfit for self-government, despite the fact that Texas courts had ruled that Mexicans had the right to naturalize (Pickus 2005, 68).

The history of American immigration and citizenship is filled with instances when certain qualities were deemed necessary, if not sufficient,

---

[10] To this day, immigrant men of eligible age – documented and undocumented – are required to register (Wong and Cho 2006).

for gaining membership in the American community. The public demanded the maintenance of what Aleinikoff calls "communities of character," and the government often responded by erecting suitable barriers to admission (1990). Birthplace, residence, religious beliefs, language ability, and knowledge and sentiment about America and its institutions were all considered important qualifications for becoming American, and many of them were required by law. Echoes of these debates about where community boundaries should be drawn can be heard centuries later. As naturalization laws have become more inclusive in determining who can become a citizen, public perceptions of who is "truly American" have continued to evolve, but not necessarily in the same direction.

THE IMAGINED AMERICAN COMMUNITY

Deutsch defines a nation as a community of individuals who perceive themselves as a group, regardless of the fact that they do not actually know one another (1953). Identification as a people is based on a sense of belonging or kinship; some definitions of the concept of nation emphasize a shared common history, customs, origins, land, and language, but there are too many exceptions to the rule to believe there is a single all-encompassing definition (Miller 1995). Anderson's classic description of a nation as an "imagined community" is more appropriate, given that the boundaries of a nation – particularly with regard to who makes up its members – are constantly in flux (1983); as such, the ties that bind individuals together in a national community exist primarily in their minds.

The nation-state is easier to picture because the boundaries of a country define the limits of its sovereignty. However, the official borders of any geographic area – be it a nation, state, county, or neighborhood – began as imagined lines. A river might have appeared to be a good dividing line between states, for example, or using degrees of latitude might have created a simple, straight border between countries. Nevertheless, there are no natural or preordained boundaries of nations; these territories are all defined (and redefined) by a history of politicking. Daniel Webster, in his concern over the secession of the South, asked "Where is the line to be drawn?...What is to remain American? What am I to be? An American no longer?" (Greenfeld 1992, 473). Shklar (1998b) asks a similar question:

What boundaries mark a democratic people off from others? Few if any territorial boundaries have ever been chosen by a people. ... Are there no defensible borders, so that the people are, as has been plausibly argued, all mankind? (127)

Although some political theorists present normative arguments in favor of a global citizenship or cosmopolitanism (see, for example, Nussbaum 1996), the vast majority of Americans draw boundaries and think of themselves in parochial terms – as Americans. Besides expressing "closeness" to America, almost half the Americans surveyed in the 1996 General Social Survey said that being an American is "the most important thing in their life," and an overwhelming majority agreed that they would rather be an American than a citizen of any other country (Citrin et al. 2001).

How does one become categorized as an American (by oneself, by others, and by the state)? What meaning underlies a sense of American national identity? In contrast with countries that have a more circumscribed, kinship-based definition of their nation, the American People is a symbolic and protean being. A commonly touted answer to "who is an American?" is ideological – anyone who believes in the American Creed and the American Dream is an American (Aronovici 1920; Gleason 1980; Hochschild 1981; Huntington 1981; McClosky and Zaller 1984; Merelman et al. 1998). The emphasis is on self-definition, which is cited as a factor in American exceptionalism (Schaar 1981); belief in American rights and freedoms *makes* one an American, and the United States is often considered a civic nation, not an ethnic one [although Yack (1996) criticizes this distinction].

However, this ideological liberal description ignores equally prevalent cultural and political traditions in our national identity (Karst 1989). Smith (1997) instead describes three separate yet coexisting definitions of American identity. Each is as authentic and American as the "rags to riches" stories of Horatio Alger, which are exemplars of Smith's first definition, the liberal tradition. Civic republicanism is the second vein in American culture, emphasizing the need for citizen participation and engagement for a healthy, self-governing nation. The third American tradition is ethnoculturalism; the racism that Myrdal saw as so contradictory to the ideals of the nation in *The American Dilemma* (1944) is therefore not an anomaly, but a cornerstone of American culture. For most of the nation's history, a substantial proportion of individuals living on American soil were ineligible for citizenship, and "American citizenship as nationality" is rife with past examples of bigotry and exclusion based on a number of different dimensions (Shklar 1991; Smith 1993).

These traditions date back to the founding of the nation. In the *Federalist Papers*, Jay described Americans in the following manner, combining all three aspects of liberalism, republicanism, and ethnoculturalism:

[Americans are] one united people – a people descended from the same ancestors, speaking the same language, professing the same religion, attached to the same principles of government, very similar in their manners and customs, and who, by their joint counsels, arms, and efforts, fighting side by side throughout a long and bloody war, have nobly established their general liberty and independence. (Rossiter 1961, 38)

Believing in individual rights and community participation, in other words, has not always been enough to be considered an American, a belief echoed centuries later by Huntington (2004).[11] Of course, Jay's description was fictional, even in his time, but this fact only emphasizes the importance of imagined boundaries centuries ago as well as today.[12]

What are the effects of inclusion in the American community on the government benefits one can receive, as well as on one's acceptance and welcome by fellow Americans? Social identity theory argues that identification as a group member leads to ingroup favoritism and biases, which can be explained as a mechanism to maintain or boost one's self-esteem (Brown 1986). Identification with a nation, therefore, implies a sense of belonging or attachment to the national community, with a resulting desire to further its interests and pride in its accomplishments (Smith 1993). Researchers have found that different conceptions of "who is an American" are indeed related to notions of patriotism and nationalistic chauvinism (Citrin et al. 2001).

Given my argument that the definition of community influences policy preferences, people who think of their community as composed of other Americans should support policies that benefit Americans at the expense of citizens of other countries. If the resource to be divided or fought over is an international good, then the relevant Them or outgroup might be a foreign country and its citizens. Americans jealously guard their interests and goals across a number of international arenas, ranging from their relative status in the United Nations to their medal count compared to other national competitors in the Olympics. And, as mentioned in Chapter

---

[11] Greenfeld writes that to be an American requires acknowledging all three traditions (1992).
[12] The controversy in 2006 over the Spanish-language version of "The Star-Spangled Banner" highlights the fact that patriotism is often seen as coming in one language only. "Nuestro Himno" was immediately labeled the "illegal alien anthem" despite its relatively faithful translation of the song's first stanza (Montgomery 2006). A Gallup poll conducted around the same time showed that more than two-thirds of Americans believed the song should be sung only in English (Carroll 2006).

1, Americans consistently favor decreasing the amount of money sent "outside" for foreign aid.

However, if the resources to be divided are domestic goods and services, then the relevant outgroup may be individuals residing within the United States who could benefit at the expense of members of the American community or ingroup, namely non-Americans or people perceived to be un-American. Identifying this outgroup is necessary if Americans are to make the intergroup comparison that may lead to competitive beliefs and behaviors (Brewer 1999).

Social identity researchers have also discovered that negative sentiments toward the outgroup are not a necessary counterpart to ingroup favoritism. There is evidence, for example, that the core of prejudice "is not the presence of strong negative attitudes toward minority outgroups but the *absence* of positive sentiments toward those groups" (Brewer 1999, 438; emphasis in original). In other words, while negative and positive biases that favor fellow community members at the expense of others may occur simultaneously, the relationship between them is contingent and not inevitable. Hatred or a desire to harm "foreigners," however defined, is not a necessary or sufficient requirement for an individual to exhibit moral parochialism in favor of other members of one's American community; categorizing someone as "outside" is sufficient.

Identification as a member of a national community is obviously not the same thing as defining the limits of that community. For example, in studying the former, Lilli and Diehl (1999) adapt a collective self-esteem scale to operationalize the concept of national identity, creating five subscales to measure membership and identification, private and public views about the nation, and comparisons with other outgroups. Social identification refers to the self-perception of membership in a group and the meaning or content of that membership, assuming clear (and static) group boundaries. However, group boundaries are not always as sharply defined as Tajfel's "underestimators" and "overestimators" of dots (Tajfel 1970). A native-born and a naturalized citizen may both self-identify as Americans, but have differing views on who *else* is an American.

In Chapters 1 and 2, I argued that recognition by others is not necessary for an individual's own sense of community. Similarly, the boundaries of a person's community – including who else belongs within its boundaries – may not be recognizable to others. An individual's definition of her community explains both (1) if she herself belongs and (2) who else belongs as a member, situated within the community borders. The first might explain who she is and what is in her community's interest, while the latter explains the reach of her community's interest, i.e., who else is in the community whose welfare is at stake. Who one includes as a part of Us affects the extent of one's bounded morality or particularism, whether that is limited to one's self or to "people like me." Just as an individual perceives the limits of a neighborhood (that may vary from the boundaries imagined by his neighbor), so it is with a nation. In the next section, I examine the conceptions of national community that Americans may have with regard to other people, beginning with the issue of immigration.

THE AMERICAN COMMUNITY: WHO BELONGS

Immigration in this country is an issue whose political salience waxes and wanes depending in part on the economy (Citrin et al. 1997; Higham 1988). In 1994 in California, where the recession was slow to end, the state's voters passed Proposition 187 in an attempt to end social services to undocumented immigrants (Schrag 1999). The governor at the time, Pete Wilson, was a proponent of the initiative to "Save Our State," arguing that states should not have to pick up the tab for educational and medical services for illegal immigrants, who were the problem and responsibility of the federal government. California's largesse, in Wilson's view, should be restricted to Californians. These immigrants' illegality was not the only issue. During that same period of widespread economic distress, two-thirds of the Americans surveyed in the 1994 General Social Survey agreed that legal immigrants should not be eligible for government assistance immediately upon their arrival in the United States.[13]

The following year, Peter Brimelow (1995, 256) highlighted the limits of his moral parochialism in *Alien Nation*:

... any general moral obligation to minister to strangers is met, and more than matched, by the specific and even stronger moral obligation to protect our own family. And on the political level, the equivalent of the family is the nation-state. ... So I suggest that the critics of immigration adopt a name that has a long and honorable role in American history. They should call themselves – Patriots.[14]

---

[13] Besides more general arguments that immigrants lower wages for all Americans (although this issue is up for debate: see Jacoby 2006, for example), some fiscal and social arguments are more targeted. For example, Borjas argues that immigrants reduce the wages of black workers, reduces their employment rate, and leads to an increase in the incarceration rate of African Americans (Borjas et al. 2006).

[14] This notion of patriotism exhibited by those who enforce the community's borders is echoed in the name of the volunteer group that argues it does the job of the Border Patrol: the Minutemen Militia.

Concerns over who is an American and who is part of our family – and therefore, who should receive the advantages, privileges, and benefits of community membership – are not limited to Republicans such as Pete Wilson or conservative pundits such as Brimelow, nor do they fluctuate a great deal over time. In 1996, President Clinton ran a campaign ad in California that focused on the issue of illegal immigration. The voice of the narrator explained that Clinton had increased border patrols and deportations and ended welfare for illegal immigrants. The ad showed grainy black and white photos of people running across a San Diego freeway, of a man climbing down a rope over a fence along the United States–Mexico border, and of Immigration and Naturalization Service (INS) agents shining their flashlights and arresting a Latino man. The aliens all appeared to be Mexican. Just as the commercial ended with the statement, "Only President Clinton's plan protects *our* jobs, *our* values," the camera pans – in color – to a smiling white mother reading to her little boy (who is also white). Clinton's ad drew lines between Us and Them, and it argued that *our* jobs, values, and social services should be reserved for Americans. Furthermore, the 1996 welfare reform law signed by Clinton made this line tangible, as *legal* immigrants became ineligible for various kinds of federal welfare assistance.

Congressman Frank Riggs explicitly stated this distinction in support of the welfare law: "[T]he message that we are sending here, and we are clearly stating to our fellow citizens [is] that we really are going to put the rights and the needs of American citizens first" (Aleinikoff 2002, 167). Aleinikoff argues that the concept of national membership sets boundaries and dictates that power should be exercised to benefit its members. This distinguishes it from the language of the Constitution, which includes aliens and citizens as subsets of the broader category of "persons" (Aleinikoff 2002, 168, 172).

The perception of how an American should act is one factor in how an individual defines a member of the American community. Ideally – at least in the minds of many elites concerned about solitary bowlers (Putnam 2000) – members should be politically participatory, actively engaged in their neighborhoods, well-informed about the state of affairs, and patriotic. Critics of multiculturalism worry about the behavior of immigrants: whether immigrants are assimilating to the idealized standards of civic engagement, whether they are maintaining dual citizenship, and whether they have divided loyalties. They fear immigrants may not act as these civic republicans believe Americans should act (Krikorian 2004; Renshon 2001). These concerns echo debates in the late nineteenth and early twentieth centuries about whether immigrants could make good citizens and become good Americans. For example, one critic wrote the following:

> No one can be called a true American who retains a particle of direct personal tradition not native to this country. Immigrants, however worthy, bring other than American traditions from their old countries. ...Only when these traditions have faded into dim knowledge of whence a family came – without any definite personal memories – can full American nationality declare itself. (Wendell in DeWolfe Howe 1924, 254)

Furthermore, it is not obvious that all native-born Americans are seen as full members of the community. Part of America's ethnocultural tradition was the exclusion of African Americans from first-class citizenship, and this exclusion persisted despite their willingness to fight for the nation in times of war (Krebs 2004). In the late twentieth century, as a result of the civil rights struggles, discrimination on the basis of color or national origin was outlawed. Nevertheless, a color-based image of the quintessential American continues. Devos and Banaji (2005), for example, find that "American" is often equated with "white" in their experiment-based research.

Also, people may believe that those who are "truly American" should act in certain specific ways, regardless of nativity. Just as one may believe that community members should speak a common language, one may also believe that other characteristics or behaviors are necessary for being truly American. If an individual breaks the law, for example, is he really a member of the community? Even if someone does not actually break the law, but only breaks from tradition – by refusing to stand during the playing of the national anthem, for example – some may see that individual as un-American, falling outside the bounds of the national community.[15]

Shklar (1998a) questions the notion that membership alone can be equated with a common national identity.

> What are these "shared understandings" on which everything is based? To be sure, we may speak the same language, but that is no guarantee of sharing. We

---

[15] The ACLU has a series of civil liberties ads that are eye-catching, mainly because they feature prominent American celebrities and the headline "I am not an American." These words would be unusual in normal times, but particularly so post-9/11. For example, the quote that accompanies Kurt Vonnegut's picture is "I AM NOT AN AMERICAN who thinks my government should secretly get a list of books I read."

curse each other and pronounce death sentences upon one another in the same language in which we speak to our friends and fellow club members. (384)

"Club" comes from her description of Walzer's portrayal of nations as such (Walzer 1981), for which "self-determination is their right." Some Americans, in other words, may perceive their nation as an exclusive club or team, whose members should share a particular group identity – perhaps race – and a shared culture – perhaps expressed in English only. "Objective" boundaries of citizenship may play a role in a court of law, but in the larger political arena, some Americans may perceive the national community as an exclusive club whose doors should only be opened to applicants who fulfill certain desirable characteristics.

Now we turn to the data. Analyses in this chapter illustrate how differing definitions of the American community affect policy preferences. Imagine the circle in Figure 4.1, where legal definitions of "American" form the outer circle, but the inner box represents who we think is a "true" American. Because I am interested in who else belongs in the community, I have to move away from the respondent-focused closeness questions to questions that can capture respondents' views of who falls outside the community boundaries. I will show in the next section that people's sense of the American community is often, in fact, smaller than that circumscribed by law. The drawing of a smaller community affects Americans' attitudes about who and what should be allowed into the country, as well as who should benefit from the nation's resources.

MEASURING THE BOUNDARIES OF THE IMAGINED AMERICAN COMMUNITY

To assess people's normative conceptions of their national community, previous research asked individuals to state the importance of a number of traits in making someone a "true American" (Citrin et al. 1990; Citrin et al. 2001; Merelman et al. 1998). The research indicates that different conceptions of American identity affect attitudes about policies concerning immigration, language, and multiculturalism.

I examine these questions using data from the 1996 and 2004 General Social Surveys (GSS). These national surveys asked respondents the following questions:

Some people say the following things are important for being truly American. Others say they are not important. How important do you think each of the following is...

1) To have been born in America,
2) To have lived in America for most of one's life,
3) To be a Christian,
4) To be able to speak English,
5) To have American citizenship,
6) To feel American,
7) To respect America's political institutions and laws,
8) To have American ancestry [asked only in 2004].

The response options were "very important," "fairly important," "not very important," and "not important at all." In defining national identity – and, thus, who belongs in the ingroup – these questions also provide a measure for determining where the boundaries of the American community are imagined to be. These boundaries reflect in part the role of the past history of American institutions and context in shaping who is seen as the quintessential American. Figure 4.2 shows the responses regarding how important each of these traits are to being "truly American."[16] Each trait grew in importance over the eight years between the two surveys.[17]

About one in five Americans surveyed thought that *all of these characteristics* are "very important" in making someone "truly American," and less than 1 percent said that none of these is important.[18] Furthermore, the fact that a quarter of the 1996 respondents (and 35 percent of 2004 respondents) believe that native-born Christians who have lived in the country all their lives are the prototypical "true American," belies the myth of the melting pot. Alternatively, people may believe in Zangwill's melting pot (1909), but think that what forms in the bottom of the crucible is not always a "true American." The gallery of individuals who are not "true Americans" includes American icons such as Muhammad Ali, Bob Hope, and Albert Einstein; Ali is not Christian, Hope was not born in the United States, and Einstein naturalized and was a dual U.S. and Swiss citizen.

Each of the traits listed in the question constricts the "circle of We" to a smaller imagined American community than that defined by law. Although respect for America's laws and the ability to speak English are

---

[16] See Citrin et al. 2001 for a more detailed discussion of these individual items.
[17] One might hypothesize that the events of September 11, 2001 may have led to this increased support (Davies et al. 2008), although there are numerous other possibilities that cannot be ruled out.
[18] Some 19 percent said all seven characteristics listed were "very important" in 1996; 27 percent of respondents in 2004 said those seven were "very important," and 19 percent said all eight (including having American ancestry) were "very important."

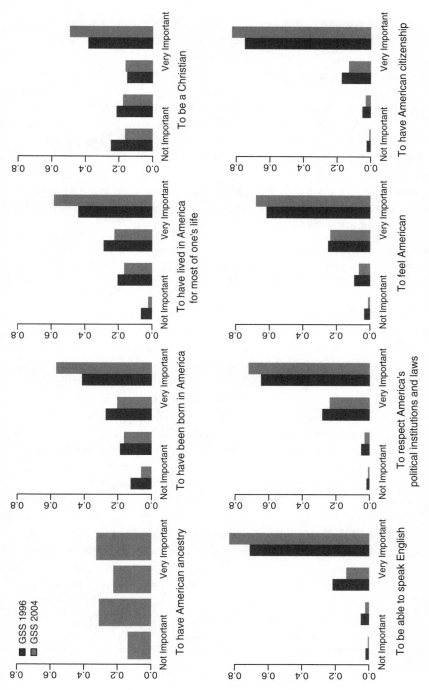

FIGURE 4.2. Who Belongs in Our National Community? Many believe "true Americans" must have both ascribed and acquired traits.

Source: 1996 and 2004 General Social Survey.

requirements for naturalization, and citizenship technically makes someone an American, the courts have not drawn the lines of the American community to coincide precisely with citizenship.[19] None of these traits is necessary for being considered part of the national community from a legal standpoint. For example, the state cannot discriminate on the basis of alienness (see *Graham v. Richardson*); the government has a responsibility to educate children, regardless of citizenship (see *Plyler v. Doe*); and it also has an obligation to provide all citizens the right to vote, regardless of language ability (see the language minority provisions in Sections 203 and 4(f)(4) of the Voting Rights Act).[20]

Society has not always been as generous as the courts about membership in the community. Wiebe (1980) describes the following historical response to immigrants:

A time-honored device was exclusion: draw a line around the good society and dismiss the remainder. Just as the defenders of the community and the men of power late in the nineteenth century each had denied their enemies a place in the true America, so worried people in the twentieth also separated the legitimate from the illegitimate. (156)

The reason for the restricted boundaries may have changed, but the fact of moral parochialism in favor of only the "good society" or "true community" has a historical legacy that continues to this day. Even if the boundaries are not drawn around only the "good," and citizenship does not necessarily make one a member in everyone's eyes, some would argue that naturalization, taking the step from noncitizen to citizen, is important "to forge a communal sense of obligation" (Pickus 1998, 125).

As factor analyses in earlier studies have shown, the seven traits depicted in Figure 4.2 cluster in two areas (Citrin et al. 2001). In 1996, the first three items – concerning birthplace, tenure, and Christianity – tap more exclusionary sentiments, while the remaining four are more assimilationist in character.[21] Although a factor analysis shows that these items load on two separate factors, the factor loadings shift significantly depending on what items are included in the analyses and which dataset

---

[19] Of course, there are native-born American citizens who do not respect the laws, and Puerto Ricans – many of whom do not speak English – are American citizens by birth.

[20] This shrinking and extension of rights and privileges to noncitizens exists in other countries (see for example, Soysal 1994) and over time in the United States.

[21] In 2004, the "speaking English" item loaded with the more exclusionary sentiments, along with the "American ancestry" item.

is used, as is the wont of factor analysis in general.[22] The theoretical arguments made about multiple traditions is compelling (Schildkraut 2007; Smith 1993), but while the distinctions are conceptually clear, empirically the picture is fuzzier. Because I am interested in *any* constriction of the national community – even if that requirement is only that someone feel American – I have created one additive index of American community for respondents' conceptions of their national community, ranging from the most inclusive (requiring none of these traits) to the most exclusive (requiring all).[23]

So, what leads people to have more exclusionary attitudes about who is a "true American"? Using both the 1996 and 2004 GSS datasets, I analyze the relationship between some basic demographic predictors and visions of the American community. In addition to education, age, income, and gender, I also include in the models whether the respondents are immigrants (or children or grandchildren of immigrants), their citizenship status, and their partisanship and ideological self-identification. Because of the small number of Asians in the samples, the models I present here are restricted to non-Hispanic white, black, and Hispanic respondents.

For the same reason that tenure was an important predictor for attitudes about geographic community in Chapter 3, tenure in the United States may influence respondents' attitudes about who a "true American" is. For example, an immigrant who has naturalized recently may be skeptical that being born in America is necessary for being part of the American community. Similarly, the grandchild of Jewish or Buddhist immigrants may have grown up hearing stories about how their family members came to the United States and worked hard to succeed, and doubt the importance of being Christian to being "truly American."

Citizenship status may also have an effect on attitudes about who counts as a community member or not. Although citizenship does not demarcate the limits of the government's attention and distributional concerns, those who have naturalized or who were born citizens may

---

[22] In 2004, "feeling American" and "respecting America's political institutions and laws" loaded together, while all the other items loaded on a separate factor. This was the case whether or not "having American ancestry" was included.

[23] In the Web Appendix, the models are replicated with "assimilationism" and "ethnoculturalism" subscales separately. For the 2004 data, I also reran the models using a 7-item (excluding the ancestry item) national community measure.

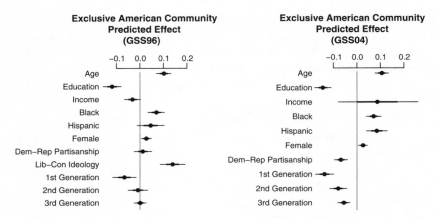

FIGURE 4.3. The Relationships Between Imagined American Community and Personal Attributes.
Source: 1996 and 2004 General Social Survey.

believe they have stronger claims for deciding who falls inside or outside the American community's borders.

Partisanship and ideological self-identification are included in the models because it is possible that Democrats and liberals could have relatively expansive views of the American community, while Republicans and conservatives could have stronger beliefs that certain attitudes and behaviors are necessary for being "true Americans." When one thinks of immigration critics such as Peter Brimelow and Samuel Huntington, for example, their major concerns are about the assimilability of immigrants who look, speak, and worship differently from Anglo-Saxon Protestant Americans. Because the question concerning ideology in the 2004 GSS was not on the same ballot as the American community and immigration items, only partisanship is included in the models of the 2004 data.

As Figure 4.3 shows, the better educated a respondent, the more likely she is to have a more inclusive or expansive view of her American community, which is consistent with previous research on both tolerance and prejudice. Women and the elderly are more likely than men and the young, however, to believe that people need to fulfill certain qualifications to be "true Americans." This pattern is consistent with attitudes toward immigration (see, for example, Citrin et al. 1997). Blacks and, surprisingly, Hispanics are likely to have a more restrictive view of the American community than are whites. The finding for African Americans is consistent with previous research (Citrin et al. 1990). One possible explanation for the finding concerning Hispanics is how the question about who is a true

American is interpreted; as Schildkraut has argued (2007), the wording can imply both a prescriptive (i.e., what the respondent thinks) and a descriptive view (i.e., what the respondent thinks most Americans think) of the true American. As predicted, conservatives and Republicans have a narrower conception of who belongs than do liberals and Democrats. Surprisingly, the immigrant generation of the respondent had only a small effect in 1996 but a marked effect in 2004: in 1996, only immigrants were different from fourth-generation Americans in their views of what qualities are necessary for being a true member of the community, but by 2004, first, second, and third generation immigrants are all distinguishable from fourth-generation-plus Americans in their more inclusive views of what makes someone truly American.[24] This general pattern of results holds when the more assimilatory versus nativist components of the scale are analyzed separately, and whether the seven-item or eight-item index is used for the 2004 data.[25]

MEASURING THE EFFECTS OF THE IMAGINED AMERICAN COMMUNITY: IMMIGRATION, PROTECTIONISM, AND RIGHTS OF CITIZENSHIP

Do attitudes about who is part of the American community predict political attitudes and policy preferences? I first look at three policy areas that are closely related to ideas of our nation's borders and boundaries: immigration, refugee policy, and protectionism. The GSS asked respondents for their preferences about the level of immigration to this country, about whether stronger measures are needed to exclude illegal immigrants, and whether political refugees should be allowed to stay.[26] One would expect that individuals who imagined their American community more narrowly would be more inclined to exclude foreigners, regardless of whether they are immigrants – documented or not – or refugees. I also created a Protectionism Index from three survey questions concerning the

---

[24] When the model was rerun, adding in whether a respondent is Christian or not, religion had a significant effect: Christians were more likely to have a more exclusionary view of their national community. This is true, even when the requirement to be Christian is removed from the American community index. When citizenship of the respondent was included in the model instead of immigrant generation, it had no effect on how the American community was perceived.

[25] See Web Appendix for the analyses of the subscales. This change over time in the effect of immigrant generation may be caused by the same phenomenon that increased support for all of these requirements – and may possibly be a result of 9/11.

[26] The refugee question was only asked in 1996.

importation of foreign products, the purchase of land in America by foreigners, and TV programming preferences for American programs (over
programs from other nations). If I am correct about the way one's imagined community works, the narrower the perception of the American
community, the greater will be the desire to maintain American control
over all goods and services.[27]

I regressed the policy preferences on the American Community index,
with controls for respondents' basic demographic characteristics (education level, age, income, gender, and race), citizenship, immigrant generation, party identification, and political ideology (for 1996 only). Previous
research, as well as the contemporary political debate, has indicated
that these variables are pertinent factors in predicting attitudes about
immigration (Citrin et al. 1997; Espenshade and Calhoun 1993). Greater
education and a liberal ideology, for example, more often lead to pro-
immigration attitudes. One might also hypothesize that being an immigrant or the child of an immigrant would lead to more liberal attitudes
about immigration and refugee policies because of personal experience or
group interest. The American Community Index ranges from 0 to 1, with
a high score indicating the most restrictive definition of who is "truly
American."[28]

People's conception of their American community was a strong predictor of their attitudes on all of these issues, as can be seen in Figure 4.4.
The more exclusive an individual's sense of who a "true American" is –
regardless of education, immigrant status, or ideological predisposition –
the more likely he or she is to want to decrease the number of immigrants
to America and support stronger measures to keep illegal immigrants out.

[27] The exact question wordings are as follows:

1) Do you think the number of immigrants from foreign countries who are permitted
   to come to the United States to live should be increased a lot, increased a little, left
   the same as it is now, decreased a little, or decreased a lot?
2) America should take stronger measures to exclude illegal immigrants. (Agree
   strongly to Disagree strongly)
3) How much do you agree or disagree that refugees who have suffered political repres-
   sion in their own country should be allowed to stay in America? (Agree strongly to
   Disagree strongly)
4) America should limit the import of foreign products in order to protect its national
   economy. (Agree strongly to Disagree strongly)
5) Foreigners should not be allowed to buy land in America. (Agree strongly to
   Disagree strongly)
6) American television should give preference to American films and programs. (Agree
   strongly to Disagree strongly)

[28] All variables, including the dependent variables, are coded to range from 0 to 1.

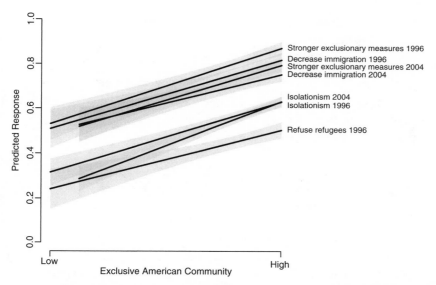

FIGURE 4.4. The Relationships Between Imagined American Community and Immigration and Isolationism Policies. Those Americans with more exclusive visions of the national community are more supportive of measures to keep out noncitizens – legal and illegal immigrants and refugees – and non-American products and investors.

Source: 1996 and 2004 General Social Survey.

More restrictive definitions of who belongs in the American community also had a strong effect on opposition to the presence of political refugees in the country. Finally, support for the list of traits of a "true American" also led to attitudes in favor of limiting the import of foreign products, prohibiting foreigners from buying land in the United States, and giving preference to U.S. programming on television. For each of these policy preferences, respondents' definitions of their American community had the largest effect of all the predictors in the models, more than educational level, immigrant status, or political predispositions (see Appendix for the full models). The more exclusive is one's sense of who belongs in the community, the more one wants to restrict the flow of outsiders into the area where that community resides. Controlling for potential interests and ideological or partisan concerns, those individuals with a vision of a smaller circle of who counts as a "true American" were also more likely to want national resources – possible jobs, services, land, and products – to be protected from those outside the borders of the national community.

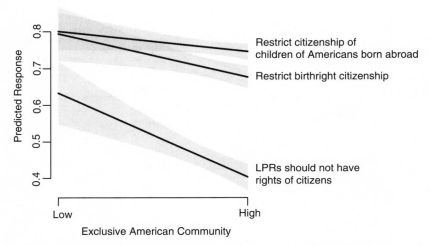

FIGURE 4.5. The Relationships Between Imagined American Community and Citizenship Rights. Those Americans with more exclusive visions of the national community are more opposed to birthright citizenship, granting citizenship to children of Americans born abroad, and extending citizenship rights to legal permanent residents.
Source: 2004 General Social Survey.

Perceptions of the American community can also have an effect on judgments about who should receive the benefits of membership and who should be allowed to become community members. Respondents in the 2004 GSS were asked to agree or disagree (strongly or not) with the following statements:

1) Children born in America of parents who are not citizens should have the right to become American citizens.
2) Children born abroad should have the right to become American citizens if at least one of their parents is an American citizen.
3) Legal immigrants to America who are not citizens should have the same rights as American citizens.

Figure 4.5 presents the results of the analyses. Again, more restrictive attitudes about who belongs in the American community are strongly related to questions about *jus soli* (birthright citizenship), *jus sanguinis* (citizenship via blood), and extending rights to noncitizens (an extension that Soysal believes leads to a postnational citizenship). Although these questions do not mention explicit benefits and goods that are given to community members, they do capture attitudes about who should be given the rights of citizenship. And respondents who have more exclusionary beliefs about who belongs in the American community also have more stringent requirements for who should be eligible for citizenship benefits, above and beyond the effects of partisanship or their own immigration experience. *Jus sanguinis* and *jus soli* are embedded in the laws of the nation, yet it follows that if one believes that being born in America is necessary for being "truly" American (questioning both the laws and myths of the immigrant nation), then one may also believe that birthright citizenship should not be taken as a given.

One might argue that attitudes about the American community are simply capturing group affect. Perhaps an individual opposes increasing the number of immigrants in the United States simply because she does not like immigrants. The 1996 and 2004 GSS have items that can roughly capture affect toward immigrants; while there is no feeling thermometer or stereotype question asked about immigrants, respondents were asked whether they believed more immigrants would result in higher economic growth, higher unemployment, more crime, and greater tolerance of cultural differences.[29] Although attitudes about immigrant impact are not the same as group likeability, it does capture interests (e.g., worry about losing jobs and economic prosperity) and fears of Balkanization. I reran the models with this additional predictor for the models in Figures 4.4 and 4.5, and the overall pattern of results did not change. (See Web Appendix for results.) Attitudes about where an individual's American community boundaries are drawn are not simply measures of immigrant affect or xenophobia. However, I do not want to overemphasize this distinction, because affect can be part of why people imagine these boundaries where they do.

Of course, it is also possible that the group whose likeability is in question is "Americans" – members of the national community – rather than the outsiders. If an individual has very strong positive affect about an ingroup, she may not want it to change (through immigration, for example). To test this idea, I reran the models in Figures 4.4 and 4.5 with additional controls for attitudes about the United States (see Web Appendix for results). I first created an index of national chauvinism

---

[29] Respondents were asked to agree or disagree (strongly or not) to the following four statements in 1996: Immigrants increase crime rates; immigrants are generally good for America's economy; immigrants take jobs away from people who were born in America; immigrants make America more open to new ideas and cultures. In 2004, the "ideas and cultures" item was not asked, so the immigrant impact scale for 2004 is composed of only 3 items. All items were recoded such that negative attitudes were scored high.

from four survey questions in both the 1996 and 2004 GSS.[30] Even with the addition of very strong group affect measures, having more expansive or restrictive views of the American community still had an effect on attitudes about individuals and goods crossing community borders, and about who should be granted rights of citizenship. As an alternative group affect measure, for the 2004 data, I created an additive index of ten items asking respondents if they felt a sense of pride in American democracy, its political influence in the world, its social security system, its armed forces, its history, its equal treatment of groups in society, and its achievements in economics, sports, science, arts, and literature. This captures patriotism more than the national chauvinism of "my country right or wrong," since it measures the degree of pride in one's nation (Kosterman and Feshbach 1989).[31] Even with the addition of this measure of affect to the 2004 models in Figures 4.4 and 4.5, the relationship between respondents' views of where the American community boundaries should be drawn and policies concerning immigration, protectionism, and rights remained largely the same.[32] So, one can safely conclude that the measure of national community is not simply a proxy for how people feel about America or Americans in general. Controlling for national chauvinism and patriotism, notions of who belongs in respondents' imagined American communities are related to their policy preferences, ranging from ideal immigration levels to control over the television airwaves to birthright citizenship.

The measures of the boundaries of the American community used thus far indicate whether *others* belong in the respondent's community, not an individual's self-placement. The policy variables, after all, do not pertain to how to help or redistribute resources among other community members, i.e., Americans, as would be comparable to the analyses in Chapter 3. Instead, they look at *who* – immigrants or refugees – or *what* – products,

---

[30] Respondents were asked to agree or disagree with the following statements: I would rather be a citizen of America than of any other country in the world; the world would be a better place if people from other countries were more like the Americans; generally speaking, America is a better country than most other countries; and people should support their country even if the country is in the wrong. This idea has also been called foreign assimilation (Davies et al. 2008), nationalism (de Figueiredo and Elkins 2003), and uncritical or blind patriotism (Huddy and Khatib 2007). De Figueiredo and Elkins do find a strong relationship between nationalism and hostility toward immigrants. So, even controlling for this national chauvinism, how people define the American community still has an effect on immigration attitudes.

[31] I will return later in the chapter to look at the direct relationship between this patriotism measure and definitions of community.

[32] This holds true also if de Figueiredo and Elkins's (2003) seven-item pride index is included instead.

TV shows, or foreign landlords – should be allowed *into* the community. As a point of comparison and to create more parallel models with the previous chapter, I reran the models in Figures 4.4 and 4.5, regressing the same dependent variables on the "closeness to America" measure used in the previous chapter instead of the national community measure (see Web Appendix for results). Controlling for the same demographic and political characteristics, defining one's community as America (measured with the "closeness" item) has little to no effect on these attitudes about immigration, isolationism, and refugees. And although closeness to America is related to greater support for birthright citizenship and citizenship for children born abroad to American parents, it is working in the opposite direction from having a more constrained view of the national community.[33] In other words, although self-identification as part of the American community had little impact on attitudes about who or what should enter the country and only a slightly more inclusive view of who should be considered a member at birth, attitudes about who or what else belongs in the American community consistently did. Setting boundaries of self-inclusion is separate from decisions of exclusion, and they can have different effects on decisions about redistribution of resources to others within that community.

It is perhaps not too surprising that how Americans imagine their national community affects who and what they want coming through their country's borders or airspace. If "true Americans" are native-born, English-speaking Christians, for example, the presence of foreigners and their demands on our government's resources are unwelcome, irrespective of whether they are Mexican immigrants or Bosnian refugees (or even Japanese cars and Canadian TV shows). This is true for any definition of the American community that excludes some perceived "outsiders" residing within the geographical borders of the United States. It is possible, therefore, that conceptions of national community may also affect other policy preferences that are not so explicitly concerned with foreign politics and borders.

MEASURING THE EFFECTS OF THE IMAGINED AMERICAN COMMUNITY ON DOMESTIC POLITICS

More restrictive attitudes about who belongs to the American community may affect domestic politics along a number of dimensions. Specifically,

---

[33] This is consistent with Elkins and Sides (2007), who find that state attachment facilitates unity in divided societies.

I expect that those who are perceived as not quite true "red-blooded" Americans can also be excluded from the benefits and protections of the nation. The lines defining who is an American may still clash, for example, with the "color line" (Devos and Banaji 2005; Perea 1998). Many Japanese Americans born in the United States were interned in camps during World War II despite their citizenship (Hatamiya 1993; Muller 2001), and similar concerns over the loyalty (and rights) of Arab Americans have been voiced in response to the September 2001 terrorist attacks.

In her interviews of working-class Americans, Lamont (2002) found that

...American workers draw moral boundaries against the poor and African-Americans in the name of work ethic and responsibility; immigrants who partake in the American dream are more easily made part of 'us' than African Americans, although anti-immigrant boundaries are present in the interviews (179).

I will test whether a constrained notion of the American community excludes African Americans regardless of immigration status.

In addition to race and ethnicity, contemporary identity politics in the United States focuses on sexuality. Changes in attitudes and policies have only occurred recently (Yoshino 2006). In 1975, the U.S. Civil Service Commission announced it would no longer exclude homosexuals from government employment, but in 1982, a number of states passed laws forbidding the placement of children for adoption or foster care with gays. In 1990, policies restricting the immigration of lesbians and gays to the United States, which had been in place since 1917, were finally rescinded. And it was only in 2003 that the Supreme Court struck down state laws that banned private consensual sex between adults of the same gender.

In surveys from 1973 to 1996, a majority of Americans thought that sexual relations between two adults of the same sex was "always wrong" (Yang 1997). Also, according to a 2007 Gallup poll, 94 percent of Americans said they were willing to vote for a qualified black president, but only 55 percent were willing to vote for a qualified gay president (Jones 2007). Although the notion that *all* Americans (born in the United States) can grow up to be president is promulgated in grade school, there are individuals who are not seen as full members of that American community with equal opportunities and status.

Race and homosexuality are ascriptive characteristics that may place an individual outside another's conception of her national community; there are also acquired group identities – based on attitudes or actions – that may place one outside the fold. Attitudes can set one apart from the mainstream as much as one's sexuality. In the 1940s and 1950s, being communist was equated with being un-American.[34] Communism and socialism have become much less salient in the last decade, but racists, atheists, and militarists are still perceived as relatively threatening and are targets of intolerance (Marcus et al. 1995). Even those who would grant these groups the right to march or protest may be hesitant to invite them into their homes; it is unclear if members of these minority groups are imagined as part of the American community or not.

Behavior can also place one outside the fold. In thirteen states around the country in 2004, ex-felons were denied the right to vote.[35] Even after serving their sentences, former criminals are viewed by some as unworthy members of society, perhaps beyond rehabilitation or redemption.[36] Punitive attitudes about criminals in general may lead to their placement outside the national community in the minds of some Americans.

To test the hypothesis that attitudes about the American community affect policies concerning domestic groups, I look at a range of policies that do not require choices to be made between Americans and foreigners.[37] The policies concern the government's right to ask about sexual orientation before giving someone a security clearance; gay marriage; the rights of gays, atheists, militarists, and racists to make public speeches, teach, and place their books in libraries (these were combined to create four three-item indices of tolerance for each group); government programs to help blacks; antimiscegenation laws; spending on law enforcement; and capital punishment. Although law enforcement spending and capital punishment do not measure attitudes towards ex-felons specifically, they do capture tendencies toward maintaining laws and boundaries, punitiveness, and what criminals deserve in our society. These regression models

---

[34] It should be noted, however, that the House Committee on Un-American Activities was originally established in the 1930s to investigate Nazi and Ku Klux Klan activities.

[35] According to the Brennan Center, thirteen states permanently disenfranchise ex-felons. However, at least in some states, there is the possibility of applying for reinstatement, although the process is difficult.

[36] Legislators have tried in numerous ways to make it easier to recognize such "outsiders." For example, Megan's Law in California ensures that there is a registry of sex offenders' addresses that the public can access online. And Ohio's legislature proposed in 2007 special fluorescent green license plates for the cars of convicted sex offenders, to go along with the special yellow license plates with red lettering required for convicted drunken drivers' cars (Driehaus 2007).

[37] While attitudes about immigration and refugee policies may be affected by attitudes about immigrants and refugees who are officially American, i.e., naturalized citizens, the policies shown in Figure 4.4 themselves refer explicitly to newcomers.

were run with the same controls as in the models for Figures 4.4 and 4.5 (education, age, income, gender, race, citizenship, party identification, and political ideology). Because of when questions were asked, almost all of the analyses in this section were run for the 1996 data only. When possible, I replicated the analyses using the 2004 dataset.

One might suggest that the measure of the American community overlaps with related concepts, such as authoritarianism, racial prejudice, or homophobia. I believe these concepts are connected and that the latter two are simply different examples of how people draw community boundaries to exclude members of certain ethnic, racial, or sexual minorities; racial prejudice and homophobia are also obviously indicators of group affect. However, because in this chapter I am primarily interested in the effects of how people perceive their *national* community above and beyond these other prejudices or values, I add a number of these controls to the models when possible and rerun them to test the robustness of the findings. Given the different ballots on which questions were placed, it was not possible to include all controls for all questions. As the addition of the measures results in a dramatic loss of cases, I present the original, simpler models in the figures that follow.

Although the GSS does not contain measures of authoritarianism, it did ask about the importance of obedience and thinking for oneself as traits in children. These two items were combined to create an additive index of what might be considered authoritarian predispositions (Feldman and Stenner 1997). The correlation between the authoritarianism scale and the American community measure is .19 ($p < .001$).

Racial prejudice is an index of four items, in which respondents explain why there are political, economic, and social differences between whites and blacks. Are the reasons blacks on average have "worse jobs, income, and housing than white people" a result of structural inequalities (i.e., discrimination or a lack of educational opportunities that are necessary to rise out of poverty), or is it related to blacks' inferiority (i.e., having "less in-born ability to learn") and lack of ambition (i.e., a lack of motivation or will power to pull themselves up out of poverty)? Those who attributed the racial gap to racial inferiority rather than larger societal inequities scored "high" on the scale. The correlation between racial prejudice and the American community measure is .24 ($p < .001$).

And, to measure homophobia, respondents were asked whether they believed sexual relations between two individuals of the same sex was wrong or not. The American community index and the homophobia measure are correlated at .37 ($p < .001$).

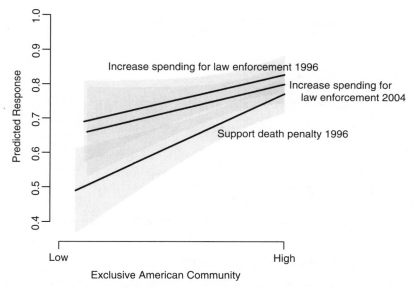

FIGURE 4.6. The Relationships Between Imagined American Community and Policies that Affect Criminals. Those Americans with more exclusive visions of the national community are more supportive of capital punishment and spending to fight crime.

Source: 1996 and 2004 General Social Survey.

The results of the analyses show that the index of American community predicted attitudes about these domestic policies almost as well as the foreign policy ones. Figure 4.6 shows that the more restricted were people's perceptions of who belongs in the national community – including those who "respect America's political institutions and laws" – the more likely they were to support the death penalty and increased spending for law enforcement.[38] In other words, even controlling for political predispositions, those individuals who believe that certain beliefs and behaviors are necessary to make someone truly American are more inclined to uphold the most extreme penalty for breaking the laws of the land; furthermore, the more constrained an individual's view of the American community, the more he is willing to spend to ensure that its laws and rules are enforced.[39] The addition of ethnocentrism and authoritarianism did not change the results much; neither measure is statistically significant, and the American community index remained one of the strongest

[38] The results hold true for capital punishment, even for the "Assimilation subscale" purged of the item concerning the importance of "respect for America's political institutions and laws."

[39] This finding concerning spending on law enforcement was replicated in 2004.

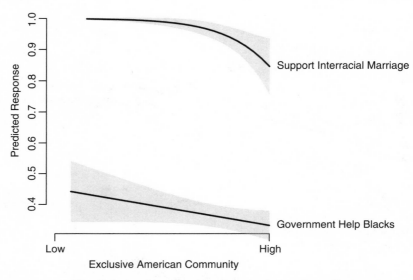

FIGURE 4.7. The Relationships Between Imagined American Community and Policies that Affect African Americans. Those Americans with more exclusive visions of the national community are more supportive of antimiscegenation laws and more opposed to government programs to help blacks.
Source: 1996 General Social Survey.

predictors of attitudes about crime and criminals.[40] (See Web Appendix for results.)

The perceived boundaries of national community are also related to attitudes about policies concerning African Americans. Among whites, even controlling for ideology and partisanship, there is a tendency for those with more restrictive normative conceptions of who an American is to be more likely to oppose government programs to help blacks (p<.05 for a one-tailed test) (see Figure 4.7). And whites with more exclusionary attitudes about who belongs in the American community are much more likely to support laws against marriages between blacks and whites.

When racial prejudice is added to the model for interracial marriage, respondents' imagined national community still has a powerful effect (even greater than the prejudice variable) on attitudes. In other words, above and beyond a white respondent's ethnocentrism, ideology, and education, the more restrictive her view of who is a "true American," the more she supports antimiscegenation laws. When racial prejudice is

[40] It was not possible to include measures of homophobia in these models.

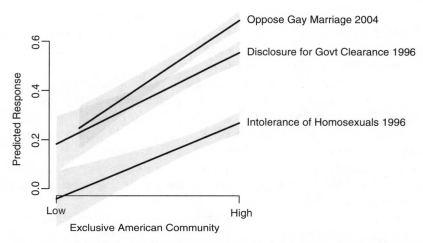

FIGURE 4.8. The Relationships Between Imagined American Community and Policies/Attitudes that Affect Homosexuals. Those Americans with more exclusive visions of the national community are more supportive of measures requiring disclosure of sexual orientation for government clearance, are more opposed to gay marriage, and are more intolerant of homosexuals.
Source: 1996 and 2004 General Social Survey.

added to the model for government programs to help blacks, the effect of the national community measure disappears and prejudice is the overwhelming predictor of aid. For this policy, white prejudice about blacks has a much stronger relationship than a scale of qualities that make someone a true American. However, this finding also suggests that attitudes about membership in the national community are strongly related to ethnocentrism. Although the correlation between these two variables is only .24, they work together in interesting ways, particularly when it comes to predicting attitudes about government programs aimed at helping minorities who might not be recognized by fellow citizens as equal members. It is clear that ethnocentrism is a way of manifesting attitudes about the national community, or vice versa.[41] (See Web Appendix for results.)

Preferences for policies concerning gays were also affected by definitions of the American community: Figure 4.8 shows that the more individuals believed that there were particular characteristics that were very

[41] It was not possible to add measures of homophobia to the model. I did include a measure of authoritarian tendencies, but it had no relationship with the dependent variable.

important for making someone a "true American," the more they also believed sexual orientation should be disclosed for government clearance. This effect remains even when controls for homophobia and authoritarian tendencies are added to the model.

The 2004 GSS asked respondents about their opinions on gay marriage. The results of the analyses follow the same pattern: attitudes about who belongs in the American community have a strong relationship to attitudes about whether "homosexual couples should have the right to marry one another." Respondents with more constricted views of their imagined American community were also more likely to oppose the rights of gays and lesbians to marry, above and beyond the effects of education and party identification.[42]

Images of the American community are also related to expressed intolerance for gays, controlling for education among other variables. The measures of the American community index do not include any questions directly asking about sexual orientation or behavior. Nevertheless, the sense that certain attributes are necessary for membership in the community affected where boundary lines were drawn; both the American community and homophobia measures capture attitudes about people who fall inside and outside boundaries of obligation. Even when measures of homophobia and authoritarian tendencies are added to the model, how people imagine their national community is still a strong predictor of intolerance of homosexuals. In fact, images of the "true American" have a stronger effect on intolerance of gays and lesbians than does the homophobia measure (despite the obvious overlap between the intolerance and homophobia measures in their shared target group).[43] (See Web Appendix for results.)

This relationship extended to tolerance of other groups as well. A constricted sense of who belongs in the American community is strongly related to less tolerance of atheists, racists, and militarists (see Figure 4.9). It appears that they are not perceived to be "true" members of the community.

---

[42] I am unable to replicate this model adding measures of homophobia because the questions were not on the same ballot of the 2004 GSS as the measures for national community.

[43] I also reran the "basic" model with controls for religious attendance, religious affiliation, and strength of affiliation, because attitudes about homosexuality in particular may be influenced by religious beliefs. The national community index was still a statistically and substantively significant predictor of greater intolerance toward gays in these models.

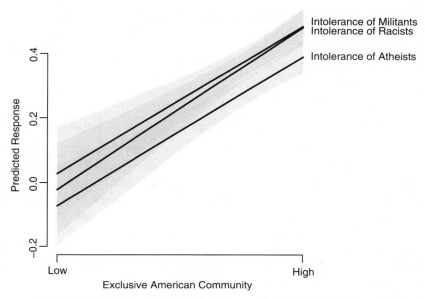

FIGURE 4.9. The Relationships Between Imagined American Community and Tolerance of Atheists, Militarists, and Racists. Those Americans with more exclusive visions of the national community are more intolerant of atheists, militarists, and racists.
Source: 1996 General Social Survey.

For the tolerance measures for atheists, militarists, and racists, the addition of ethnocentrism and homophobia measures to the models did not affect the overall impact of the American community measure.[44] (See Web Appendix.) In other words, controlling for dislike of Them (defined in terms of sexuality and race), more constricted notions of where national community boundaries are drawn are still related to greater intolerance of deviant groups in society. If one has an image of who is a "true" community member, the less likely one is to tolerate aberrant beliefs and behavior. This confirms the finding in Chapter 3 that there is a relationship between feeling a sense of (geographical) community and intolerance of a book expressing deviant views.

So, for some Americans, not only are non-English speakers and non-Christians not "truly American," it seems that criminals, African Americans, gays, and other groups with non-mainstream attitudes and

---

[44] Because of the different split samples in the General Social Survey, I was not able to add controls for authoritarianism into any of the models of tolerance.

behaviors may also be considered outside the national community.[45] They are not seen as full and equal members of the American community, and therefore should not be accorded the same benefits, such as job opportunities and free speech rights.

MEASURING THE LIGHT SIDE OF THE IMAGINED AMERICAN COMMUNITY

Having a more exclusionary vision of one's national community certainly has a number of negative correlates or consequences. Nevertheless, its effects are not necessarily one-sided. As I noted in Chapter 3, feelings of geographic community can lead to a greater sense of loyalty and to increased participation and sacrifice on behalf of the community. Here I test whether perceptions of who belongs in the American community also have these beneficial qualities. In particular, I look at the relationship between people's views of their national community and their trust in government and sense of citizens' obligations.

I hypothesize that the greater one's identification or sense of belonging in the community, the greater one's sense of obligation to that community. Do respondents who have a clear view of what it takes to be a true member of the community feel more obligated to act on behalf of the community than respondents whose view of the American community is more inclusive (or at least not defined by the traits listed in the GSS questionnaire)? The 2004 survey instrument contained a battery of ten questions asking about citizen obligations. Respondents were asked the following:

There are different opinions as to what it takes to be a good citizen. As far as you are concerned personally on a scale of 1 to 7, where 1 is not at all important and 7 is very important, how important is it...

  1) Never to try to evade taxes.
  2) Always to obey laws and regulations.

Together, these two were created into an index of Obligation to Obey Laws.

  3) Always to vote in elections.
  4) To keep watch on the actions of government.
  5) To be active in social or political associations.
  6) To try to understand the reasoning of people with other opinions.
  7) To choose products for political, ethical or environmental reasons, even if they cost a bit more.
  8) To be willing to serve in the military at a time of need.

[45] This is perhaps not surprising, given contemporary American views about atheists (Edgell et al. 2006).

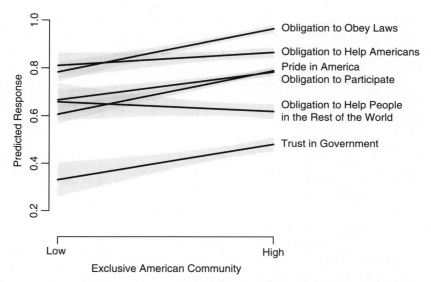

FIGURE 4.10. The Relationships Between Imagined American Community and Political Obligations, Patriotism, and Trust in Government. Those Americans with more exclusive visions of the national community are more likely to believe they must fulfill obligations to be a good citizen (except for an obligation to help those in need abroad), express more pride in the United States, and are more trusting of the national government.
Source: 2004 General Social Survey.

These six items were added together in an index of Obligation to Participate.

   9) To help people in America who are worse off than yourself.
   10) To help people in the rest of the world who are worse off than yourself.

All variables were recoded to range from 0 to 1, and the models run for each variable are similar to those run for the other figures in this chapter.[46]

Perceptions of American community are related to belief in all of these citizen obligations *except* that of helping people in the rest of the world (see Figure 4.10). In other words, respondents with narrower conceptions of the national community were more likely to believe good citizens (i.e., ideal members of the community) should be politically engaged, civic-minded, law-abiding, empathetic, ethical, and generous to other members of the community. The one exception is that a more constricted view of

---

[46] The analyses were also run separately for each of the items composing the indices and similar results were obtained. For simpler presentation of the results, the two Obligation Indices were created.

the American community was not related to the notion that one must be generous to people outside the community – "in the rest of the world" – who are worse off. One's duties and obligations extend only to the border of one's community.

The GSS also gauged respondents' feelings about different aspects of their country. It asked, "How proud are you of America in each of the following?"

1. The way democracy works;
2. Its political influence in the world;
3. America's economic achievements;
4. Its social security system;
5. Its scientific and technological achievements;
6. Its achievements in sports;
7. Its achievements in the arts and literature;
8. America's armed forces;
9. Its history; and
10. Its fair and equal treatment of all groups in society.

These items were combined together in an additive Patriotism Index. Figure 4.10 shows that how people imagine their American community is related to their pride in their country's achievements and accomplishments. The more restricted one's sense of one's national community – the clearer one's vision of what types of people belonged within and outside of the community boundaries – the prouder one felt about the nation as a whole.

Respondents were also asked whether they agreed or disagreed with the statement, "Most of the time, we can trust people in government to do what is right." The results of the analyses show a pattern similar to that from Chapter 3: those respondents who had a clear vision of their community were more likely to have faith in the institutions governing that community.[47]

---

[47] Defining one's nation as one's community – as measured by the closeness to America question – is positively related (controlling for the same independent variables as the models in Figures 4.6 through 4.10) to being willing to spend more on law enforcement (in 2004 but not 1996), being more opposed to gay marriage, expressing patriotism, trusting in government officials, and being supportive of many of the citizen obligations listed. The effects, however, are neither as strong nor as consistent as those for the "true American" measures of national identity. The dependent variables in this chapter are less about providing benefits for Us, and more about restrictions on Them; the disparate impact of placement of the self compared to others within community boundaries may reflect this distinction. Reynolds et al. (2000) explain that there is

An imagined American community that is smaller than what might otherwise be dictated by citizenship laws or court rulings has both negative and positive effects. While it leads to more exclusionary and intolerant attitudes toward those American residents who do not have certain traits (including ascribed ones), it also comes hand in hand with a greater sense of obligation to the community, a greater pride in the community's accomplishments, and a greater trust in the government that is leading the community.[48] It does not, however, lead to any obligation to individuals in need outside the community boundaries.

DISCUSSION AND CONCLUSION

Where an individual draws the boundaries of his or her American community affects a wide range of attitudes and beliefs. It is an important predictor of attitudes toward immigration, including the notion of America as a melting pot and ideas about what kinds of effects immigrants have on the economy, unemployment, and culture (Citrin et al. 1997). It also affects support for a broader range of public policies. Perceptions of where community boundaries are drawn predict whether someone will choose to close our borders to outsiders, and whether civil liberties should be extended to those who legally reside within those boundaries. Clearly, our national community – perceived in the minds of average Americans – is not defined simply by lines on a map or by legal definitions; the psychological boundaries may have their roots in their objective counterparts, but they appear to be influenced by a host of historical, environmental, and experiential factors.

These results provide empirical support for Smith's contentions that there is an ethnocultural strain in American political attitudes. Furthermore, given the strong evidence that a sizable minority possesses a restricted view of the American community, and that this attitude has an effect on policies concerning a range of groups across American society, these analyses provide alternative explanations for segmented assimilation and two-tiered pluralism (Hero 1992; Zhou 1997). The choices for assimilation are not all on the side of immigrants if the host society

an asymmetry in intergroup discrimination, depending on whether the experimental task is the distribution of positive resources or negative consequences. Ingroup favoritism is more evident in the former situation than in the latter, at least in laboratory experiments.

[48] It is an unanswered question whether this belief is, in fact, followed by action. A correlate of a more exclusive conception of the American community is nationalism, which is negatively related to vote turnout (Huddy and Khatib 2007).

will not include them in the national community, above and beyond any economic limitations. After all, why should immigrants try to become American if they are doomed to fail from the start by their birthplace or by their religion?

Imagined geographic communities – at the local as well as the national level – are clearly important considerations in understanding how ordinary people think about both domestic and foreign policies in the United States. In Chapters 3 and 4, I have shown how we can measure the boundaries of geographic communities and their effects on policy preferences. Self-placement within a local community has political ramifications, as does regard for others at the national level. Perceptions of community can lead to acts of duty and obligation, and they can also close the door on opportunities, resources, and rights for those seen as outside community boundaries.

Citizenship is often described as defining membership in the nation, but this chapter has shown that citizenship does not guarantee that one is considered a member of the community, nor does employment or political participation. Ordinary Americans do not think that all citizens are "true Americans." Restrictive definitions of our American community – defined by specific beliefs, language, birthplace, and residence – lead to isolationist policy attitudes. They also lead to strong beliefs that Americans have duties to be engaged and help others in their imagined national community before considering the welfare of those outside community boundaries.

5

Blurring the Color Line

In 1993, Billings, Montana, suffered a rash of hate crimes. Racist graffiti was painted on the home of a Native American family, skinheads threatened the services of an African American church, and a brick was thrown at a Jewish family's home, breaking a window displaying a menorah. In response, residents of Billings (of different races and religions) volunteered to paint over the graffiti, they went to the church's services to show support and provide protection, and thousands placed menorahs in the windows of their homes.

The story of this town is unusual enough that it was made into a documentary film, and it provides a vivid example of how the expanding of community boundaries beyond objective group lines can occur.[1] In Chapter 4, I showed how the shrinking of community boundaries to only "true Americans" leads to attitudes restricting who can enter the country and who should benefit from the rights and opportunities of community membership. The opposite is also possible: an enlarged perception of one's community can prompt greater support for government programs to benefit individuals who are not objective ingroup members.

Race provides a good case for studying the potentially shifting boundaries of community and of obligation (Wong 1999). Researchers may understand that race does not exist as an unconstructed reality (Diamond 1994),[2] but they argue that people continue to see it as fixed and objective

---

[1] The story of Billings spurred a campaign that has spread to other towns, called "Not In Our Town," which is also the title of the film. http://www.pbs.org/niot/.

[2] Some research publications, such as *Nature Genetics*, have policies to avoid the pitfalls of "the use of race and ethnicity as pseudo-biological variables" ("Census, Race, and Science" 2000, 98; Malik 2005). While some scientists are uncomfortable with any

nonetheless, justifying a continued research focus on issues of descriptive representation, race consciousness, and shared fate, for example. Researchers recognize, too, that race ought to be thought of as a continuum, yet they argue that ordinary people make decisions based on racial dividing lines, however such lines are drawn in people's minds. Average Americans may indeed be color conscious – in the ways delineated by scholars – but it is not a foregone conclusion that they draw the community boundaries between Us and Them to coincide with race.

The events in Billings provide a compelling anecdote to support the claim that race does not have to dictate community boundaries. In this chapter, I use national survey data to examine systematically whether community boundaries extend beyond racial lines, and when they do, what effect they have on politics. I look at three cases in particular: 1) whites and their inclusion of both whites and blacks in their community; 2) blacks and their inclusion of blacks and whites in their community; and 3) the inclusion by non-Hispanic whites, African Americans, Hispanics, Asian Americans, and black Caribbeans of each other in their communities.[3]

I rely on a variety of data sources and use multiple measures to capture people's sense of community; these allow me to trust that the results I show here are robust and are not merely a reflection of chance processes within a single survey item or sample. To the extent possible, I replicate the analyses using similar operationalizations of community across cases. I use measures of closeness to different groups as indicators of whether individuals are drawing the lines of their communities beyond those of their ingroup, as explained in Chapter 2. To strengthen my results I examine the effects of community using data from four different national surveys sampling the views of multiple racial/ethnic groups over 20 years. I examine the relationships between how people imagine their community and their attitudes about patrolling community borders, investment in these communities, and actions to benefit these communities. In the end, my consistent findings of the association between individuals' perceptions

use of "race," they agree that "the frequencies of certain allelic variants or mutant genes among people who share a geographic origin or culture have medical value" (Schwartz 2001, 1393). Furthermore, the FDA's recent decision to allow a race-targeted heart medication – and the research leading up to this decision – has led to a debate about whether this policy could enforce the idea that race is genetically determined, not socially constructed (Duster 2005; Kahn 2005; Wood 2001).

[3] In this chapter, I use the terms "African American" and "black" interchangeably. When I use the term "Caribbean," I am referring to black Caribbeans in particular. "White" is a shorthand for "non-Hispanic white," and all Hispanics, regardless of race, are considered "Hispanic" or "Latino."

of their communities and their policy attitudes lead me to conclude that when individual Americans draw the boundaries of their communities beyond the confines of their objective racial identity, their policy attitudes may benefit all members of their community, not simply those who share the same race. Of course, there is the potentially dark side of community as well: those with imagined communities that encompass more than their own ingroup may overlook inequalities between ingroups and outgroups.

HISTORICAL AND INSTITUTIONALIZED BOUNDARIES OF RACIAL COMMUNITIES

The history of racial community in the United States is a story of slowly expanding boundaries, although not one of steady growth. At times, the boundaries shrank substantially before again spreading outward. When the country was established, it was clear that American Indians were not considered part of the American community. Although blacks were counted as within the boundaries – albeit sometimes as property – they were generally not considered community members.[4] Membership was not an issue of equality or status alone; women and children were not considered equal to adult men, yet they were generally considered part of the community. Women, for example, fell within the realm of obligation and responsibility, above and beyond the way that men felt about the care of their property (at least for most of the population).

Of course, "race" has evolved a great deal from the eighteenth century to the twenty-first. Immigrants from China, for example, originally were considered part of an inferior, yellow race, despite their role in building the transcontinental railroad that made travel and commerce within the nation as a whole more widely available (Takaki 1989). The Irish were considered an inferior race, and at times were barred from serving in the nation's armed forces (Chambers 1987); Jews and Italians were also not considered white and suffered economically, socially, and politically as a result (Ignatiev 1995; Jacobson 1998). Once citizenship became attached to either being white or black after the Civil War amendments, many people tried to argue that they were, in fact, white and were therefore members of the American community. As Haney-Lopez (1996) documents, very few plaintiffs argued they were black, but depending on a variety

---

[4] Moral inclusion did occur during Reconstruction, when African Americans were no longer outside the scope of justice (Opotow 2008).

of legal arguments – including common sense, legal definitions, scientific definitions, and judicial decree – people of Lebanese, American Indian, South Asian, Mexican, etc., descent all argued that they were white and were therefore entitled to community membership. Although the definition of white (according to the Supreme Court) changed over time, it was not endlessly elastic. American Indians were granted citizenship in the 1920s and Asian immigrants were finally allowed to naturalize in the 1950s, but neither group was considered white.

"Scientific" efforts to define racial community have also existed throughout American history. The "one drop" rule that determined whether one was black is only one variation, and at various times, the U.S. census has gathered data on quadroons, octaroons, mestizos, and the like (Skerry 2000). Any deviation from "pure white" blood could limit one's social, political, and economic rights.[5] Ironically, the debate over the scientific determination of one's race continues today, with a growing interest in and tendency to use genetic tests to determine one's ancestry. Some of it is personal curiosity – for example, the *New York Times* ran a story about a light-skinned African American woman, who was tired of being called "yellow," who showed that her roots could be traced to West African kingdoms (Harmon 2005) – while others are driven by more political concerns – for example, Black American Indians who are trying to prove that they can, in fact, trace their roots genetically to certain tribes and should therefore be considered equal members, despite their ancestors' having been categorized separately as a result of the Dawes Act a century ago (Koerner 2005).

However, being a member of a racial community is not the same as being of a particular race. Both, I would argue, are social constructs, but a community does not have to be composed of one race; homogeneity is not a defining characteristic. In other words, it does not require one to act as Griffith did (as documented in his memoir, *Black Like Me*), passing as black (via drugs that darkened his skin) to experience what life is like as an African American. One can walk in another's shoes less literally, and whites and blacks, for example, can see each other as members of each

[5] As a result, some individuals tried to pass if it was physically possible (i.e., if their outward appearances made them look "white," then they tried to live as though they were members of the white racial community). Of course, appearance alone was not always the determining factor. Gregory Williams, for example, tells the opposite story in his memoir, *Life on the Color Line* (1995): until the age of 10, he believed he was a white child with white parents. Only after his mother left and his father moved his family back home did Williams realize his father was black, not Italian. Because everyone in his father's hometown knew his father and grandmother as black, from then on Williams was treated as black despite looking as if he were white.

other's community. In that sense, the civil rights movement changed the terrain of American racial politics and of how racial communities were defined.

The principle of "separate but equal" was established in the Supreme Court case *Plessy v. Ferguson,* 163 U.S. 537 (1896), and it was the law of the land through much of the Jim Crow era. Whites and blacks lived in separate worlds, attending separate schools, sitting in different areas on buses and trains, and having very little contact with each other as equals; politics was an all-white arena. With the beginning of the civil rights movement, acceptance of this status quo waned among African Americans, and their struggle began to gain legitimacy in the eyes of the law as well as in the hearts and minds of white Americans. One of the major accomplishments of the movement was the end of *de jure* segregation – a clear example of beliefs often following actions (some were voluntary, but some were constrained by laws and by federal forces sent to enforce them). *Brown v. Board of Education* was only one milestone in the long struggle, and some would argue today that de facto segregation in today's public schools, for example, is only one sign that little progress has been made (Orfield 2006). Although racial prejudice has not disappeared (Kinder and Sanders 1996; Schuman et al. 1997), it is widely accepted among social scientists that the socially desirable attitudes and actions are those that are nonracist and nondiscriminatory (Sniderman et al. 2000). Whether people privately believe what they publicly espouse is a matter of debate (Thernstrom and Thernstrom 1999), but the fact that the public discourse has changed is a dramatic shift in the past half century.

The civil rights movement encouraged other sociopolitical movements that have gained Hispanics and Asian Americans equal rights, and the notion of a "rainbow coalition" became possible. Immigration laws became less ethnically and racially restrictive, and other minority groups – defined racially or simply numerically – have also gone on to fight for equal rights. The argument is not that everyone is the same, but that members of all races are part of the same larger community. An individual can have a very strong identity as an Asian American without restricting her sense of community only to Asian Americans; she may feel that members of other races also fall within the boundaries of her community, and feel toward them a sense of obligation and duty.

THE IMAGINED NATURE OF RACIAL COMMUNITIES

The United States has been described as "two nations" (Hacker 1995), divided by a color line (DuBois 1968), or as a "nation within a nation"

(Higginbotham 1993).[6] Blacks and whites occupy different worlds in many ways, including how they perceive politics and economics (Bobo and Kluegel 1993; Kinder and Sanders 1996; Schuman, Steeh, Bobo, and Krysan 1997) and where they live (Massey and Denton 1993). When one considers the effects of recent immigration on the country's demography, the picture becomes even more complex (Farley 1999; Massey 2000). Hollinger (1995) has described the current political situation as being determined by the ethno-racial pentagon of whites, blacks, Latinos, Asians, and Native Americans. Awareness of the numerous ethnicities that fall under the umbrella categories for each race could easily lead one to think of America as a kaleidoscope, a colorful but fragmented country.

Race sets a divide across numerous facets of American life. Political redistricting plans, affirmative action programs, and attempts to stop racial profiling all depend on keeping counts of different racial groups; how many people of a particular race live where, are hired by whom, and are pulled over by the police? Shared ethnicity and race are also effective at increasing political participation and mobilization (Leighley 2001; Shaw et al. 2001). This awareness of race has parallels in American art and culture. Bookstores have different sections for Latino literature, African American women writers, and Native American history, to name just a few. A debate about the existence and necessity of a "black theater" has been reported on in several articles in the *New York Times* (Grimes 1997; Jefferson 1997; Rich 1997). Movies are often criticized for promoting racial and ethnic stereotypes (Schwartz 1994), TV viewing patterns among white and black Americans show that there are indeed "different worlds" (Sterngold 1998), and reality shows have pitted races against each other (Ross 2006). Even surges and dips in the American economy have had disparate impacts on different racial groups. Concerns about discrimination in hiring and promotion, income inequality, and glass ceilings continue to exist (Conley 1999; Oliver and Shapiro 1997), even in times of low unemployment and strong economic growth.

Nevertheless, this picture is overdrawn. Race does not create rigid or automatic boundaries in politics or culture. Redistricting along racial lines occurs only after race and behavior have coincided; the federal courts require that polarized voting be evident, not just the presence of different racial or ethnic groups (Aleinikoff and Issacharoff 1993). Furthermore,

[6] The first use of "nation" in "nation within nations" can refer to any number of groups, including African Americans, Latinos, or Hawaiians.

in the 2006 session, Chief Justice John Roberts asked, "What's the difference between 'being one' and 'looking like one'?" in reference to a majority Latino district in Texas (Greenhouse 2006). Cross-racial coalitions also form, with black and white activist groups intersecting (Dawson 2001; Sonenshein 1993). Literature, too, is not so easily divisible into races and ethnicities: "passing" occurs by fictional characters and by authors themselves. Pop culture is crossing color lines as well (Halter 2000), with white suburban boys listening to hip-hop (Croal 1999) and fashion designers deciding that "ethnic is in" (White 1997). Nike advertisements only emphasize the all-encompassing adulation of athletes in our culture. "Be like Mike" was not simply directed at black males, and "I'm Tiger Woods" is repeated by a rainbow coalition of aspiring young golfers. Finally, in the economic realm, the rise of the black middle class, of Asian professionals, and of immigrant-run small businesses ensures that class and race are not synonymous.

Interracial marriage makes it even more complicated to keep track of a person's race, further blurring racial lines (Farley 1999; Harris and Sim 2002). One component of the debate about the 2000 census concerned the use of a multiracial category (Hirschman et al. 2000; Skerry 2000).[7] Crouch envisions a future America of interracial children (1996), and *Time* magazine's picture of the "new face of America" was a computer-generated picture of a woman of a multiracial and multiethnic background (Gitlin 1995).

The multiplicities of races and ethnicities complicate the world that ordinary people experience. When high school students in California drew maps of their school in terms of who hangs out where, an immigrant youth's map named cliques like "Vietnamese who speak English," "Afghans," "Fijian Boys," and "Americans"; an American-born student's map of the same school named "white skaters," "band kids," "ESLers," and "Asians, Blacks, and Latinos" (Olsen 1997, 42, 61). Race and ethnicity seem to be in the eye of the beholder (Lamont and Molnar 2002).

No matter the context, the boundaries of race are unclear. Many researchers have documented the arbitrary basis of race and changing categories over time, depending on the different views of scientists, judges, legislatures, and society (Haney-Lopez 1996; Omi and Winant 1986). The "I know it when I see it" standard for pornography is even less reliable when applied to race; when in-person surveys are conducted

---

[7] The U.S. census also reinforces the idea that self-description is what matters, even for individuals who claim only one race; the practice of census enumerators deciding the race of individuals ended decades ago.

and interviewers are given the opportunity to state the respondent's race, there is never a complete match between the interviewers' opinions and those of the respondents themselves (Waters 1990). Waters, for example, describes the Office of Management and Budget's directive that for people of mixed origins, "the category which most closely reflects the individual's recognition in his community should be used for purposes of reporting" (Waters 1998). It is an interesting (and open) question as to which actually has more relevance in political attitudes and behavior: how one sees oneself, or how one is perceived by others. In this chapter, as in the book as a whole, I focus on how people see their own community.

Although race is a construct that exists only in the imagination of Americans, it is still not an optional identification for most blacks, Hispanics, and Asians in this country, nor is it one from which white Americans are likely to opt out (Feagin and O'Brien 2003; McDermott and Samson 2005). Nevertheless, even if we have not yet achieved a "postethnic America" (Hollinger 1995), the choice of those for whom I feel responsible and whom I am willing to help are decisions that may or may not be free from considerations of color. There has been no systematic examination and scholars do not know whether people tend to draw the boundaries of their communities to include only people of their own race.[8] If, in fact, the divisions between Us and Them are not cast in stone along the lines of the ethno-racial pentagon, race and community may interact dynamically, perhaps in some cases reinforcing strict boundaries and associated social ills (as when people tend to help hurricane victims of the same race) but in other cases moving beyond such confines (as reported in numerous stories following September 11). Because people's perceptions of their communities may lead them to feel a sense of responsibility for other community members, I argue that heterogeneous communities, which are composed of people of more than one race, enable the passage of policies that benefit minority groups in our democracy.

Figure 5.1 provides a simple diagram of how a community can expand to include both blacks and whites in theory. In a world (Figure 5.1a) where racial group boundaries are impermeable and ingroup identity and consciousness are the only possible motivations or sources of preferences, then person A belongs to a different group altogether than person B. However, I argue that people's communities can transcend racial group boundaries, such that the boldfaced box can represent person A's

---

[8] Belonging to the same ingroup, of course, does not guarantee ingroup favoritism. Navarro (2006) describes situations where Latino workers feel particularly shocked by a lack of empathy from their Latino employers.

FIGURE 5.1. Community from the Perspective of Person A. In (a), the circles represent "objective" racial groups. In (b), the bold box represents A's imagined community, which includes individuals of a different race.

perception of his transracial community of whites and blacks:[9] in this case, A believes that B and he both belong in the same community, despite recognizing that they are of different races.[10]

One danger in research on racial politics in the United States is treating each racial group as a new case, wholly unique and deserving of its own set of concepts and theories; this elevates area studies at the expense of comparative politics. However, it would also be naïve and misleading to believe that individuals of different races are interchangeable. Because of the asymmetry of power between whites and blacks in the United States over the past several centuries, for example, crossing racial borders and defining one's community to include individuals of different races can have different implications and ramifications, depending on the individual in question. "Passing" has almost always meant racial minorities trying to be perceived as white to receive the benefit of that dominant racial status. The famous Kenneth and Mamie Clark experiment in which black schoolchildren were more likely to want to play with white dolls than with black dolls, is another case of socialization into an easily recognized power structure that favors one group over another (Clark and Clark 1958). Although racial identification and pride on the part of blacks and other racial minorities are seen as empowering – both personally and politically – racial pride on the part of whites today would raise the specter of aberrant white supremacists wearing sheets.

[9] I want to emphasize that this bold-faced community exists in the minds of individual Americans. The overlapping oval does not, in this case, represent a physical community of mixed-race Americans. Although multiracial Americans may indeed believe their community (and identity) to be made up of more than one racial group, I am interested here in the communities perceived by any individual, regardless of what box or boxes he would check on a census form.

[10] According to social identity theorists, A would be expressing both ingroup identification (i.e., closeness to his ingroup) and outgroup sympathy (i.e., closeness to his outgroup).

With these caveats in mind, I am interested in how people define their communities to transcend objective racial lines, and how these communities may be similar in their political effects, regardless of the race of the individuals defining them.

MEASURING THE BOUNDARIES AND EFFECTS
OF RACIAL COMMUNITIES

To provide some evidence that closeness to outgroup members bears on attitudes about those individuals as well as on group-specific political issues surrounding them, I conduct three studies. In each study, I test (1) whether this phenomenon – the extension of community boundaries beyond objective group membership – occurs at all, and since I find it does, (2) who is more likely to believe their community extends beyond their "objective" racial group,[11] and (3) what the effects are on political judgments about racial politics. I test these relationships across different surveys, with different populations, using slightly different measures, and the substantive findings are replicated in each case: when a white, black, Latino, or Asian American extends the boundaries of her community beyond her objective racial or ethnic ingroup, she is more inclined to support policies that benefit others, regardless of their race, and less likely to believe racial/ethnic groups are in competition with one another. The first study looks at white respondents and whether they include blacks in their community, the second study looks at black respondents and whether they include whites in their community, and the final study looks at how respondents belonging to five different racial/ethnic categories view each other.

For the sake of clarity in the following discussions, I will refer to individuals who feel a psychological attachment or closeness to their ingroup as "identifiers."[12] If people's community and sense of community obligation are restricted to other members of some perceived primordial racial or ethnic group, then tribalism and ethnocentrism will be the norm, as

---

[11] Given that race is a social construct, "objective" racial group seems an oxymoron. However, given that I am interested in communities that may transcend racial ingroups and outgroups, I treat self-identification on a survey or census as an individual's "objective" race or racial ingroup.

[12] I believe "closeness" (to ingroups and outgroups) defines the boundaries of people's communities. However, in this chapter I will also use "identity" as well as "closeness" because (1) this term references previous research, and (2) it is shorter and less awkward to use than constantly referring to "an individual who defines his or her community to include other individuals who are of the same 'objective' racial group."

has been shown in the extensive social science literature on race (see for examples, Bobo and Tuan 2006, Kinder and Sanders 1996, Sidanius and Pratto 1999). If instead there is heterogeneity of races within a person's imagined community, then the emotional ties and sense of duty that accompany community membership will lead to political judgments that go beyond the effects of prejudice, partisanship, ideology, and other general values.

STUDY 1: WHITES' INCLUSION OF WHITES AND BLACKS IN THEIR COMMUNITY

The data for my analyses in Study 1 were collected in the 1996 American National Election Study (NES) and the 1996 General Social Survey (GSS). I use both surveys for the following reason: while they each contain survey items measuring "closeness" to blacks, the question wordings and response options vary. If I am able to replicate my results across both surveys, I will have more faith in the robustness of my findings. For this study, I limit my analyses to the 1321 white respondents in the NES sample and 741 white respondents in the GSS sample who were asked the "closeness" questions.

The NES survey instrument included a battery of questions concerning "closeness" to different groups in American society.[13] Among the groups listed were whites and blacks, and respondents were allowed to name as many or as few groups as they liked (for more information on the groups listed and the reliability and validity of these items, see Wong 1998). It is a common response to feel close to a group of which one is an "objective" member. For example, 45 percent of whites in the NES indicated that they felt close to whites – these respondents are "identifiers." There was also a small group of whites whose sense of community extended beyond racial lines: 7 percent of white NES respondents felt close to blacks.

The GSS version of the closeness question is slightly different. Respondents were asked, with no preamble as to the meaning of "close," "In general, how close do you feel to blacks?" "And in general, how close do you feel to whites?"[14] Sixty-eight percent of whites in the GSS sample felt close to whites, and 28 percent of whites felt close to blacks. Both

---

[13] See Chapter 2 for an in-depth discussion of the group closeness question.
[14] Respondents were asked to place themselves on a 9-point scale, where 1=not at all close, 5=neither one or the other, and 9=very close. The plurality of white respondents chose the midpoint of the scale for closeness to whites (29 percent) and for closeness to blacks (50 percent).

of these figures are about 20 percentage points higher than their counterparts in the NES, which is most likely because of the differences in
response options and question format.

What leads to a sense of racial community that extends beyond one's
"objective" group? Are some individuals more likely to have flexible
visions of their community than others? To begin, I examine some of the
same factors that are used to predict people's racial identity as well as
their geographic communities.

Who Draws the Boundaries of Their Communities to Include Outgroups?

Who tends to identify with their ingroup and who tends to feel close to
their outgroup? I analyzed the effects of age, education, income, gender, and region (a dummy variable for South/non-South) on white identification for both the NES and GSS data (see Figure 5.2). Tate (1993)
used these predictors in her analyses of black identification and linked
fate. Only age has a significant effect for whites in the NES data, with
younger respondents being more likely to feel close to whites. When the
9-point GSS closeness scale is regressed on the same factors, only gender
approaches levels of significance (p<.10), with women slightly more likely
than men to feel close to whites. When closeness to blacks is regressed
on the same indicators as above, income is a significant predictor for the
NES sample (see Figure 5.2). Poorer whites are more likely to feel close
to blacks than are wealthier respondents. Unfortunately, it is not possible with these analyses to discern if this closeness is a result of empathy
with others who are also less well-off in society, or a result of contact
because of residence.[15] Age matters for both the NES and GSS samples,
with the young more likely to feel close to blacks. Despite research that
links education with racial liberalism and tolerance, there is no relationship between education and closeness to blacks in these samples. From
the different (and many null) results that arise from the analysis of two
national surveys conducted in the same year, it is clear that there is no

---

[15] These analyses do not give us much information about what leads to racial identification among whites. However, Hartigan (1999) found that in Detroit, poor whites
living among blacks were more likely to be aware of feelings of shame and empathy.
I did rerun the 1996 GSS models adding in whether blacks lived in the white respondents' neighborhoods. It appears that contact (or at least proximity) may have some
effect: whites with black neighbors were more likely to express closeness to blacks than
respondents in more homogeneous settings. Having black neighbors had no effect on
white identification. (Results in Web Appendix.)

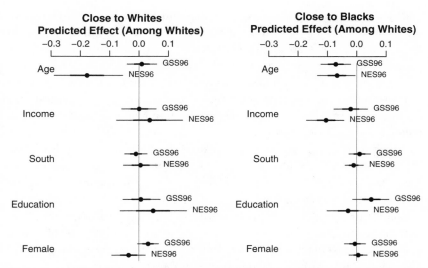

FIGURE 5.2. The Relationships Between Closeness to Whites and Blacks and Personal Attributes.
Source: 1996 National Election Study and 1996 General Social Survey, white respondents only.

simple story that explains either white identification or white closeness to blacks.[16]

What is the relationship between whites who feel close to whites and whites who feel close to blacks? It is possible that they are one and the same, or that they are mutually exclusive groups. In other words, there may be certain types of individuals who feel closer to all groups – and therefore say that they feel close to both blacks and whites – or white identifiers may be completely different from whites who feel close to blacks. The NES data show that a majority (53 percent) of whites feel close to neither whites nor blacks, 40 percent feel close to whites only,

---

[16] Using the NES surveys conducted every four years from 1972 to 2000, Wong and Cho (2005) looked at whether age, education, income, gender, and urbanicity predict whites' feelings of closeness to both whites and blacks. They found that although overall levels of closeness remained relatively stable over the time period, the factors leading to greater feelings of closeness fluctuated over time and no coherent story emerged. In the end, they speculated that experiential factors leading to identity and closeness to outgroups, such as interracial contact and geographic context, need to be measured and evaluated in greater depth; they might be able to provide a more reliable story than basic demographic factors. For example, Dixon (2008) finds that national news watching alone coincides with people being more likely to draw on negative stereotypes of blacks in their judgments.

and 5 percent feel close to both whites and blacks.[17] The same cross-tabulation yields slightly different results from the GSS data: 31 percent feel close to neither group, 41 percent feel close only to whites, and 27 percent feel close to both whites and blacks.

These data show that there is an overlap in feelings of closeness to the two racial groups, and that almost no white respondents feel close only to blacks and not to whites. When most white respondents feel close to members of their outgroup, it is in addition to closeness to their ingroup. In other words, white identification does not preclude a psychological attachment to blacks. This finding is important in so far as it shows how a community of both whites and blacks may exist in the minds of white Americans, as shown earlier in Figure 5.1. The finding that white identification is fairly common, in other words, should not give white suprema-cists hopes for increasing their ranks; one can be a white identifier and also feel close to blacks. However, on the other end of the spectrum, very few white Americans would choose to forswear their race as evidence of their "loyalty to humanity" and declare themselves "race traitors" (Ignatiev and Garvey 1996). Although a liberal observer might admire generally the sentiment of making an individual-level effort to change the social hierarchy in the United States, it seems unlikely – and perhaps is psychologically unhealthy – to expect whites to disavow their own racial identity and imagine their communities as exclusively consisting of blacks.

Feelings of closeness, however, do not necessarily imply good feelings. An individual may not necessarily like all the members of her community, just as she may not like every member of her family, but she is still likely to feel a sense of responsibility toward her crazy cousins or unpleasant community members. In the next section, I examine the political effects of people's boundaries of community. I also distinguish the effects of how people draw their communities from the effects of group affect and like-ability, ideology, and values.

Community Boundaries, Distance, and Policy Attitudes

Does a narrow, as opposed to a broad, conception of racial community matter for political attitudes and behavior? Past research has shown that

---

[17] Obviously, 5 percent is a small proportion of whites who feel close to blacks. It both indicates that a cross-racial community is a possibility and that social desirability is clearly not leading whites to believe that feeling close to blacks is the only nonracist response option.

black identification matters for political beliefs and behavior, at least partially because of the perception among African Americans that they have shared interests (Dawson 1994). The question I ask here is whether white identification and a broader definition of community by whites has similar effects. If white identification leads to greater support for distance between racial groups and greater opposition to policies that help blacks, then it would appear that the effects of white identity and black identity are similar, at least in their emphases on ingroup benefits in a zero-sum policy world. If white identification does not predict racially conservative viewpoints, then this would mean that not only is the level of racial identity lower for whites than for other racial minorities (Gurin et al. 1999), its salience and impact on political attitudes are also different. Furthermore, a transracial definition of community by whites could have the same political impact as white identification, or it could have a contrasting effect.

The main question is whether definitions of community affect whites' policy preferences. Why, for example, should whites support affirmative action for blacks? One might argue that whites could support the policy out of self-interest, to avoid threats and fear, but there is little or no evidence that this theory of appeasement could explain the attitude of most white supporters of the policy. Reasons grounded in self-interest and group interest cannot explain the bulk of such support unless whites consider the achievement of racial diversity as in their interest. Ideology or partisanship, however, could explain why whites would support a government policy that – by leveling the playing field – removes the advantages accrued to whites in employment and promotions, college admissions, and the like (Sniderman et al. 2000). The Democratic Party is seen to represent the interests of African Americans, at least relative to the Republican Party in the late twentieth and early twenty-first centuries (Carmines and Stimson 1989; Frymer 1999), and liberals are greater proponents of equality of outcomes.

Are there other reasons why certain white respondents would favor policies to benefit individuals who are members of the "objective" outgroup? I argue that if whites' communities are not restricted to racially identical others, if blacks are considered to be part of a white individual's community, then he will feel a sense of responsibility to help the members of his community, regardless of whether they share his race. This is not simply a matter of affect or *liking* an outgroup; in a world where racial group interests do not conflict, liking someone could, in fact, lead to preferences for helping those one likes. However, a sense of duty and responsibility need not extend to all those one likes; such a sense of obligation is reserved for the members of one's community, particularly if the situation is potentially zero-sum and one must choose to help either a community member or one who is not.

I do not, however, assume that there is no racial divide in public opinion; the marked difference in policy preferences of whites and blacks has been well documented (Kinder and Sanders 1996; Kinder and Winter 2001). Nevertheless, white Americans do not speak with one voice, and where they draw community boundaries may explain some of the variance in their opinions.

Because my major interest in this chapter is whether a sense of community affects attitudes about whether racial groups can come together and also about racial policies, I begin by regressing respondents' attitudes about the maintenance of boundaries between racial groups on feelings of closeness to whites and blacks, controlling for their demographic characteristics, partisanship, and ideology. I also examine models of policy preferences. The results in Figure 5.3 show analyses from both the 1996 GSS and NES. The GSS included a number of questions that tap social distance, which one could think of as policing racial boundaries:

1. (Negroes/Blacks/African-Americans) shouldn't push themselves where they're not wanted. (Agree or disagree)
2. How about having a close relative or family member marry a black person? Would you be very in favor of it happening, somewhat in favor, neither in favor nor opposed to it happening, somewhat opposed, or very opposed to it happening?
3. Now I'm going to ask you about different types of contact with various groups of people. In each situation would you please tell me whether you would be very much in favor of it happening, somewhat in favor, neither in favor nor opposed to it happening, somewhat opposed, or very much opposed to it happening? Living in a neighborhood where half of your neighbors were blacks?
4. Do you think there should be laws against marriages between (Negroes/Blacks/African-Americans) and whites?

I created an additive Index of Social Distance from these four items.[18]

The GSS also asks about support for government efforts to alleviate the effects of racism:

Some people think that (Blacks/Negroes/African-Americans) have been discriminated against for so long that the government has a special obligation to

[18] In a confirmatory factor analysis, they all load on a single factor.

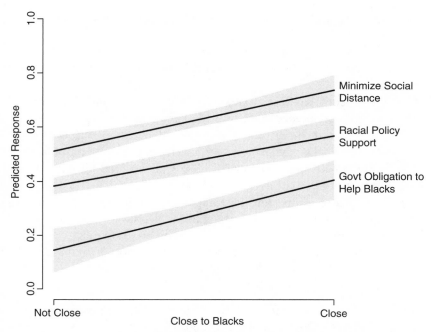

FIGURE 5.3. The Relationships Between Closeness to Whites and Blacks and Policy Preferences. Whites who include African Americans in their community are more likely to want to minimize social distance between racial groups and support a wide array of government programs intended to benefit blacks.
Source: 1996 National Election Study and 1996 General Social Survey, white respondents only.

help improve their living standards. Others believe that the government should not be giving special treatment to (Blacks/Negroes/African-Americans). Where would you place yourself on this scale, or haven't you made up your mind on this?

The NES asked respondents a similar question, as well as other policy questions:

1. Some people feel that the government in Washington should make every effort to improve the social and economic position of blacks. (Suppose these people are at one end of a scale, at point 1.) Others feel that the government should not make any special effort to help blacks because they should help themselves. (Suppose these people are at the other end, at point 7.) And, of course, some other people have opinions somewhere in between, at points 2,3,4,5, or 6. Where would you place YOURSELF on this scale, or haven't

you thought much about this? (This question was asked both pre- and post-election.)

2. Should the government in Washington see to it that black people get fair treatment in jobs or is this not the federal government's business?

3. Some people say that because of past discrimination, blacks should be given preference in hiring and promotion. Others say that such preference in hiring and promotion of blacks is wrong because it gives blacks advantages they haven't earned. What about your opinion – are you FOR or AGAINST preferential hiring and promotion of blacks?

4. Some people think that if a company has a history of discriminating against blacks when making hiring decisions, then they should be required to have an affirmative action program that gives blacks preference in hiring. What do you think? Should companies that have discriminated against blacks have to have an affirmative action program?

For the NES items, I created an additive index of racial policy support.[19]

The analyses of the GSS data in Figure 5.3 show that whites who include blacks in their community are more likely than those whites whose communities were composed only of ingroup members to oppose both social practices and laws that would create greater interpersonal distance between whites and blacks.[20] Whites with communities that extended beyond "objective" racial lines were also more likely to believe the government had special obligations to alleviate the suffering of African Americans, above and beyond any effects of partisanship and ideology.[21] In fact, closeness to blacks has a stronger relationship with the policy attitude than either party identification or ideological self-identification,

---

[19] These survey items all loaded on a single factor and the reliability score was above .8.

[20] I reran the model, adding in a measure for whether blacks lived in the white respondents' neighborhoods. Reporting having a black neighbor had no effect on social distance judgments, and closeness to blacks still had the largest effect of all predictors in the model.

[21] Because the GSS measure of closeness is not dichotomous, I am able to test whether feeling close to blacks or not feeling close to blacks alone is driving the effect of this variable. Regression diagnostics show that the linearity assumption is not violated. In addition, I recoded the closeness to black question as three dummy variables and reran the model from Table 2. The interpretation of the results is the same: including blacks in one's community leads whites to be largely indifferent to racial boundary-drawing, and not including blacks leads whites to patrol borders (familial, territorial, and political) between races.

which are the more typical predictors of racial attitudes and policy preferences.

The models using the NES data also show that whites who feel close to blacks were more likely to support government aid to blacks, affirmative action programs, and the provision of fair job opportunities for blacks, compared to whites who did not feel close to blacks. In other words, even controlling for ideological self-identification and partisanship, whites who drew the boundaries of their community beyond color lines were more likely to support policies that would benefit African Americans and less likely to support attitudes and policies that patrol racial boundaries. The effect of white identification, in contrast, was small in the NES model and indistinguishable from the null hypothesis of no effect in the GSS models. Therefore, I find little evidence to support theories of race consciousness that would link white identification with clear white group interests and negative attitudes toward blacks. Instead, inclusion of blacks within one's community – operationalized here as whites feeling close to blacks – tends to lead to support for programs to help these community members, above and beyond the effects of ideology and party identification.

Because people's values can also affect their policy preferences, I tested (when possible) whether beliefs about equality or helping others would eliminate the effect of how people imagine their communities. I reran the NES model from Figure 5.3 with measures of egalitarianism, humanitarianism, and economic individualism as controls (Feldman and Steenbergen 2001).[22] Closeness to blacks still had a strong predictive

---

[22] Humanitarianism is an index created from the following four survey items. "Please tell me how much you agree or disagree with each [of the following statements]: (1) One should always find ways to help others less fortunate than oneself. (2) A person should always be concerned about the well-being of others. (3) It is best not to get too involved in taking care of other people's needs. (4) People tend to pay more attention to the well-being of others than they should." Egalitarianism is an index created from the following six survey items. "I am going to read several statements. After each one, I would like you to tell me whether you agree strongly with the statement, agree somewhat, neither agree nor disagree, disagree somewhat, or disagree strongly. (1) Our society should do whatever is necessary to make sure that everyone has an equal opportunity to succeed. (2) We have gone too far in pushing equal rights in this country. (3) One of the big problems in this country is that we don't give everyone an equal chance. (4) This country would be better off if we worried less about how equal people are. (5) It is not really that big a problem if some people have more of a chance in life than others. (6) If people were treated more equally in this country we would have many fewer problems." Economic individualism is an index created from the following. "(1) Next, I am going to ask you to choose which of two statements I read comes closer to your own opinion. You might agree to some extent with both, but we want to know which one

effect on policy preferences even with the addition of these values as variables in the models. (See Web Appendix for results.) In other words, a community that crosses racial boundaries leads to support for government policies to help blacks, above and beyond the effects of ingroup interests, partisanship, ideology, and abstract beliefs about equality, individualism, and altruism.

One other obvious alternative explanation for why whites welcome blacks in their families and neighborhoods or support government programs to help African Americans is that they simply like blacks. Although group affect and prejudice do play a large role in racial politics, how people imagine their communities is not simply a proxy for likeability. To test this hypothesis, I reran the models in Figure 5.3 with controls for group affect. With the GSS data, I control for both stereotypes of blacks and whites.[23] For the NES data, I reran the models with stereotypes of blacks and whites, and also with feeling thermometer scores for whites and blacks.[24] (See Web Appendix for results.) As with values, the addition of controls for group likeability or prejudice did not eliminate the effect of how people imagine their communities. Not surprisingly, the effect size of closeness to blacks became smaller – given the correlation between feelings of closeness and affect toward an outgroup – but these replications provide clear evidence that understanding who people include in their communities is not simply another way of capturing group affect. Because group affect can be part of why people draw their community boundaries where they do, adding affect into the models is an extremely

is closer to your views. One, the less government, the better; or Two, there are more things that government should be doing? (2) One, we need a strong government to handle today's complex economic problems; or Two, the free market can handle these problems without government being involved. (3) One, the main reason government has become bigger over the years is because it has gotten involved in things that people should do for themselves; or Two, government has become bigger because the problems we face have become bigger. (4) One, it is more important to be a cooperative person who works well with others; or Two, it is more important to be a self-reliant person able to take care of oneself."

[23] The survey items asked respondents to place whites and blacks on seven-point scales of intelligence, laziness, and wealth. I created additive indices from these items for each racial group.

[24] The standard measure for affect toward groups in the National Election Studies is the feeling thermometer, which asks respondents to rate an individual or group on a scale from 0 to 100. A high score means that the respondent feels "warmly" toward the group, and a low score indicates negative feelings or "coolness." The 1996 NES also asked a battery of questions to measure stereotypes about whites and blacks. Respondents were asked to rate whites on seven-point scales of intelligence, trustworthiness, and laziness, and were then asked a set of corresponding questions for blacks. I created an additive index from the stereotype items.

conservative test of the effect of community, and more likely than not, it is biasing the results of the community measure downward.

I also ran one final replication, with the idea that either contact or living near blacks would explain the GSS social distance variable. To that end, I included in the original model a question that asked respondents "Are there any (Negroes/Blacks/African-Americans) living in this neighborhood now?" Again, the finding for community definition is robust; while having a black neighbor does diminish a white respondent's feelings of social distance from blacks, whether she feels close to blacks still has a significant effect on determining where she patrols the boundaries of her community.

Summary

From the analyses in this study of white respondents, it appears that some whites do draw their community boundaries to include blacks, and that feeling close to blacks – "in their ideas, and interests, and feelings about things" – matters for whites' attitudes toward blacks, for their beliefs about interactions and contact between racial groups, and for certain policy preferences.[25] These whites are more likely to support a variety of programs targeted to help African Americans and minimize distance between whites and blacks, above and beyond group likeability, racial prejudice, ideology, partisanship, and values like egalitarianism, humanitarianism, and individualism. A community defined by one's ingroup, on the other hand, has a very limited impact on such politically relevant variables, and even when its effects are statistically significant, they are much smaller in magnitude than closeness to blacks. Racial identification is fairly common among whites (although not universal), but there is little evidence among white respondents that it has much of an effect on their racial and political attitudes.

The limited political impact of white identification may be caused by the fact that whites' group interest is not at stake for the policies examined. Stoker (1996) shows that even for affirmative action policies, whites do not necessarily perceive a conflict of interest between whites

---

[25] To put this in perspective, the percentage of whites who felt close to blacks in 1996 is roughly the same percentage of whites who expressed the most negative stereotypes of blacks (coded as the bottom quartile on an index of items asking whether blacks are hard-working, intelligent, and trustworthy). Also, see Walsh (2007) for a much more nuanced discussion of the mixed effects of interaction and discussions between whites and blacks.

and blacks. She also finds that "whites' concern for blacks' interests is largely contingent on the happenstance of shared interests" (1996, 27). I do not have measures for the role that perceptions of zero-sum outcomes played in policy attitudes for these data, but it is certainly possible that the whites who feel close to blacks are more concerned about advancing blacks' interests – interests they share with fellow community members – than are whites who do not feel close to blacks.

Furthermore, despite the commonality of white identification, it is not a central or salient political identity (Wong and Cho 2005). As I showed in Chapter 2, white identity is almost never chosen as a primary identity; "whites" are only chosen along with other groups in the closeness battery, even if "blacks" are not also selected. In other words, although many white respondents feel close to whites but not blacks, this does not automatically mean their white identity is central in their political judgments.

The findings here suggest that broadening one's "circle of We" and extending feelings of attachment beyond racial lines has a distinct effect on the public opinion of whites in the United States. The effects of this broader sense of community are, in fact, as strong, if not stronger, than those of racial identification for whites. The weak role of racial identification may be unique for whites because of the dominant or majority status of this group in the United States, or perhaps because it is bound up with national identity (Devos and Banaji 2005). The effect for community, however, has its strongest test in this case: whites have no need to build broader coalitions with outgroups to create a numerical majority nationally. Even in a hypothetical world without the residential and occupational segregation that exists in this country, only about one in eight people that an American meets would be black. In a time when media images of African Americans are oftentimes negative or, at best, stereotypical (Gilens 1999; Gilliam and Iyengar 2000), strong or weak ties (e.g., contact) would seem to be necessary in order to counteract media portrayals to create a transracial community for whites (Allport 1954). Nonetheless, whites who include members of their racial outgroup in their community favor outlooks and policies that are intended to help *all* members of their communities.

STUDY 2: BLACKS' INCLUSION OF BLACKS AND WHITES IN THEIR COMMUNITY

One difficulty in replicating the same analyses of whites (as in Study 1) for blacks is that the meanings of public policies are quite different, depending on whether the respondent belongs to the majority/dominant group in society or not. A white man who extends his community to include blacks may feel obligated to help blacks (e.g., to support government aid to blacks). The converse story is not as logical: a black man who extends his community to include whites may feel obligated to help whites, but this is most likely unrelated to his opinion about government aid to blacks.[26] Surveys also do not ask about policies explicitly designed to aid whites; asking a respondent in contemporary America about a "government program to help whites" would be perceived as either nonsensical or offensive. Therefore, it is difficult to compare identical policy models for blacks and whites because the meaning of the models of policy preferences would not be comparable.[27]

Ideally, one would have questions that asked respondents about policies that were not explicitly zero-sum, in order to best replicate the position of white respondents in Study 1. What are relevant in a study of blacks' sense of identity and community are survey items that might place whites and blacks in a competitive or antagonistic position. Therefore, in this study of African Americans' attitudes, I focus on attitudes about possibilities of conflict, desires for cross-racial cooperation, and policy preferences.

The data for my analyses in Study 2 come from the 191 black respondents in the 1996 NES and the 1150 respondents in the 1984 National Black Election Study (NBES). The NBES also contained measures of closeness, with a question wording similar to the NES closeness items:

Please tell me if you feel very close, fairly close, not too close, or not close at all to the following groups. How close do you feel in your ideas and feelings about things to... Whites in this country? Black people in this country?

The response options are different (four categories, ranging from "very close" to "not close at all," compared to the dichotomous NES item),

---

[26] Of course, extending one's community could also reflect a desire for more power, passing, and assimilation in a way different from whites feeling close to blacks.

[27] I did repeat the same analyses concerning policy attitudes from Study 1 for the blacks in the NES sample (results not shown here). When attitudes about racial policies – government aid to blacks, affirmative action, and job opportunities for blacks – were regressed on closeness to whites and blacks, party identification, ideology, and demographic controls, closeness to whites has no effect on policy attitudes. Black identification is significant only for attitudes about the government helping blacks and affirmative action. However, due to a very small sample size – even smaller than that reported in Figure 5.4 due to the addition of political predispositions as controls – it is difficult to interpret, much less generalize from, these results, even if they were appropriate comparisons to the models shown in Figure 5.3.

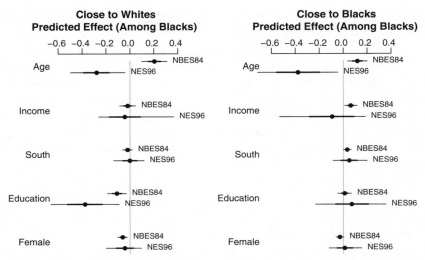

FIGURE 5.4. The Relationships Between Closeness to Blacks and Whites and Personal Attributes.
Source: 1984 National Black Election Study and 1996 National Election Study, black respondents only.

however, and the NBES item does not explicitly mention "interests" as the NES item does.[28]

Who Identifies?

Who are the black identifiers? The NES results show that 77 percent of the black respondents feel close to blacks. Age is related to identification, such that younger blacks are more likely to feel close to blacks than older blacks, but otherwise, it is difficult to discern what characteristics lead blacks to identify or not. Regressing closeness to blacks on measures of age, income, education, gender, and region produced few significant predictors (see Figure 5.4). Who are the black identifiers in the NBES data? Ninety-three percent of the sample felt "very" or "fairly" close to blacks, and regression results indicate that the older, wealthier, and Southern

---

[28] I choose here to use the same operationalization of racial identification as I used in the study for whites. Much work has been done on black identity using multiple measures (see, for example, Sellers et al. 1997; 1998), particularly with the National Black Election Study (Dawson 1994; Gay and Tate 1998; Herring et al. 1999; Tate 1993). However, because I am interested in comparing black respondents' psychological attachment to both blacks and whites with that of white respondents, for this analysis I use the same operationalization for black identity that I did for whites in Study 1.

respondents were more likely to feel close to blacks than the young, the poor, or non-Southerners.

Who are the blacks who feel close to whites? The NES data show that 19 percent of the black respondents felt close to whites, whereas the NBES data indicate that 64 percent of blacks felt "very close" or "fairly close" to whites. Again, this difference may be caused by the differences in question wordings and response options. Regressing closeness to whites on age, education, income, gender, and region shows us that for the NES sample, younger respondents and less educated blacks are more likely to feel close to whites than better educated or older ones (see Figure 5.4). The same analysis using the NBES data shows that men, the older respondents, and the less educated are more likely to feel close to whites than women, youths, and respondents with more education. As with the white respondents in the previous study, it is difficult to discern a clear pattern using basic demographic factors as indicators for predicting who someone includes in their community – members of their ingroup, members of their outgroup, both, or neither.

With the NES data, a cross-tabulation of black identifiers with blacks who feel close to whites indicates that 22 percent of blacks feel close to neither group, 59 percent feel close to blacks only, and 19 percent feel close to both. Clearly, the overlap between feeling close to whites and feeling close to blacks is greater among black than white respondents in the NES. The NBES pattern is markedly different, with a greater percentage of respondents feeling "very" or "fairly" close to *both* blacks and whites: 5 percent feel close to neither, 31 percent feel close to blacks only, and 63 percent feel close to both. These results comparing closeness to ingroup and outgroup are similar to the ones in the previous study: feeling close to an outgroup occurs only *in addition* to feeling close to one's ingroup.[29] Sidanius and Pratto (1999) explained that deference or outgroup favoritism is a "special case of asymmetrical ingroup bias," such that subordinates actually favor dominants over their ingroups; both the NES and NBES results show that this deference is indeed rare.

The main question of interest is how the group closeness measures relate to racial attitudes and political preferences. Therefore, I now turn to analyses that test the effects of community sentiment for African Americans. The 1984 NBES included a wide array of questions about race relations and policies. I created three indices to capture attitudes

[29] I am not making a temporal argument, however, that outgroup closeness follows ingroup identification.

about the likelihood of racial borders being transcended in one's community – including beliefs that the system is too unfair for blacks and whites to act as equal community members and attitudes about black nationalism – and policy preferences. To measure beliefs about whether there is a level playing field for whites and blacks to come together as equal community members, I create an additive perceived inequality index out of the following three items.[30]

1. Do whites as a group have too much influence, just about the right amount of influence, or too little influence [in American life and politics]?
2. This country would be better off if we worried less about how equal black people and white people are. (agree/disagree)
3. Discrimination against blacks is no longer a problem in the United States (agree/disagree)

Blacks who include whites in their communities tend to have more positive views about the state of racial equality in the United States (see Figure 5.5). They are more likely than blacks who do not feel close to whites to believe that discrimination is no longer a problem, that the country should worry less about equality, and that whites do not have too much influence. The effect of including whites in their community is much more powerful than that of racial identification, which does work in the opposite direction. Those respondents who would include both whites and blacks in their community are less likely to think racial prejudice and discrimination are as bad as those who feel close only to other blacks. Depending on how one views the state of the nation's racial inequality, this could be interpreted as a dark side of community, potentially blinding one to intergroup inequities.

One response to such ongoing prejudice and discrimination is an emphasis on black power and autonomy (Ture and Hamilton 1992), rather than depending – fruitlessly, they would argue – on the federal government (or whites) to intervene to help African Americans. NBES respondents were asked to agree or disagree with the following four items that relate to the issue of black power and self-reliance:[31]

1. Black children should study an African language.
2. Blacks should always vote for black candidates when they run.

---

[30] All three items load on a single factor in a confirmatory factor analysis.
[31] Again, all items load on a single factor. Black nationalism has been measured using the NBES in a number of different ways, partly because of the vagaries of factor analysis

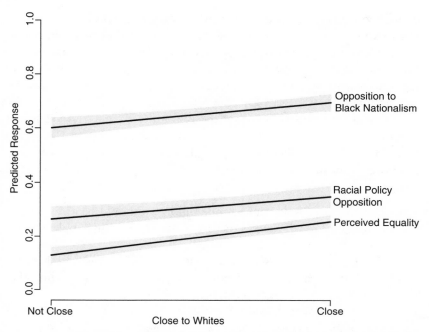

FIGURE 5.5. The Relationships Between Closeness to Blacks and Whites and Political Attitudes. African Americans who include whites in their community are less likely to perceive inequality as a problem, are more likely to oppose black autonomy at the cost of integration, and are less likely to support a wide array of government programs intended to benefit blacks.
Source: 1984 National Black Election Study.

3. Black people should shop in black-owned stores whenever possible.
4. Blacks should not have anything to do with whites if they can help it.

I created an additive index of nationalism from these four items. Figure 5.5 shows that black identification is a strong predictor of support for black autonomy and creating some distance between blacks and whites. Closeness to whites, on the other hand, is a significant predictor of negative attitudes about black nationalism. Blacks who include whites

as a tool. See, for examples, Davis and Brown (2002) for a ten-item single factor model and Brown and Shaw (2002) for an eight-item two dimensional model. I choose a much simpler operationalization because for the purposes of this analysis, a broad measure (or multiple measures) is not needed.

in their communities are less likely to believe that blacks should shop in black stores whenever possible, and they are also less likely to think that blacks should avoid all contact with whites. These results make intuitive sense, given that someone who has a multiracial community would see little reason to support attitudes and actions that encourage racial segregation.

The final set of questions from the NBES that I analyze refer to the role that the government and other institutions can play in remedying racial inequality via policies to help blacks and other minorities. The policies range from specific policies targeted at employment to more general programs:[32]

1. Because of past discrimination, minorities should be given special consideration when decisions are made about hiring applicants for jobs. (agree/disagree)
2. The government in Washington should make every possible effort to improve the social and economic position of blacks and other minority groups. (agree/disagree)
3. The government should not make any special effort to help blacks and other minorities because they should help themselves. (agree/disagree)
4. Some people feel that the government in Washington should make every possible effort to improve the social and economic position of blacks and other minority groups. Suppose they're at number 1 on a scale. Others feel that the government should not make any special effort to help minorities because they should help themselves. Suppose they're at number 7. And, of course, other people have opinions somewhere in between. Where would you place yourself on this scale, or haven't you thought much about this?

These four items were used to create an additive index of racial policy support. As shown by past research on black identity and Figure 5.5, black identifiers are more likely to think that the government and its policies should make efforts to improve the position of blacks. Blacks who drew multiracial communities to include whites were less likely than black identifiers to support government efforts and affirmative action programs, although it should be noted that this is a matter of degree. Relative to blacks who did not feel close to whites, respondents with a more inclusive community – feeling close to both blacks and whites – were

---

[32] In a confirmatory factor analysis, all four policy items loaded on a single factor.

less supportive, but as is clear from the model, are still on average in favor of these policies and programs.

Again, because there could be concern that drawing community boundaries is simply a matter of group likeability, I reran the three models with an additional variable that captures respondents' views of whites' intentions toward blacks. Respondents were asked, "On the whole, do you think most white people want to see blacks get a better break, or do they want to keep blacks down, or don't they care one way or the other?" While the question does not ask directly about how much whites are liked, it is implicit that if a group as a whole is perceived as having malevolent intentions, then that group is not well-liked.[33] The addition of this stereotype measure does not change the overall results of the models in Figure 5.5; it is not a significant predictor of either black nationalism or policy preferences, although it does have a relationship with attitudes about inequality in the United States. And, drawing community boundaries to include racial outgroup members continues to be significantly related to how blacks view the playing field, how they see their interactions with whites, and what policies they prefer.

Summary

Although closeness to whites among African American respondents had little effect on policy opinions from the NES survey, analyses of NBES questions that placed whites and blacks in opposition indicated that the inclusion of whites within a black respondent's community affected his or her political outlook. Respondents who feel close to whites are less likely to believe that whites have too much influence and that blacks should try to segregate themselves.

Blacks who expand their community to include whites also believe less strongly that blacks needed to rely only on themselves – looking after their own political and economic interests – or that whites are consciously racist. Closeness to whites did tend to lead to more racially conservative policy views, relatively speaking; however, it should be noted that the majority of blacks who expanded their community to include whites still have liberal racial attitudes. For example, they continue to see discrimination as a problem, they support affirmative action programs, and they believe that the government should work to improve the social and economic position of blacks, even controlling for ideological and partisan

---

[33] The NBES did not include a feeling thermometer for whites.

predispositions. The solutions sought by those blacks whose communities include blacks and whites are more likely to emphasize intergroup cooperation, and they are more likely to trust the government to create policies to address problems of prejudice and discrimination.

The results in this study emphasize why we need to examine different policy consequences for the effects of racial identity for whites and blacks. Different racial groups in society are not simply mirror images of each other, and we need to be aware of the social and numerical statuses of the different groups in research on the political ramifications of ingroup identity and outgroup closeness. In the next study, I turn to look at the relationships between multiple groups in American society, using the same measures of community and political attitudes for each group.

STUDY 3: NON-HISPANIC WHITES, AFRICAN AMERICANS, HISPANICS, ASIAN AMERICANS, AND BLACK CARIBBEANS' INCLUSION OF EACH OTHER IN THEIR COMMUNITIES

The NES, GSS, and NBES allow us to examine in depth the effect of group closeness for whites and blacks across a number of racial attitudes and policy preferences. However, it would be helpful to conduct the same set of analyses for different racial groups using one dataset, to set aside any concerns that differences in specific question wording, timing of the survey, or sampling could show similar effects of community boundaries because of coincidence. Therefore, I turn to the 2004–2005 National Politics Study (NPS). The NPS is a national telephone survey, conducted before and after the 2004 presidential election in both Spanish and English (depending on the respondents' preferences), of non-Hispanic whites, Latinos, Asian Americans, African Americans, and Caribbean blacks. Because of the large subsamples of racial minorities, and the fact that the survey contains questions of group closeness and intergroup competition between all five groups in the sample, I am able to compare (1) the factors that lead respondents of different races to feel close to members of multiple racial outgroups; (2) explore in more depth the potential relationships between feelings of closeness, contact with outgroup members, and racial context; and (3) the political effects of where racial community boundaries are drawn for respondents of different races, without concern that the questions are asymmetric because of question wording differences. I am able to look at how people patrol the boundaries of their communities (however they are perceived), how invested they feel in those communities, and what actions they take or policies they support on behalf of community members.

The NPS asked all respondents, "How close do you feel to each of the following groups of people in your ideas, interests, and feelings about things?" Respondents were asked of all groups, including their own – non-Hispanic whites, blacks, Hispanics, Asian Americans, and Caribbeans – and the order was randomized. The question wording is very similar to that of the NES, and again allows respondents to draw the boundaries of their community beyond their "objective" racial group. Figure 5.6 shows the relationships between closeness to ingroups and outgroups, and demographic characteristics and the contexts of respondents. Context in this case is measured by percentages for the various racial groups in a respondent's 2000 census tract.

As has been evident in the analyses of who expresses closeness in Studies 1 and 2, there are no basic demographic factors that consistently lead respondents to feel close to ingroups or outgroups. There is some indication that the presence of an outgroup in a respondent's environment is related to more affirmative answers of closeness to that outgroup. So, for example, whites who live among more Hispanics and Caribbeans are more likely to feel close to the two minority groups, compared with whites who live in more homogeneous settings. For blacks, living among more whites and Hispanics also coincides with more closeness to these groups; Hispanics, who live among more Asians and Caribbeans are more likely to include them in their communities; and Asians who have more white neighbors are more likely to place whites within the boundaries of their racial communities.[34]

Respondents in the NPS also were asked to agree or disagree with the following questions:

1) I would approve if someone in my family married a person of a different racial or ethnic background from mine.
2) Whites and racial and ethnic minorities can never be really comfortable with each other, even if they are close friends.
3) The problems of Blacks, Hispanics, and Asian Americans are too different for them to be political allies or partners.

These three items answer the question of whether racial groups are or should be distant from one another, with the idea that if they are too

---

[34] For black, Caribbean, and Hispanic respondents, living among more ingroup members is also related to greater closeness to one's ingroup.

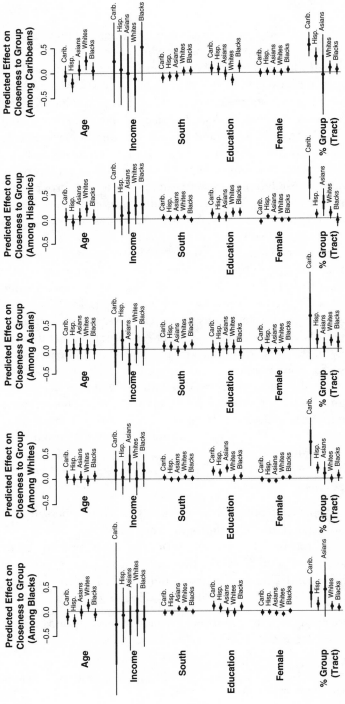

FIGURE 5.6. The Relationships Between Closeness to Ingroups and Outgroups, Racial Context, and Personal Attributes, by racial group of the respondents.

Source: 2004–5 National Politics Study.

distant, then social and political cooperation will be difficult if not impossible. The advantage of these questions is that they can be asked of all racial groups with relatively the same meaning. For each of these three items, I regressed it for each racial group separately, with closeness to a single group at a time, along with basic demographic characteristics as the predictors.[35]

The results of the analyses shown in Figure 5.7 clearly indicate that how people draw their communities is related to how they view marriage between racial groups, controlling for partisanship and ideology; this relationship is strongest for white respondents. Among whites, including blacks, Caribbeans, Hispanics, and Asians in their communities is associated with a greater acceptance of interracial marriage and is the biggest predictor except for age. Although none of the predictors reached standard levels of statistical significance for Caribbean or Asian respondents, closeness to blacks, Caribbeans, and Asians among Hispanic respondents was also significantly related to greater support for intermarriage. For African American respondents, closeness to Caribbeans, Hispanics, and Asians were also related to support for marriage across races. Racial identity, by contrast, had little to no effect for respondents of any race, despite the argument that strong identifiers would be more supportive of maintaining clear boundaries between ingroups and outgroups.

Figure 5.8 shows the results for the question of whether racial groups are too different from each other to be good allies. For white respondents, including Asians, blacks, Hispanics, and Caribbeans in their communities is related to greater support for intergroup cooperation in politics, and this effect is stronger than that of partisanship and ideological self-identification. This relationship is also significant for blacks who feel close to Asians and Hispanics; Caribbeans who feel close to blacks; and Hispanics who feel close to African Americans. Expansion of one's community beyond objective ingroup lines is related to greater optimism about the possibilities of "rainbow coalitions," above and beyond party identification and ideology. Although the results for the question about whether racial groups can be comfortable with each other are not shown here for reasons of space (see Web Appendix), the pattern is similar and most consistent again for whites.

Again, to set aside concerns that I am simply capturing how much respondents like a particular group, I reran the models for each racial

---

[35] These three items did not hold together, so the models were run separately for each question.

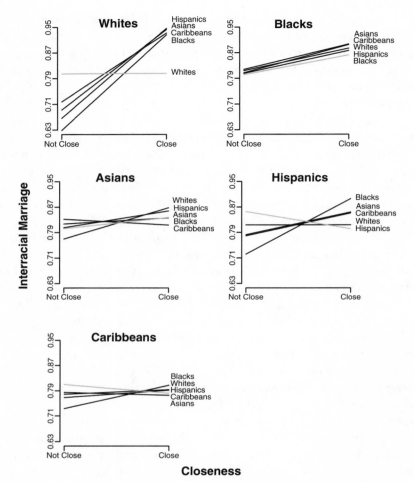

FIGURE 5.7. The Relationships Between Closeness to Ingroups and Outgroups and Support for Interracial Marriage, by racial group of the respondents. The more inclusive one's imagined community, the greater one's support for a family member marrying someone of a different race or ethnicity.
Source: 2004–2005 National Politics Study.

group separately, including closeness to a single outgroup and group stereotypes of that outgroup as predictors, along with the demographic controls.[36] The overall results lead to the same conclusion that how

---

[36] Respondents were asked the following: "I have some more questions about different groups in our society. Imagine a seven-point scale on which the characteristics of the people in a group can be rated. In the first question a score of 1 means that you think

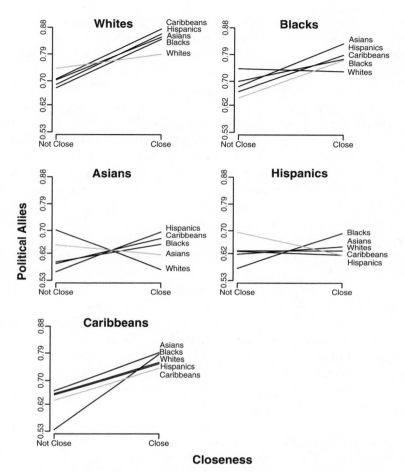

FIGURE 5.8. The Relationships Between Closeness to Ingroups and Outgroups and Support for a Rainbow Coalition, by racial group of the respondents. The more inclusive one's imagined community, the greater one's belief that African Americans, Latinos, and Asian Americans can be political allies.
Source: 2004–2005 National Politics Study.

almost all of the people in that group tend to be lazy. A score of 7 means that you think that most people in the group are hardworking. A score of 4 means that you think most people in the group are not closer to one end or the other, and of course, you may choose any number in between. Where would you rate Whites in general on a scale of 1 to 7, where 1 indicates lazy, 7 means hardworking, and 4 indicates most Whites are not closer to one end or the other?" Respondents were also asked about African Americans, Hispanics, Asian Americans, and Caribbeans, and the order with which the groups were presented was randomized.

communities are drawn matters. In fact, the coefficients for the closeness measures were consistently larger than those for the stereotype items. Of course, even if there is no distance sensed between racial groups, competition may still prevent cooperation among groups.

Researchers have studied intergroup competition across and between a range of groups – including European immigrants, Latinos, Asians, and blacks (Borjas 2006; Kim 2000; Olzak and Shanahan 2003) – and possible situations and consequences, like competition over scarce resources, status, elections, and leadership of protest movements (Levine and Campbell 1972; Olzak 1992; Sonenshein 1993; Ture and Hamilton 1992). If racial groups are seen to be in competition with one another, then the possibility of multiracial communities becomes more distant.

The NPS survey asks respondents about their views of interracial group competition in two different arenas: politics and economics. They are asked the extent to which they agree or disagree with the following statements, "More good jobs for [outgroup] means fewer good jobs for people like me" and "The more influence [outgroup] have in politics, the less influence people like me have in politics." These questions were previously used in the Los Angeles County Social Survey (LACSS), as well as in other research on intergroup conflict (Bobo and Hutchings 1996). For the sake of simplicity, I present results for a competition index, where the political and economic competition questions have been added together for each outgroup.[37] Again, a major advantage of these questions is that they are parallel for all groups.

As with the analyses using the other datasets, I included in the models as predictors both closeness to respondents' ingroups as well as closeness to their outgroups (in separate models), for each outgroup competition question.

Figure 5.9 presents the results for white respondents' perceptions of competition with blacks, Hispanics, Asians, and Caribbeans. (What is represented is the effect of outgroup closeness from four separate models.) As whites expanded the boundaries of their racial communities to include members of racial groups other than their own, they became less likely to see politics and the job market as a zero-sum game between their ingroup and outgroups. In other words, a white individual who felt very close to blacks was much less likely to see African Americans as taking jobs or political influence away from whites, compared to another

---

[37] I also reran the models for the two types of competition separately. While there are small differences, the overall story was similar for all groups. (See Web Appendix for these regression results.)

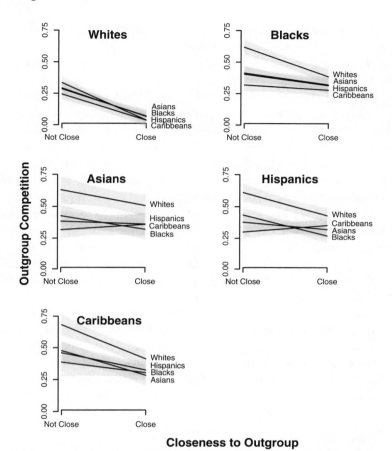

Closeness to Outgroup

FIGURE 5.9. The Relationships Between Closeness to Ingroups and Outgroups and Intergroup Competition, by racial group of the respondents. The more inclusive one's imagined community, the less likely one believes racial groups are in competition with each other politically and economically.
Source: 2004–2005 National Politics Study.

white individual who excluded blacks from her community. This effect of broadening community boundaries remains statistically and substantively significant, even with controls in the models for age, education, gender, income, region, partisanship, and ideological self-identification, and ingroup identification. I replicated the models, and the findings hold even when outgroup affect is added to the models. In other words, even controlling for one's like or dislike of a group, including that group in one's community creates a sense that everyone is struggling together. Politics and the job market are not seen as a dog-eat-cat world.

A similar pattern emerges for black respondents. Black respondents who include whites in their community are much less likely to see that whites and blacks are at odds when it comes to politics and jobs. Although the effect of expanding community boundaries also leads to lesser feelings of intergroup competition with Hispanics, Caribbeans, and Asian Americans, it is not as large as when the outgroup asked about is whites. Nevertheless, even controlling for affect toward whites, Asians, Caribbeans, and Hispanics, the make-up of African American respondents' communities still had an effect on perceptions of competition.

For Latinos, closeness to whites, blacks, and Asians leads to fewer perceptions that these groups are engaged in zero-sum games when it comes to political influence and jobs. Even controlling for dislike of these racial outgroups, Latinos who drew the boundaries of their community to include whites, blacks, and Asians perceived less competition between their ingroup and outgroups.[38] Figure 5.9 indicates that for Asian and Caribbean respondents, closeness to different outgroups had similar effects on their beliefs about intergroup competition, although they did not reach standard levels of statistical significance. All of these models included controls for partisanship and ideology, and in most cases, how people imagine their community has as strong, if not stronger, an effect on competition beliefs as these political predispositions.

Finally, I looked at the effect of how communities are drawn on policy preferences that emphasize an explicit recognition of race. The NPS asked respondents to agree or disagree with the following:

1) People are best represented in political office by leaders from their own racial or ethnic background.
2) Law enforcement should be able to stop and arrest people of certain racial or ethnic backgrounds if they are thought to be more likely to commit crimes.

Respondents were also asked two different affirmative action questions:

1) Some people say that because of past discrimination, some groups in society should be given preference in hiring and promotion. Others say that such preference in hiring and promotion is wrong because it gives some groups advantages they haven't earned. How

---

[38] Closeness to Caribbeans does seem to work in the opposite direction for Hispanic respondents, such that those who expand their communities to include Caribbeans are more likely to perceive them as political and economic competitors.

strongly do you favor or oppose preferential hiring and promotion?
Are you strongly in favor, somewhat in favor, somewhat opposed,
or strongly opposed to it?

2) Generally speaking, do you think affirmative action is a good thing
or a bad thing?

For each of these policy items, feelings of closeness to outgroups was
related to respondents expressing greater support for affirmative action
and descriptive representation, and greater opposition to profiling.
Figure 5.10 presents only the results for the preferences item, but the
pattern of results for the other dependent variables is similar, albeit
weaker. For white respondents, including any outgroup in their community increased their support for affirmative action. For black respondents,
including Asians, Caribbeans, Hispanics, and whites in their communities
goes hand in hand with greater support for preferences in hiring and promotion to compensate for past discrimination. And, for Hispanic respondents, closeness to Asians, blacks, Caribbeans, and whites corresponds
with greater support for racial preferences as a response to past discrimination. It is not surprising that how people imagine their communities
does not have as strong an effect on affirmative action preferences as
does ideology. It is significant that, controlling for political predispositions that are very salient in the policy debate, who is included in one's
community still matters.

These analyses using the National Politics Survey confirm the results
derived from the other surveys presented in this chapter. Using the same
measures for community boundaries across all groups and using the same
dependent variables measuring social and political distance, perceived
intergroup competition, and policy preferences, it provides a final test
of the robustness of the results found in Studies 1 and 2. Who people
include in their community affects their attitudes about with whom they
are in competition over jobs and politics and with whom they share these
goods.

CONCLUSION

Across racial and ethnic groups, the analyses from these studies show
that individuals do sometimes express closeness to members of their outgroup. Such outgroup closeness was expressed only in addition to group
identification, such that individuals expand their racial communities to
include members of outgroups only if the racial community first contains

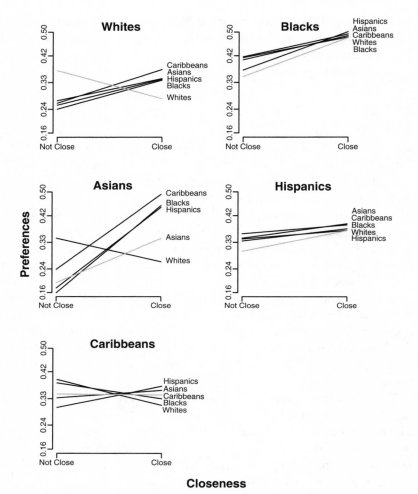

FIGURE 5.10. The Relationship Between Closeness to Ingroups and Outgroups and Support for Affirmative Action, by racial group of the respondents. The more inclusive one's imagined community, the greater one's support for preferences for hiring and promotion because of past discrimination.
Source: 2004–2005 National Politics Study.

members of the "objective" ingroup. This chapter has also shown that this extension of one's community is similar in effect to what Tajfel called the "value and emotional significance" that individuals attach to their identity. Outgroup closeness clearly leads to the type of favoritism that Tajfel studied, even when the group in question is not the respondent's "objective" ingroup. In other words, when the boundaries of one's community are drawn to include members of racial outgroups, the sense of political responsibility or obligation that one feels is then extended to those outgroup members. For example, policies that do not help ingroup members are supported – regardless of how much outgroup members are liked or not – as long as these policies help outgroup members who are contained within the boundaries of a respondent's community. Thus, "ingroups" and "outgroups" are subsets of a superordinate group, a community to which an individual belongs, and it is at the level of community that duties and obligations operate, expressed in terms of policy support. However, the superordinate groups that matter do not have to be identified by proper nouns (such as "America") to improve intergroup relations (Transue 2007).

The generality of my findings concerning the effects of community boundaries held up across samples of people, instruments, and items. When respondents expanded their community – operationalized as closeness to the outgroup – their preferences for policies tended to be in favor of helping all community members, regardless of outgroup status. Communities perceived to include both ingroup and outgroup members influenced policy decisions, even after controlling for ingroup identification and political predispositions. While some might argue this is simply evidence of the importance of groups (Converse 1964; Merton and Rossi 1968), there is no explanation for why whites would use both whites and blacks as reference groups, for example; the alternatives to an argument about transracial communities do not provide a clear rationale for why individuals should care about the welfare of "objective" outgroup members.

The findings in this chapter show that expanding the boundaries of one's community beyond one's ingroup – where the subjective boundaries of community are not constrained by the lines defined by governmental directives or common sense notions of race – does affect political decision making among ordinary Americans. The degree to which Americans expand their community boundaries varies greatly, depending on the measure used and the respondent's race; nevertheless, the smallest estimate still predicts that millions of Americans do expand their community boundaries beyond color lines.

Understanding this expanding (and possible shrinking) of community boundaries is crucial for politics – both the size of people's communities and the degree of obligation and responsibility that they feel toward other community members. How would the interests of numerical minorities be served if everyone followed only self-interest or group interest?

Although there is a racial divide in public opinion on some topics, our national politics do not pit *all* whites against *all* blacks against *all* Latinos against *all* Asians. I argue that we would have little support for policies aimed at helping numerical minorities if people's communities did not extend beyond the boundaries of their racial ingroup; pluralism would otherwise have no fighting chance. Ideology and values alone cannot account for the policy support. There are simply too few ideologues in a democracy of our size to believe that abstract beliefs about individualism or egalitarianism would lead to policies designed to help minority groups in this country (Converse 1964). Instead, it is a sense of community that creates a sense of duty and responsibility, which then lead respondents to support policies to benefit fellow community members.

6

Conclusion

How people imagine their communities sets the boundaries for the consideration of self or group interest, values, and ideology in their political lives. Who belongs inside a community and who is considered an outsider are determined by the types of its boundaries (be they relational or geographic) and where these boundaries are drawn. As Robert Frost explains in his poem *Mending Wall*, "There where it is we do not need the wall: He is all pine and I am apple orchard." This line highlights another crucial feature of communities: they are pictures in the minds of individuals. If we want to understand why people support redistributive policies, the important lines dividing "our community" and "you people" are the ones that are imagined, not the ones printed on paper or built of stone.

The images of their communities are major considerations when people make decisions, both in and out of the realm of politics. How will the actions they choose and the policies they support affect different people, and whose interests will be taken into account? The story that many social scientists tell is one motivated by interests: we want to promote our own self-interest and, often, the interests of groups to which we belong. These interests are obviously important factors in how people make high-stakes decisions, such as where their children should go to school or which job they should take. The idea of "utility" is also useful because it helps scholars understand the hierarchy of preferences, personal or political, from which individuals can make choices. However, I have demonstrated that boundaries crucially constrain the operation of interests, such that a person's self-interest or "objective" group interests can be subsumed or overridden by what is perceived to be in her community's interests. For example, I showed in Chapter 3 that people's feeling of a sense of community with their neighbors – not their personal income and how much they would have to pay – matters when making decisions about tax policies to increase local social services, from which they may or may not personally benefit. And, in Chapter 5, we saw that whites' definitions about who falls within the boundaries of community affect their opinions about affirmative action programs, irrespective of their race. A policy may not benefit an individual materially, but she may still support it because it will benefit the members of her imagined community.

A woman's community could be composed of only herself and her immediate family, but given modern conveniences, such as supermarkets, televisions, and the Internet, which force people into contact with one another physically or visually, it is hard to imagine many people whose considerations are focused inward to that extent. Sometimes a community may be nothing more than a group, but it is not constrained by "objective" definitions or a requirement that group members be homogenous along some visible dimension.[1] The prominent role of group-oriented thinking in public opinion is well documented (Converse 1964; Merton 1968), and group interest can serve both as a proxy for self-interest and as a motivation independent of one's material concerns. However, the question of which groups in particular are relevant is often simply announced or assumed by the researcher, and the boundaries of these groups are largely understood to be impermeable. For example, many political discussions involve talk of monolithic groups, such that "blacks argue that ...", "women support this ..." and "Americans believe...."[2] The presidential primary race between Hillary Clinton and Barack Obama in 2008, treated as the ultimate example of identity politics, only heightened this type of conversation among news reporters. The day after the Democratic National Convention ended, John McCain chose Alaska Governor Sarah Palin as the Republican vice presidential nominee. To hear the pundits' frenzied focus on women voters, from one day to the next, an alien might wonder if American women would vote for anyone with two X chromosomes. Taking the concept of community into account provides a more realistic picture of how the group-oriented thinking of individuals affects political judgments. Research by social identity and reference group

---

[1] Even microtargeting, which can lead to political mail directed to Target-shopping soccer moms who regularly vote and read *Newsweek*, is still focused on "communities" defined by outsiders.

[2] Outside the realm of American politics, one could add as an example to the list, "Chewa and Tumbuku think ..." (Morrison et al., cited in Posner 2004).

theorists is fundamental, but we need to add to it by acknowledging that the relevant groups or communities can be both smaller and larger than what is defined objectively or by an outsider. Because communities are imagined in the minds of ordinary people, individuals can determine for themselves how salient and central various group-based considerations are in their political decisionmaking.

People's communities also add to the stories researchers tell of the effects of ideology and values on public opinion and actions. Scholars over the past 50 years have shown the strong effects of these values and predispositions on attitudes and behavior (see, for examples, Converse 1964, Feldman and Steenbergen 2001, McClosky and Zaller 1984), but I have shown that even these principled stands often operate corralled by community boundaries. Chapter 5 showed that people's imagined communities have an effect on racial policy, for example, regardless of their belief in egalitarian or humanitarian values. Egalitarianism and individualism can also explain support for certain U.S. public policies, but these values do not often apply to all humans on earth equally. It is a very rare American who willingly lowers her family's standard of living to a significant degree to help a stranger in another country lead a better life, choosing a Values Without Borders lifestyle. Those who remind us of moral duties may speak of "one world," and globalization may ensure that people's livelihoods around the world are tied together, but that does not mean that the boundaries of people's interests and the boundaries encompassing the range of the application of their values will also fall away.

RATIONALE FOR PRIORITIZING ONE'S COMMUNITY

In Chapter 1, I discuss the existence and commonality of ethical particularism, but why should people favor members of their community? One simple explanation is ingroup favoritism, much like what social psychologists have found in minimal group experiments (Gaertner and Insko 2000; Tajfel 1970). Even if the favoritism does not result in advantages for the self, promoting group interest is, nevertheless, a more common response than choosing an egalitarian distribution of goods. What makes a relationship "special," justifying what Dagger (1985) calls moral parochialism? The communities that people imagine may prompt a feeling of obligation or moral duty to help community members, much as the duty of parents to care for small children (Garrison 1998; Stein et al 1998). Children are expected to give to parents because the latter are entitled to help; providing needed assistance is one of the strongest and most fundamental social expectations of kinship (Hanson et al. 1983; Seelbach and Sauer 1977). The obligation to help is not based on altruism but on a principle of right action. Coming to the aid of community members can be seen as a moral principle independent of inclination, likeability of recipients, general values, and emotions that imposes the obligation (Obler 1986, 422). Those within the borders of my community are "in" and deserving of help, while those on the outside are beyond the limits – practical or moral – of concern. When tradeoffs must be made, community members are favored. Because I can add people to my community and remove them from it, my sense of obligation or loyalty to the community can remain steady, and I do not have to worry about ambivalence or cognitive dissonance between feeling attached to my group but not its leaders, or some other such scenario. And because my community is as *I* imagine it – people who are like me in some way (and the homogeneity along this dimension is defined only be me) – then I can feel happily tied to them.[3] I may want to assist them because we are tied together. This could be seen as group interest writ large, although only to the extent that the group is the community as I imagine it. Interest can be loosely construed to mean I benefit via empathy if someone else in my community benefits. One could argue that Dawson's group utility heuristic applies to all communities – but only in the very loosest sense (1994). What happens to other community members will affect me to a certain extent, although when Dawson developed the concept, discrimination by outgroup members – not necessarily a sense of community or fraternity within the group – is what tied blacks of different social classes together.

This prioritizing of community members occurs at a number of different levels. Dagger (1985) and Miller (1995) write of national communities, and Hoffmann is also writing about national boundaries, for example, when he explains the limited nature of obligations in *Duties Beyond Borders*:

Obligations to other people exist only if they are part of the same community. We may be interdependent with others, but interdependence is a material fact, community is a moral fact. (1981, 152)

[3] However, this simple description blithely ignores the fact that we are not unencumbered political selves. We are surrounded by political messages – implicit and explicit – that try to tell us where we should draw our community boundaries. Parties and ideologies explain what groups or beliefs "go together"; social norms and schools indoctrinate people with who is "cool" or "good"; and laws draw boundaries between groups that can be adopted wholesale as individuals' own community boundaries.

Sandel (1982) agrees that community membership generates obligations extending beyond those owed to all human beings: "[T]o some I owe more than justice requires or even permits" (1982, 179). In other words, an individual may think that it is morally good to help the needy; nevertheless, she may have vastly different opinions about social programs to benefit homeless children in America and famine victims in Ethiopia if she considers Americans, but not Ethiopians, to be part of her community.

The sphere of obligation may be defined at a much lower, subnational level. Scheffler (2001), for example, describes special obligations restricted to community members as "associative duties," and he writes that people may have such

...associative duties to their friends, neighbors, and more distant relatives; to members of the same community, nation, or clan; to colleagues, co-workers and fellow union members; to classmates, compatriots, and comrades; to members of the same religious or racial or ethnic groups; and even to members of the same team, gang, or club. (50)

These associative duties do not have to be constrained to any single community. The determining factors are individual beliefs about belonging, irrespective of whether the boundaries are drawn along lines of ethnicity, class, nationality, or the like. Regardless of how community boundaries are drawn, "virtually any kind of group or personal relationship that has significance for the people it unites may be seen by them as giving rise to associative duties" (Scheffler 2001, 51).

In addition to describing moral parochialism as a fact of human life, across a number of different types of communities, some theorists make a normative case for such particularistic obligations (Dagger 1985; Etzioni 2002), arguing why helping only those within one's community is just. Dagger, for example, runs through a number of potential (but, to him, flawed) arguments for favoring one's compatriots – necessity, efficiency, and "side effects" – before arriving at what he describes as a good rationale, all else being equal: reciprocity. From his point of view, individuals may be incapable psychologically of concerning themselves with the lives of more than a small number of fellow human beings before becoming overwhelmed. And they probably would choose to get more results from their concern and help – both in terms of benefits for their recipients and the goodwill or friendship that could result – rather than less. After all, rigidity of supply and scarcity are two of the dimensions of goods that lead to localized justice (Elster 1995). Although necessity, efficiency, and "side effects" are insufficient to justify parochialism morally for Dagger, they are nevertheless still plausible explanations for why average citizens might act to benefit community members. The images of their communities that people have in their minds may have the psychological benefit of narrowing the focus of concern. The connections felt between community members, however tenuous, may facilitate the giving and receiving of aid, and the desire to strengthen these connections may provide an incentive to fulfill these associative duties or particularistic obligations. For Dagger, though, it is the notion of reciprocity that defensibly explains who benefits: it is not the nearest or the most needy, but those who are in a reciprocal relationship with the benefactor.

In contrast to Dagger, other theorists describe moral parochialism as commonsensical and intuitive behavior, as natural as devotion to one's family. Tamir, for example, does not need reciprocity as a rationale (although she does rely on cooperation); her support for a "morality of community" rests on belonging and connection. Without these outcomes that favor members, a "community" loses meaning and anarchy is the alternative:

> Communal membership will be meaningless unless individuals...perceive fellow members as partners in a shared way of life, as cooperators they can rely on. Having developed this attitude, they cannot but care for other members... These feelings provide individuals with a reason to attend first to the needs and interests of their fellows. If the moral force of such feelings is denied, ruling out any special attention to fellow members, the social structure might collapse and we shall be left with isolated individuals and an abstract humanity. (1993, 115–16)

Shue agrees that special obligations to intimates are unassailable, since not showing priority would be seen as "grossly lacking in human feeling, as having an attitude that was impersonal to the point of being inhuman" (1988, 692).

Macedo also points to intuition and pragmatism, when he argues that cosmopolitan social justice makes no sense without a cosmopolitan state or a cosmopolitan community, "which hardly anyone seriously argues for."[4] And, he writes, "If we ask what generates and sustains powerful obligations of mutual justification and justice, the best answer seems to me to be the complex relations shared by members of political communities" (2008, 24).

---

[4] Walzer sounds a similar note when he asks where he should register to vote as a citizen of the world (1996).

COMMUNITY WITHIN COSMOPOLITAN APPEALS

By definition, values have no boundaries as to their applicability; in practice, though, they are parochial. A number of public service organizations have been placing ads in prominent magazines to encourage philanthropy and altruistic behavior. For example, the Red Cross and Keep A Child Alive (an AIDS awareness organization) have run extensive media campaigns. On their face, the advertisements appear to be making altruistic appeals to cosmopolitans. The Red Cross ad reads, for example... "I don't know your name, but I will help save your life." The message is that the Red Cross (and its donors and volunteers) does not rely on close ties to determine whom to help. The implicit idea is that viewers of the ad should be inspired to contribute (blood or money) to the "organization without borders." However, in the smaller text, the ad goes on to read, "There is a place where a complete stranger will reach out to help make everything okay. That place is called America, where we look out for each other." So, the boundaries of obligation – even altruistically inspired – are constrained by national borders.

The Keep A Child Alive ads portray various celebrities, such as Gwyneth Paltrow, Richard Gere, and Lucy Liu, with the unifying slogan "I am African." The image of a blonde woman with a few streaks of tribal-like face paint is meant to convey that everyone – regardless of geography – can and should identify with the plight of African children suffering from AIDS. However, what is interesting is the smaller print that appears in the ads: "Each and every one of us contains DNA that can be traced back to our African ancestors." So, even though the slogan sounds cosmopolitan, emphasizing that anyone (and implying everyone) can be "African," the justification for why people should care is one that emphasizes roots and boundaries. Because everyone's genetic background indicates that we all descended from African ancestors, we should all feel responsibility toward our "community" and work to prevent AIDS from killing children in Africa. One could go so far as to argue that values as expressed in everyday life are simply broader interests applied to an individual's community.[5]

---

[5] One may wonder if these ads are necessary in the first place because political bodies are constrained by geographic boundaries. For example, because Americans privilege helping Americans over helping others in need (as shown in Chapter 4), perhaps politicians feel limited by what they can do to alleviate AIDS in Africa.

Thinking about the role of communities in politics provides a new perspective on who people are thinking about and how they come to their conclusions about whom to help. Imagined communities affect which policies are favored and when people will expend time to engage in civic and political activities. My argument about the effect of community boundaries holds up across three different "cases" – with communities that pertain to geography, nation, and race – with multiple tests for each case. Different considerations exist in each case, but the overall findings remain the same: how people imagine their communities affects whom they are willing to help in the political arena, above and beyond the more common explanations of interests, ideology, and values.

GEOGRAPHIC COMMUNITY

"Not In My Backyard" (NIMBY) attitudes are spurred by imagined communities based on geographical ties. People oppose the establishment of prisons, waste dumps, and homeless shelters in their neighborhoods because these projects are seen as dangerous and undesirable. Such objections lead people to expend time and effort to protect the status quo, preserving the economic, physical, and social health of those they perceive as members of their local community (including, of course, themselves) (Fischel 2001).

NIMBY movements enhance the social capital in an area. Neighbors leave their TV sets and interact and converse with one another; they organize and strategize about how to lobby local elites; they trust and rely on one another; and they believe (at least, at first) that they can make their voices heard by political leaders and effect change for the good. By engaging with each other, people in such movements may develop or enhance their feelings of community.[6] Prosocial behavior in general is more likely when individuals regard themselves as sharing membership in a larger social unit with superordinate goals (Kramer and Brewer 1984; Sherif and Sherif 1979; Transue 2007).

Although NIMBYism is an example of what could be touted by pundits as the magical, unifying powers of a sense of community, it also clearly demarcates the boundaries of obligation. People care, help, and work for the benefit of those individuals who are believed to be part of their community. Obviously, if they are successful, someone else will have to deal

---

[6] Community psychologists, after all, find that contact with neighbors is highly correlated with a "sense of community" (see Chapter 2).

with the toxic waste or prison; but, that is not a NIMBY activist's concern, because she will not consider those "someones" to be part of her community. An activist living in Louisville, Kentucky, may not think of people living across the river in Clarksville, Indiana, as part of her geographic community. This does not, however, preclude her from thinking of Americans (including those Clarkesvillians) as part of her community, thus expanding her community boundaries. In other words, people's perceptions of their communities need not depend on geographic proximity; the Louisvillian, for example, can think of her city and nation as part of her community, blithely ignoring her county, state, and region as considerations. This perception of community is also mobile. More than 15 percent of Americans move each year, and I have shown that their understanding of their geographic community moves from place to place with them.

Although contextual factors are related to whether individuals imagine their communities to include their neighbors or city, it is socioeconomic status rather than race that affects where boundaries are drawn. For both white and black respondents, having black neighbors diminishes feelings of closeness to their neighborhood and city, indicating a perceived economic effect more than a strictly prejudicial one. Racial context is obviously intertwined with people's prejudice and political actions, but objective racial context alone – at least as measured by census-tract-level data – does not appear to map onto imagined geographic communities in a simple or clear way. What probably matters more is how political elites translate this context into messages that inspire or threaten residents of an area (Hopkins 2009).

Using national and local survey data, I demonstrate that an individual who feels a sense of community in her neighborhood is more likely to trust local political institutions, feel politically efficacious, and participate in a number of different local activities, such as joining the PTA; this is true above and beyond how much she likes her neighborhood. Drawing community boundaries around her neighborhood or county also leads to support for tax policies that will benefit her local area; she is willing to pay higher taxes in order to increase services for her community, such as local transportation, parks, and public libraries – even if she tells a survey researcher that she is ideologically conservative and should therefore be ambivalent about, if not opposed to, a large role of the state in the provision of social services.

The question of for whom one is willing to pay for services extends beyond the realm of local politics to that of the nation. The gated local community is analogous to the ever-more-fenced-in national community.

NATIONAL COMMUNITY

The demographic make-up of the United States has changed dramatically since 1965, largely because of immigration, and the fanfare surrounding the 1990 and 2000 censuses has led to numerous articles about who "We, the People" are (see, for example, *Time* special issue, Fall 1993). Although this country is a "land of immigrants," and social identities and interests have always played a role in American politics, some scholars and politicians worry about the effects of the new immigrants on national unity, job market competition, social services, and the economy overall. Much of the debate surrounding immigration reform in the past couple of decades has focused on exactly who is a citizen, what it means to be a citizen, and who is entitled to the social and economic benefits provided by the national and state governments (Karst 1989; McDonnell 1997; Schuck and Smith 1985). These questions center on whether part of the assimilation and naturalization process in the United States involves a redrawing of boundaries, whereby empathy and allegiance shift from neighbors and compatriots in the old world to neighbors in the new. And the nation (via the U.S. Citizenship and Immigration Services) refines what it means to become a legal member every time the test required for naturalization is revised. Although the boundaries of people's imagined communities do not coincide with legal definitions, ordinary Americans are not altogether immune to institutional stipulations.

Boundary drawing also affects political attitudes when people think of the nation. Those individuals who are considered to be part of a person's national community also tend to be those perceived to be worthy of aid and a share of the government's resources and benefits. NIMBYism is not the term used in this context, but immigration scholars refer to nativism, ethnocentrism, and national chauvinism as negative reactions to individuals who fall outside the boundaries of individuals' imagined national community.

I show in Chapter 4 that Americans draw the boundaries around their national community in different ways, and that the more restrictive their subjective definition of a "true American," the more strongly they desire to maintain barriers to prevent foreign goods or individuals from crossing such perceived community boundaries.[7] Furthermore, individuals who

---

[7] And, in fact, given Song's three models of civic solidarity, there is the greatest support in public opinion for liberal nationalism (requiring a shared national culture) rather than constitutional patriotism (requiring only shared ideals or principles) or deep diversity (promoting a "hard" multiculturalism) (2008; Citrin et al. 1997).

believe that "true Americans" should be native-born, English-speaking Christians are also more likely to exclude other groups of Americans, such as homosexuals and African Americans, from full rights of community membership, and to support capital punishment for those who break the rules and laws of the community. Homophobia, ethnocentrism, and perceptions of the national community are all wrapped up in Americans' attitudes about tolerance and rights for minorities, whether racial, sexual, or attitudinal. And although notions of American community overlap with ethnocentrism, homophobia, authoritarianism, patriotism, and national chauvinism, the effect of imagined communities is distinct and remains, even with the addition of these various values and prejudices.

The country may place both legal and physical walls at its borders, but imagined community boundaries are more important when it comes to individuals' political attitudes. These subjective boundaries tend to be less expansive than the law would dictate – encompassing a smaller subset of who people believe are "true" Americans – and these constricted boundaries about who belongs in the community influence the decisions people make about who is entitled to the benefits that the government can allocate, and the punishments it can mete out.

Community boundaries can also expand. At a session of the First Continental Congress, Patrick Henry expressed this sentiment when he said, "The distinction between Virginians, Pennsylvanians and New Englanders is no more. I am not a Virginian but an American" (quoted in Savelle 1962, 919). This broadening of one's community is explained in the context of racial communities in Chapter 5.

RACIAL COMMUNITY

The power of racial group boundaries was highlighted nationally during the deliberations of the juries for two court cases in Los Angeles in the 1990s. In the first case, a predominantly white jury (10 whites, 1 Asian, and 1 Hispanic) in Simi Valley acquitted white police officers accused of beating Rodney King. In the second case, a largely black jury acquitted O. J. Simpson of murder. From the accounts of national public opinion surveys, it appears that blacks were much more willing than whites to believe that Simpson was innocent of murder and to feel more disillusionment about the acquittal of the LAPD officers (Decker 1995). One difference between these two verdicts is that the Simi Valley jury was accused of outright ignorance and racism by the mainstream press, while the Simpson jury was accused of racial loyalty. Ethnocentrism and ingroup favoritism, by any other names, are still ethnocentrism and ingroup favoritism; in both cases, racial lines were prominent.

A person may also expand the boundaries of her community, instead of contracting them, so that those considered as members could include individuals who are not part of her "objective" ingroup. In this book, I find that the presence of objective outgroups in one's neighborhood make it more likely that outgroups will be included in one's imagined community, such that geography can affect how one views the centrality of race. I also use national survey data to show that whites, blacks, Latinos, and Asian Americans whose definitions of their communities cross racial lines are more willing to support government policies to benefit objective racial outgroup members; are more willing to interact with outgroups socially, economically, and politically; and are less likely to see other outgroups as engaged in zero-sum competition with their ingroup. These boundary-expanding individuals do not believe they themselves are a different race, nor are they passing; their community simply extends to individuals who belong to groups other than their own.

For the story of pluralism and coalitional politics, then, one can use perceptions of community as a new lens for reinterpreting the effects of interests and ideology (Sonenshein 1993; Ture and Hamilton 1992). Considerations of interests do not have to be restricted to those of single race groups, and ideology is not the only motivation behind multiracial coalitions. Perceptions of communities whose boundaries do not follow color lines provide interests of their own, as well as senses of duty or obligation, regardless of ideology.

My argument about perceived community boundaries and the obligations that may follow can be applied across relational and geographic communities. The concept of community also ties together research across a number of fields, even though it may bear different names depending on the context. For example, work on local politics and the "homevoter" pertain to the dynamics involved in a relatively small and contained geographic area, where there are often repeated or sustained interactions between ordinary citizens, elites, and institutions. Where people draw the boundaries of their communities has an effect on where they want to live, how happy they are in their homes, how threatened they feel by environmental hazards nearby, and how willing they are to pay to improve social and political services to their locale. The gated community is an embodiment of a community's boundaries being solidified for all to see; what might only be perceived in the minds of residents becomes an objective wall dividing members and strangers.

Similarly, research in comparative politics on ethnicity, identity, and nationalism all focus on questions of membership: who belongs and who does not belong to the nation, in the state, and within an ethnic group. Lieberman (2003) explicitly discusses the political ramifications of a "national community," particularly when it comes to taxation policy, but concerns about fixed or fluid identities (national or subnational) are all, in essence, questions of who belongs within and outside community boundaries. Elites who seek to manipulate ethnic labels are trying to shift the boundaries of the pertinent communities in individuals' voting calculus. When Smith (2003) argues for the importance and centrality of stories of peoplehood, the "people" for whom the myths and symbols should resonate depends on who perceives themselves as part of that community.

Racial and ethnic politics are all questions of ingroups and outgroups, where the boundaries drawn can determine affect, prejudice, conflict, and coalitions. However, the groups do not simply correspond with colors of the rainbow; besides the fact that almost all social scientists would agree that, "we are all constructivists now" (riffing from Nathan Glazer's book title), the multiracial check-off boxes on the 2000 census form highlight the fact that even for non-academics, Simmel's intersecting circles are a reality.

By linking the research across these disparate fields, scholars may avoid reinventing the wheel. Social psychologists studying the effects of racial stereotype threat, for example, may converse with political comparativists interested in understanding the conditions under which interactions between different ethnic groups can diminish conflict. Or they may extend their discussions to public policy scholars who are analyzing the effects of social capital on political tolerance. These phenomena should not be tossed together willy-nilly, but the mechanisms motivating individual attitudes and behavior may be similar and advances in knowledge may accumulate more rapidly with more minds joining together in a common enterprise.

Although my case studies end with a positive example of greater inclusion, I do not believe that "community" is a goal to be achieved. It is a social science concept, not a normative ideal, and the analyses in Chapters 3, 4, and 5 do not point to a "quick fix" for more expansive communities: education is related to more inclusive national communities, but not to more inclusive local or racial ones, for example, and while home ownership is related to greater attachment to one's neighborhood and city, its effect does not extend to one's national or racial communities. I worry that the simple use of the term "community" propels one into the pages of *Porch* magazine, which expounds its benefits while forgetting many of the negative consequences that go hand in hand with the positive. *Porch*'s premier issue opened with a letter from the editor:

We hope to restore the fire of community spirit without bringing us back to the barefoot and pregnant days our mothers fought so hard to wrench us out of.

We hope...some of you may feel like it is possible at the end of the day to connect, to build, to become a community again. We hope to make you laugh, and we hope you'll get out on your porch, hand a glass of wine to your neighbour, and smile.... (Kelly 2004, 10)

You can almost picture Scout Finch and Boo Radley sitting on that porch, happily sipping lemonade and building social capital.[8] And if you squint in just the right way, you might not notice that you are only looking at the white part of town, that Calpurnia is doing all of the housework, and that Tom Robinson is dead. "Community" may be a good thing for some, but it can have nasty outcomes for those who are considered outside its boundaries.

It is also not my intention to imply that expanding community boundaries is a goal to be achieved. The image of contracting and expanding communities could put one in mind of Dr. Seuss's Grinch, whose heart was "two sizes too small" until he realized the true meaning of Christmas, at which point "his heart grew three sizes that day." This image is altogether too simplistic. Plus, there is some indication that an enlarged community may lead to less sensitivity to discrimination, prejudice, and inequality within the community. The normative debate about communities – where should their boundaries be drawn, what justifies these boundaries, and what purposes do they serve – lies in the realm of ethicists and political philosophers.

The goal of this book has been to provide an empirical response to the questions and concerns of political philosophers. Where do people draw their community boundaries? How permeable or impervious are they? And what effects do these boundaries have on Americans' policy preferences and political behavior? These are questions that an empirical social scientist can address and thus contribute to the philosophical debate. The consequences of these findings also reflect on the possibility of a welfare state that treats all those under its purview equally. My results show

---

[8] These are characters in Harper Lee's *To Kill A Mockingbird*, a novel set in the South in the 1930s.

how perceptions of overlapping communities can fuel the pluralism that allows for policies that benefit numerical majorities and minorities.

There is a growing literature – primarily among economists, although growing among political scientists – that argues that diversity is linked to welfare state restrictions. According to scholars such as Alesina, Glaeser, and Sacerdote (2001), for example, the small size of the American welfare state relative to that of European countries is a result of the racial diversity in the United States. And although there is no evidence that a welfare state has actually shrunk as the result of increased immigration or ethnic diversity, Soroka et al. (2007) find that the more open a society is to immigrants, the smaller is the rate of growth of its welfare state. Putnam, too, has found similar results in linking racial diversity with a lower level of social trust (even of one's own racial group) and cooperation (2007).

The conclusions in this book do not dispute these findings; however, they provide a new way of looking at how these parochial effects are not inevitable. If the boundaries of people's communities are not drawn to coincide with race or immigrant status, for example, then there is no reason to assume that demographic diversity will automatically doom the provision of social services by the state. And, what is seen as "heterogeneity" depends on how one imagines one's community. In their study of the Netherlands, Sniderman and Hagendoorn find that "[t]olerance, not identity, provides the foundation for diversity" (2007, 16). Although I do not examine the relationship between ethnic identity and tolerance, in Chapter 4, I do show that a more inclusive imagined community is also related to greater tolerance.

Now we know (1) that people think of themselves as members of communities, (2) that these communities are imagined rather than imposed by the environment (including other people, groups, or public officials), and (3) that where community boundaries are drawn affects people's beliefs about others (both inside and outside those boundaries), political attitudes, and political and civic participation. The findings in this book raise a number of new questions, the answers to which will help fill in the details about how "community" operates in politics. First, why do people draw boundaries where they do? For example, why would a white American exclude non-English speakers from her community or include African Americans? Perceptions of community boundaries may arise from a number of different sources, including childhood socialization, one's family and social networks, the media, political elites and parties, laws, and the context in which one grows up and lives. Answering this question may also reveal the dynamics by which people's perceptions of their communities can change over time. We need to look beyond the demographics and few contextual variables presented in the models here.

Because one goal of this book was to add an empirical element to the theoretical debates about "community," a second question is how to apply these empirical findings to arguments in political theory. For example, how do these examples of the effects of community boundaries affect arguments about associative duties, special obligations, and moral parochialism? The justification for parochialism may change if one considers the actual negative consequences of moral exclusion that can occur simultaneously with giving compatriots priority.

The empirical findings of the book can also be applied to models in formal political theory, which thus far account only for self-interest and homogeneous group interests. In testing the conditions under which players cooperate, can the utility of other people be included? Does membership in a community affect trust and reputational concerns, both for players within the same community and across communities? Can observational learning about who is Us versus Them occur across games and contexts?

A third question raised by the book is how to determine the effects of overlapping communities in cases where multiple communities are salient and in conflict. How do individuals make decisions under those conditions? Although I have chosen a diverse set of cases here and studied them in relative isolation from one another to make as clear an argument as possible regarding each, I do take seriously the idea that people have overlapping communities. That these communities may sometimes come into conflict is obvious, but the surveys I have used in the book do not often ask about these policy issues in ways that highlight how different communities' interests are competing and incompatible. For example, a survey question about whether the number of immigrants allowed into the United States should be increased or decreased does not highlight concerns of environmentalists, civil rights groups, farmers, and libertarians in the wording, even though all of these interests are vocal in immigration debates in Congress.

In this book, I have taken the first step, showing that where people draw their community boundaries can have political consequences, and imagined communities are strong predictors that should stand alongside interests, ideology, and values. The boundaries that define who belongs together do not have to be tangible, such as a country's borders or a planned development's fences, but can also be imagined, flexible lines dividing a population. The individuals "like us" are included in people's conceptions of their communities; those who are different are excluded, and these judgments are consequential in determining the operation of people's sense of duty and desire to help, both personally and via public policies. Thus, political attitudes about the obligations of government to redistribute resources and decisions about political participation are "helping behaviors" that are based not only on values and calculations of self-interest, but also on assessments of broader interests that are often articulated in terms of "community." If the potential beneficiary of an opinion voiced, a meeting attended, or an initiative supported is part of my community, I am more willing to help. Because he is "my brother," "he ain't heavy," "his welfare is my concern," and he falls within the boundaries of obligation.

> ...So on we go, his welfare is my concern
> No burden is he to bear, we'll get there
> For I know he would not encumber me
> He ain't heavy – he's my brother...
>
> (lyrics from "He Ain't Heavy, He's
> My Brother," recorded by singers
> ranging from Neil Diamond,
> Al Green, Olivia Newton-John,
> and Cher to the Hollies, the
> Housemartins, the Osmonds, and the
> Everly Brothers)

Appendix

Variable coding All variables in all the models are coded to run from 0 to 1. The variables that represent percentages are limited to the 0 to 1 range but are not required to have minimum values of 0 and maximum values of 1. Unless otherwise specified, for policy or attitude variables, 0 anchors the more liberal position and 1 the conservative position.

TABLE AI.

	Alienation	Efficacy	Trust
Constant	0.34 (0.04)	0.51 (0.04)	0.33 (0.03)
Neighborhood sense of community	0.09 (0.02)	0.05 (0.02)	0.08 (0.01)
City sense of community	0.08 (0.02)	0.08 (0.02)	0.08 (0.01)
Lib-Con ideology	0.02 (0.03)	−0.02 (0.03)	0.02 (0.02)
Social trust (1=people can be trusted)			0.11 (0.01)
Age	0.05 (0.05)	−0.05 (0.04)	0.17 (0.03)
Education	0.07 (0.03)	0.08 (0.03)	0.02 (0.02)
Income	0.07 (0.04)	0.06 (0.03)	−0.01 (0.02)
Female	0.04 (0.02)	0.02 (0.02)	0.04 (0.01)
Black	−0.00 (0.03)	0.05 (0.02)	−0.08 (0.02)
Hispanic	−0.09 (0.03)	−0.00 (0.02)	−0.00 (0.02)
Married	0.04 (0.02)	0.02 (0.02)	−0.00 (0.01)
Parent	−0.02 (0.02)	0.00 (0.02)	−0.00 (0.01)
Homeowner	0.03 (0.02)	0.03 (0.02)	−0.00 (0.01)
Length of residence	−0.01 (0.04)	0.03 (0.03)	−0.05 (0.02)
South	−0.00 (0.02)	0.01 (0.02)	0.02 (0.01)
N	1,167	1,202	1,143

OLS models describing Political Trust (0=trust not at all, 1=trust a lot), Political Alienation (0=agree strongly that leaders do not care about me, 1=disagree strongly), and Political Efficacy (0=no impact at all, 1=a big impact) as a function of local sense of community (0=no sense of community, 1=sense of community) and personal attributes (SOCCAP, Chapter 3, Figure 4).

TABLE A2.

	Neighborhood Association	Neighborhood Cooperation	PTA (parents)	PTA (non-parents)	Ban Book
Constant	−3.61 (0.40)	−1.56 (0.53)	−3.54 (0.51)	−4.53 (0.73)	0.05 (0.05)
Neighborhood sense of community	0.48 (0.20)	0.66 (0.30)	0.55 (0.26)	−0.04 (0.35)	0.06 (0.02)
Lib-Con ideology	−0.27 (0.27)	−0.41 (0.40)	0.55 (0.35)	0.48 (0.53)	0.22 (0.04)
Age	1.65 (0.41)	0.52 (0.57)	4.06 (0.79)	−0.70 (0.73)	0.31 (0.05)
Education	1.08 (0.26)	−0.10 (0.39)	1.39 (0.37)	1.75 (0.48)	−0.16 (0.04)
Income	1.51 (0.30)	0.70 (0.42)	0.90 (0.38)	0.04 (0.56)	−0.15 (0.04)
Female	−0.12 (0.15)	−0.39 (0.22)	0.68 (0.20)	0.60 (0.30)	0.03 (0.02)
Black	0.63 (0.21)	0.10 (0.31)	0.02 (0.26)	−0.17 (0.47)	0.10 (0.03)
Hispanic	0.27 (0.22)	0.07 (0.32)	−0.28 (0.25)	0.15 (0.49)	0.15 (0.03)
Married	0.08 (0.16)	0.09 (0.24)	−0.17 (0.23)	0.70 (0.30)	0.02 (0.02)
Parent	0.09 (0.17)	0.14 (0.26)			0.03 (0.02)
Homeowner	0.24 (0.20)	0.24 (0.29)	0.02 (0.24)	0.18 (0.40)	−0.02 (0.03)
Length of residence	−0.21 (0.28)	−0.01 (0.43)	0.31 (0.37)	0.82 (0.56)	0.03 (0.04)
South	−0.05 (0.16)	−0.18 (0.23)	0.24 (0.20)	0.21 (0.29)	0.01 (0.02)
N	1,219	424	555	664	1,197

Logit models summarizing Participation in a Neighborhood Association (0=no, 1=yes), Cooperation with Neighbors (0=no, 1=have worked with others, and Participation in a PTA (0=no, 1=yes), and OLS model summarizing Willingness to Ban a Book (0=disagree strongly that a book should be kept out of the library, 1=agree strongly) as a function of neighborhood sense of community (0=no sense of community, 1=sense of community) and personal attributes (SOCCAP, Chapter 3, Figure 5).

TABLE A3.

	Parks Tax	Sin Tax	Easier Tax Vote	Transportation Tax	Volunteer	Attend Meetings
Constant	0.89 (0.37)	1.85 (0.44)	1.48 (0.42)	1.22 (0.40)	-0.03 (0.04)	-1.21 (0.27)
Neighborhood sense of community	0.42 (0.22)	-0.27 (0.25)	0.46 (0.25)	0.46 (0.23)	0.06 (0.02)	0.31 (0.16)
Age	-1.06 (0.40)	-1.20 (0.44)	-0.75 (0.43)	0.24 (0.42)	0.02 (0.04)	-0.09 (0.27)
Education	-0.66 (0.38)	0.68 (0.44)	-1.05 (0.41)	-0.48 (0.43)	0.21 (0.04)	0.74 (0.27)
Income	0.19 (0.35)	-0.85 (0.38)	-0.56 (0.39)	0.26 (0.38)	0.07 (0.03)	0.20 (0.24)
Female	0.08 (0.20)	0.30 (0.22)	0.29 (0.22)	-0.07 (0.22)	0.02 (0.02)	0.13 (0.14)
Lib-Con ideology	-0.81 (0.35)	-0.68 (0.41)	-1.00 (0.41)	-1.34 (0.38)	0.07 (0.03)	0.02 (0.25)
Length of residence	-0.21 (0.30)	0.21 (0.32)	-0.16 (0.32)	-0.75 (0.32)	0.05 (0.03)	0.29 (0.21)
N	418	414	362	397	855	859

Logit models describing Support for a Parks Tax (0=oppose tax, 1=favor tax), Support for a Sin Tax (0=oppose tax, 1=favor tax), Support for Making it Easier to Pass Tax Votes (0=vote no, 1=vote yes), Support for a Transportation Tax (0=oppose tax, 1=favor tax), and Attending Local Meetings (0=no, 1=yes), and OLS model describing Volunteering in One's Community (0=none in last year, 1= more than 10 hours per week) as a function of Neighborhood Sense of Community (0=no sense of community, 1=neighborhood has sense of community) and personal attributes (PPIC, Chapter 3, Figure 6).

216

TABLE A4.

	Parks Tax	Sin Tax	Easier Tax Vote	Transportation Tax	Volunteer	Attend Meetings
Constant	0.71 (0.38)	0.20 (0.37)	1.15 (0.41)	0.98 (0.38)	0.14 (0.04)	-1.00 (0.27)
Intended length of residence	0.04 (0.28)	-0.26 (0.29)	-0.19 (0.30)	-0.10 (0.29)	-0.06 (0.03)	0.30 (0.20)
Age	0.00 (0.39)	0.28 (0.41)	-1.07 (0.42)	-0.01 (0.41)	-0.05 (0.04)	-0.80 (0.28)
Education	0.48 (0.40)	0.64 (0.43)	-0.64 (0.43)	0.13 (0.42)	0.11 (0.04)	0.67 (0.29)
Income	-0.79 (0.36)	0.17 (0.38)	-0.07 (0.38)	0.34 (0.38)	0.12 (0.04)	0.52 (0.25)
Female	-0.25 (0.21)	0.61 (0.22)	-0.05 (0.22)	0.00 (0.22)	0.03 (0.02)	0.18 (0.15)
Lib-Con ideology	-0.95 (0.36)	-0.08 (0.38)	-0.69 (0.37)	-1.06 (0.39)	-0.01 (0.04)	0.08 (0.26)
Length of residence	-0.19 (0.31)	-0.61 (0.32)	-0.05 (0.34)	-0.51 (0.32)	0.04 (0.03)	-0.04 (0.22)
N	387	395	354	364	792	794

Logit models describing Support for a Parks Tax (0=oppose tax, 1=favor tax), Support for a Sin Tax (0=oppose tax, 1=favor tax), Support for Making it Easier to Pass Tax Votes (0=vote no, 1=vote yes), Support for a Transportation Tax (0=oppose tax, 1=favor tax), and Attending Local Meetings (0=no, 1=yes), and OLS model describing Volunteering in One's Community (0=none in last year, 1= more than 10 hours per week) as a function of Intended Length of Residence (0=live outside of LA County, 1=live in current neighborhood) and personal attributes (PPIC, Chapter 3, Figure 6).

217

TABLE A5.

	Parks Tax	Sin Tax	Easier Tax Vote	Transportation Tax	Volunteer	Attend Meetings
Constant	0.70 (0.40)	1.85 (0.46)	1.30 (0.43)	0.95 (0.42)	-0.03 (0.04)	-1.25 (0.28)
Neighborhood sense of community	0.40 (0.23)	-0.28 (0.26)	0.39 (0.26)	0.58 (0.24)	0.06 (0.02)	0.34 (0.16)
Identification with LA County	0.68 (0.35)	0.99 (0.47)	0.97 (0.44)	1.11 (0.46)	-0.02 (0.03)	0.47 (0.24)
Age	-0.97 (0.41)	-1.16 (0.45)	-0.75 (0.44)	0.17 (0.44)	0.03 (0.04)	-0.07 (0.28)
Education	-0.49 (0.39)	0.69 (0.47)	-0.98 (0.42)	-0.37 (0.45)	0.22 (0.04)	0.68 (0.28)
Income	0.14 (0.36)	-0.75 (0.40)	-0.43 (0.40)	0.33 (0.39)	0.05 (0.04)	0.22 (0.25)
Female	0.10 (0.21)	0.33 (0.23)	0.33 (0.23)	-0.09 (0.23)	0.02 (0.02)	0.10 (0.15)
Lib-Con ideology	-0.80 (0.36)	-0.80 (0.43)	-1.00 (0.43)	-1.19 (0.40)	0.07 (0.04)	-0.01 (0.26)
Length of residence	-0.15 (0.31)	0.01 (0.34)	-0.05 (0.33)	-0.82 (0.33)	0.06 (0.03)	0.36 (0.21)
N	398	393	347	372	810	814

Logit models describing Support for a Parks Tax (0=oppose tax, 1=favor tax), Support for a Sin Tax (0=oppose tax, 1=favor tax), Support for Making it Easier to Pass Tax Votes (0=vote no, 1=vote yes), Support for a Transportation Tax (0=oppose tax, 1=favor tax), and Attending Local Meetings (0=no, 1=yes), and OLS model describing Volunteering in One's Community (0=none in last year, 1= more than 10 hours per week) as a function of Identification with LA County (0=most identify with other, 1=most identify with LA County) and personal attributes (PPIC, Chapter 3, Figure 7).

218

TABLE A6.

	Exclude Illegals 1996	Exclude Illegals 2004	Isolationism 1996	Isolationism 2004	Decrease Immigration 1996	Decrease Immigration 2004	Disallow Refugees
Constant	0.46 (0.04)	0.53 (0.05)	0.41 (0.04)	0.30 (0.04)	0.47 (0.05)	0.56 (0.05)	0.22 (0.05)
Exclusive American community 1996	0.34 (0.04)		0.31 (0.04)		0.31 (0.05)		0.26 (0.05)
Exclusive American community 2004		0.32 (0.05)		0.39 (0.04)		0.26 (0.05)	
Age	0.07 (0.02)	0.11 (0.02)	-0.04 (0.02)	0.00 (0.02)	0.02 (0.02)	0.04 (0.02)	-0.02 (0.03)
Education	-0.04 (0.03)	0.01 (0.03)	-0.22 (0.02)	-0.13 (0.02)	-0.12 (0.03)	-0.12 (0.03)	-0.09 (0.03)
Income	0.07 (0.02)	-0.11 (0.13)	-0.01 (0.02)	-0.03 (0.10)	0.05 (0.03)	-0.02 (0.14)	0.01 (0.03)
Black	-0.05 (0.03)	-0.08 (0.02)	0.00 (0.02)	-0.00 (0.02)	-0.01 (0.03)	-0.08 (0.03)	-0.00 (0.03)
Hispanic	-0.20 (0.04)	-0.23 (0.04)	-0.06 (0.03)	-0.05 (0.03)	-0.02 (0.05)	-0.12 (0.04)	-0.04 (0.05)
Female	-0.04 (0.01)	-0.03 (0.02)	-0.01 (0.01)	0.01 (0.01)	0.03 (0.02)	0.00 (0.02)	-0.00 (0.02)
Dem-Rep partisanship	0.05 (0.03)	-0.12 (0.02)	-0.03 (0.02)	-0.01 (0.02)	0.04 (0.03)	-0.04 (0.02)	0.03 (0.03)
Lib-Con ideology	0.08 (0.04)	0.01 (0.03)	0.09 (0.03)	-0.02 (0.02)	0.03 (0.04)	0.10 (0.04)	0.10 (0.04)
First generation	-0.06 (0.04)	0.01 (0.03)	-0.09 (0.03)	-0.02 (0.02)	-0.17 (0.04)	-0.19 (0.03)	-0.12 (0.04)
Second generation	0.03 (0.03)	0.02 (0.03)	-0.01 (0.02)	-0.01 (0.02)	-0.04 (0.03)	-0.00 (0.03)	-0.03 (0.04)
Third generation	-0.01 (0.02)	-0.02 (0.02)	0.01 (0.01)	-0.02 (0.02)	0.00 (0.02)	-0.02 (0.02)	-0.01 (0.02)
N	889	1011	877	987	800	937	858

OLS models describing Stronger Measures to Exclude Illegals (0=disagree strongly, 1=agree strongly), Isolationism (0=no favoritism, 1=favor American goods and owners), Decrease Immigration Level (0=increase a lot, 1=decrease a lot, and Disallow Refugees (0=agree strongly that refugees can stay, 1=disagree strongly that refugees can stay) as a function of Exclusive American Community (0=no requirements, 1=all requirements needed to be a True American) and personal attributes (GSS96 and GSS04, Chapter 4, Figure 4).

TABLE A7.

	Children of Americans Born Abroad	Support Birthright Citizenship	Rights of Citizens
Constant	0.80 (0.04)	0.77 (0.05)	0.68 (0.06)
Exclusive American community	–0.06 (0.03)	–0.13 (0.05)	–0.26 (0.06)
Age	–0.05 (0.02)	–0.05 (0.02)	–0.10 (0.03)
Education	0.01 (0.02)	0.03 (0.03)	0.07 (0.03)
Income	0.10 (0.10)	–0.11 (0.14)	–0.06 (0.16)
Black	–0.00 (0.02)	0.03 (0.03)	–0.00 (0.03)
Hispanic	–0.00 (0.03)	0.13 (0.04)	0.08 (0.04)
Female	0.01 (0.01)	0.02 (0.02)	–0.04 (0.02)
Dem-Rep partisanship	0.01 (0.02)	0.09 (0.02)	0.08 (0.03)
First generation	0.06 (0.02)	0.08 (0.03)	0.10 (0.04)
Second generation	0.05 (0.02)	0.06 (0.03)	0.04 (0.03)
Third generation	0.05 (0.01)	–0.00 (0.02)	–0.01 (0.02)
N	1016	1014	1009

OLS models describing Support Citizenship of Children of Americans Born Abroad (0=strongly disagree, 1=strongly agree), Support Birthright Citizenship (0=disagree strongly, 1=agree strongly), and LPRs should have Rights of Citizens (0=disagree strongly, 1=agree strongly) as a function of Exclusive American community (0=no requirements, 1=all requirements needed to be a True American) and personal attributes (GSS04, Chapter 4, Figure 5).

Appendix

TABLE A8.

	Support Death Penalty	Law Enforcement 2004	Law Enforcement 1996
Constant	0.48 (0.08)	0.62 (0.10)	0.60 (0.08)
Exclusive American community 1996	0.30 (0.08)		0.15 (0.08)
Exclusive American community 2004		0.16 (0.09)	
Age	−0.11 (0.04)	0.03 (0.04)	−0.02 (0.04)
Education	−0.17 (0.05)	0.04 (0.05)	0.04 (0.05)
Income	0.14 (0.04)	−0.37 (0.24)	−0.05 (0.04)
Black	−0.09 (0.05)	0.06 (0.05)	0.03 (0.05)
Hispanic	−0.01 (0.07)	0.10 (0.07)	0.08 (0.07)
Female	−0.13 (0.03)	0.04 (0.03)	0.03 (0.03)
Dem-Rep partisanship	0.20 (0.05)	−0.00 (0.04)	0.03 (0.05)
Lib-Con ideology	0.15 (0.07)		0.08 (0.07)
First generation	−0.16 (0.07)	−0.13 (0.06)	−0.07 (0.06)
Second generation	0.12 (0.05)	−0.02 (0.05)	0.07 (0.05)
Third generation	0.02 (0.03)	0.01 (0.04)	−0.05 (0.03)
N	880	518	488

OLS models describing Support Death Penalty (0=oppose, 1=favor) and Increase Spending for Law Enforcement (0=spending too much, 1=spending too little) as a function of Exclusive American Community (0=no requirements, 1=all requirements needed to be a True American) and personal attributes (GSS96 and GSS04, Chapter 4, Figure 6).

TABLE A9.

	Antimiscegenation Laws	Govt Programs for Blacks
Constant	6.73 (1.34)	0.64 (0.06)
Exclusive American community	−5.59 (1.39)	−0.12 (0.07)
Age	−1.35 (0.45)	0.04 (0.03)
Education	2.69 (0.69)	0.01 (0.04)
Income	0.35 (0.52)	−0.08 (0.04)
Female	−0.06 (0.32)	0.02 (0.02)
Dem-Rep partisanship	−0.51 (0.52)	−0.07 (0.04)
Lib-Con ideology	0.08 (0.81)	−0.30 (0.06)
South	−0.38 (0.32)	−0.05 (0.03)
N	523	556

Logit model describing Oppose Antimiscegenation Laws (0=oppose interracial marriage, 1=support it) and OLS model describing Support Govt Programs to Help Blacks (0=Oppose programs, 1=Support programs) as a function of Exclusive American Community (0=no requirements, 1=all requirements needed to be a True American) and personal attributes (GSS96 white respondents only, Chapter 4, Figure 7).

	Oppose Gay Marriage	Disclosure for Govt Clearance	Intolerance of Homosexuals	Intolerance of Atheists	Intolerance of Militarists	Intolerance of Racists
Constant	0.39 (0.06)	0.09 (0.07)	0.01 (0.07)	-0.07 (0.07)	-0.06 (0.08)	0.05 (0.08)
Exclusive American community 1996		0.37 (0.07)	0.31 (0.07)	0.46 (0.07)	0.50 (0.08)	0.46 (0.08)
Exclusive American community 2004	0.50 (0.06)					
Age	0.14 (0.03)	0.19 (0.03)	0.17 (0.03)	0.21 (0.04)	0.25 (0.04)	0.08 (0.04)
Education	-0.11 (0.03)	-0.04 (0.04)	-0.29 (0.04)	-0.28 (0.04)	-0.26 (0.05)	-0.17 (0.05)
Income	0.21 (0.16)	0.02 (0.04)	-0.09 (0.04)	-0.09 (0.04)	-0.07 (0.04)	-0.06 (0.04)
Black	0.12 (0.03)	0.04 (0.04)	-0.00 (0.04)	0.06 (0.04)	0.07 (0.05)	0.06 (0.05)
Hispanic	-0.03 (0.04)	-0.03 (0.06)	0.07 (0.06)	-0.03 (0.07)	-0.02 (0.08)	0.10 (0.08)
Female	-0.08 (0.02)	-0.12 (0.02)	-0.02 (0.02)	0.02 (0.03)	0.01 (0.03)	0.01 (0.03)
Dem-Rep partisanship	-0.32 (0.03)	0.13 (0.04)	0.07 (0.04)	-0.04 (0.04)	-0.01 (0.05)	0.00 (0.05)
Lib-Con ideology		0.14 (0.06)	0.07 (0.06)	0.13 (0.06)	0.16 (0.07)	0.07 (0.07)
First generation	0.09 (0.04)	-0.06 (0.05)	-0.04 (0.06)	0.09 (0.06)	0.20 (0.07)	0.15 (0.07)
Second generation	-0.03 (0.04)	0.06 (0.05)	-0.07 (0.04)	0.04 (0.05)	-0.10 (0.05)	-0.11 (0.05)
Third generation	-0.08 (0.03)	-0.06 (0.03)	-0.04 (0.03)	-0.05 (0.03)	-0.07 (0.03)	-0.05 (0.03)
N	1004	920	590	589	589	589

OLS models describing Oppose Gay Marriage (0=strongly agree homosexuals should have right to marry, 1=strongly disagree), Disclosure for Government Clearance 1996 (0=govt should not ask about sexual orientation, 1=govt should), Intolerance of Homosexuals 1996 (0=tolerant, 1=intolerant), Intolerance of Atheists, Intolerance of Militarists, and Intolerance of Racists as a function of Exclusive American Community (0=no requirements, 1=all requirements needed to be a True American) and personal attributes (GS96 and GS04, Chapter 4, Figures 8 and 9).

TABLE AII.

	Obey Laws	Participate	Help Americans	Help Rest of the World	Patriotism	Trust in Govt
Constant	0.71 (0.03)	0.60 (0.03)	0.73 (0.04)	0.58 (0.05)	0.63 (0.03)	0.34 (0.05)
Exclusive American community	0.21 (0.03)	0.14 (0.03)	0.06 (0.04)	-0.04 (0.05)	0.21 (0.03)	0.17 (0.05)
Age	0.02 (0.01)	0.07 (0.01)	0.02 (0.02)	-0.04 (0.02)	0.04 (0.01)	-0.03 (0.02)
Education	-0.01 (0.02)	0.09 (0.02)	0.00 (0.02)	0.10 (0.03)	0.02 (0.01)	0.12 (0.03)
Income	0.12 (0.07)	-0.05 (0.08)	-0.11 (0.10)	-0.16 (0.14)	-0.07 (0.07)	0.14 (0.13)
Black	-0.02 (0.01)	-0.02 (0.01)	0.04 (0.02)	0.12 (0.03)	-0.05 (0.01)	-0.06 (0.03)
Hispanic	0.05 (0.02)	0.02 (0.02)	0.06 (0.03)	0.12 (0.04)	0.01 (0.02)	0.04 (0.04)
Female	0.04 (0.01)	-0.02 (0.01)	0.05 (0.01)	0.05 (0.02)	-0.02 (0.01)	-0.05 (0.02)
Dem-Rep partisanship	-0.02 (0.01)	-0.01 (0.01)	0.06 (0.02)	0.05 (0.02)	-0.10 (0.01)	-0.09 (0.02)
First generation	0.04 (0.02)	0.02 (0.02)	0.01 (0.02)	0.09 (0.03)	0.04 (0.02)	0.07 (0.03)
Second generation	-0.02 (0.02)	-0.00 (0.02)	-0.01 (0.02)	0.03 (0.03)	0.02 (0.01)	-0.03 (0.03)
Third generation	-0.00 (0.01)	0.00 (0.01)	0.01 (0.02)	0.02 (0.02)	0.00 (0.01)	-0.03 (0.02)
N	1026	1013	1027	1025	858	1027

OLS models describing Obligation to Obey Laws (0=no obligations, 1=maximum obligations), Obligation to Participate (0=no obligations, 1=maximum obligations), Obligation to Help Americans (0=no obligation, 1=obligation to help), Obligation to Help People in the Rest of the World (0=no obligation, 1=obligation to help), Patriotism (0=minimum, 1=maximum), and Trust in Government (0=strongly disagree that we can trust people in Washington,1=strongly agree) as a function of Exclusive American Community (0=no requirements, 1=all requirements needed to be a True American) and personal attributes (GSS04, Chapter 4, Figure 10).

TABLE AI2.

	Racial Policy Suport	Minimize Social Distance	Govt Help Blacks
Constant	0.09 (0.04)	0.50 (0.06)	0.28 (0.08)
Close to whites	−0.04 (0.02)	−0.06 (0.05)	0.03 (0.07)
Close to blacks	0.18 (0.03)	0.23 (0.05)	0.26 (0.06)
Age	0.08 (0.04)	−0.16 (0.03)	0.02 (0.04)
Education	0.15 (0.04)	0.20 (0.04)	0.14 (0.05)
Income	−0.03 (0.03)	0.03 (0.03)	−0.07 (0.05)
Female	0.01 (0.02)	0.04 (0.02)	−0.01 (0.03)
South	−0.01 (0.02)	−0.08 (0.02)	−0.04 (0.03)
Dem-Rep partisanship	0.12 (0.03)	0.03 (0.04)	−0.16 (0.05)
Lib-Con ideology	0.26 (0.05)	−0.03 (0.05)	−0.18 (0.07)
N	608	286	298

OLS models describing Racial Policy Support (0=op-pose policies, 1=favor), Minimize Social Distance (0=maximize distance, 1=minimize), and Government Obligation to Help Blacks (0=no special treatment, 1=government help) as a function of Closeness and personal attributes (NES96 and GSS96 white respondents only, Chapter 5, Figure 3).

TABLE AI3.

	Perceived Equality	Oppose Black Nationalism	Racial Policy Opposition
Constant	0.25 (0.03)	0.72 (0.04)	0.34 (0.05)
Close to whites	0.13 (0.02)	0.10 (0.03)	0.08 (0.03)
Close to blacks	−0.07 (0.03)	−0.19 (0.03)	−0.16 (0.04)
Age	−0.04 (0.03)	−0.10 (0.04)	0.04 (0.05)
Income	−0.06 (0.02)	0.07 (0.02)	0.05 (0.03)
South	0.02 (0.01)	−0.02 (0.01)	0.01 (0.02)
Education	−0.10 (0.02)	0.04 (0.03)	−0.04 (0.03)
Female	0.01 (0.01)	−0.00 (0.01)	0.02 (0.02)
Dem-Rep partisanship	0.01 (0.02)	0.02 (0.03)	0.05 (0.04)
Lib-Con ideology	0.03 (0.02)	0.01 (0.02)	0.05 (0.03)
N	600	592	521

OLS models describing Perceived Equality (0=low, 1=high), Opposition to Black Nationalism (0=favor, 1=oppose), and Racial Policy Opposition (0=support policy, 1=oppose) as a function of Closeness (0=not close at all, 1=very close) and personal attributes (NBES84 black respondents only, Chapter 5, Figure 5).

TABLE AI4.

	Intermarriage (Close to Whites)	Intermarriage (Close to Blacks)	Intermarriage (Close to Hispanics)	Intermarriage (Close to Asians)	Intermarriage (Close to Caribbeans)
Constant	0.87 (0.07)	0.71 (0.06)	0.73 (0.06)	0.78 (0.06)	0.78 (0.06)
Age	-0.41 (0.05)	-0.42 (0.05)	-0.40 (0.05)	-0.42 (0.06)	-0.41 (0.06)
Income	-0.20 (0.19)	-0.19 (0.18)	-0.19 (0.18)	-0.23 (0.18)	-0.23 (0.19)
South	-0.02 (0.03)	-0.03 (0.03)	-0.03 (0.03)	-0.03 (0.03)	-0.02 (0.03)
Education	0.18 (0.04)	0.18 (0.04)	0.15 (0.04)	0.12 (0.04)	0.16 (0.04)
Female	0.04 (0.02)	0.03 (0.02)	0.05 (0.02)	0.05 (0.02)	0.04 (0.02)
Dem-Rep partisanship	0.04 (0.04)	0.02 (0.04)	0.03 (0.04)	0.03 (0.04)	0.05 (0.04)
Lib-Con ideology	-0.17 (0.05)	-0.16 (0.05)	-0.17 (0.05)	-0.17 (0.05)	-0.16 (0.05)
Close to whites	0.00 (0.05)				
Close to blacks		0.30 (0.04)			
Close to Hispanics			0.28 (0.04)		
Close to Asians				0.25 (0.04)	
Close to Caribbeans					0.21 (0.04)
Black	-0.04 (0.09)	0.12 (0.09)	0.08 (0.09)	0.05 (0.09)	0.04 (0.09)
Asian	0.07 (0.11)	0.29 (0.11)	0.24 (0.10)	0.20 (0.11)	0.23 (0.11)
Hispanic	-0.02 (0.09)	0.06 (0.08)	0.16 (0.08)	0.04 (0.08)	0.05 (0.08)
Caribbean	-0.01 (0.11)	0.12 (0.10)	0.11 (0.11)	0.08 (0.10)	0.11 (0.11)
Age x black	0.30 (0.09)	0.33 (0.09)	0.30 (0.09)	0.32 (0.09)	0.32 (0.09)
Age x Asian	0.35 (0.12)	0.36 (0.12)	0.34 (0.12)	0.36 (0.12)	0.36 (0.12)

Age x Hispanic	0.07 (0.10)	0.08 (0.10)	0.05 (0.10)	0.08 (0.10)	0.06 (0.10)
Age x Caribbean	0.13 (0.11)	0.13 (0.11)	0.13 (0.11)	0.14 (0.11)	0.14 (0.11)
Income x black	0.36 (0.76)	0.51 (0.78)	0.47 (0.75)	0.51 (0.76)	0.42 (0.76)
Income x Asian	0.08 (0.29)	0.08 (0.28)	0.08 (0.28)	0.13 (0.28)	0.14 (0.37)
Income x Hispanic	0.34 (0.27)	0.30 (0.26)	0.32 (0.27)	0.37 (0.27)	0.32 (0.28)
Income x Caribbean	-0.16 (0.36)	-0.20 (0.35)	-0.17 (0.35)	-0.14 (0.35)	-0.13 (0.36)
South x black	-0.05 (0.04)	-0.03 (0.04)	-0.03 (0.04)	-0.04 (0.04)	-0.03 (0.04)
South x Asian	0.06 (0.05)	0.07 (0.05)	0.08 (0.05)	0.07 (0.05)	0.07 (0.06)
South x Hispanic	0.02 (0.04)	0.04 (0.04)	0.04 (0.04)	0.03 (0.04)	0.03 (0.04)
South x Caribbean	0.07 (0.05)	0.07 (0.05)	0.08 (0.05)	0.07 (0.06)	0.07 (0.06)
Education x black	-0.12 (0.06)	-0.13 (0.06)	-0.09 (0.06)	-0.06 (0.06)	-0.10 (0.06)
Education x Asian	-0.26 (0.08)	-0.25 (0.08)	-0.23 (0.08)	-0.20 (0.08)	-0.23 (0.08)
Education x Hispanic	-0.04 (0.06)	-0.07 (0.06)	-0.03 (0.06)	0.01 (0.06)	-0.04 (0.06)
Education x Caribbean	-0.16 (0.08)	-0.16 (0.07)	-0.13 (0.07)	-0.10 (0.08)	-0.14 (0.08)
Female x black	-0.03 (0.03)	-0.03 (0.03)	-0.05 (0.03)	-0.04 (0.03)	-0.03 (0.04)
Female x Asian	-0.00 (0.04)	0.00 (0.04)	-0.01 (0.04)	-0.01 (0.04)	-0.01 (0.04)
Female x Hispanic	-0.02 (0.03)	-0.01 (0.03)	-0.03 (0.03)	-0.03 (0.03)	-0.02 (0.04)
Female x Caribbean	-0.06 (0.04)	-0.06 (0.04)	-0.08 (0.04)	-0.08 (0.04)	-0.06 (0.04)
Party x black	-0.05 (0.06)	-0.05 (0.06)	-0.04 (0.06)	-0.05 (0.06)	-0.07 (0.07)
Party x Asian	-0.08 (0.07)	-0.08 (0.07)	-0.08 (0.07)	-0.08 (0.07)	-0.11 (0.07)
Party x Hispanic	-0.04 (0.06)	-0.03 (0.06)	-0.02 (0.06)	-0.03 (0.06)	-0.05 (0.06)
Party x Caribbean	0.02 (0.08)	0.04 (0.08)	0.03 (0.08)	0.04 (0.08)	0.01 (0.08)
Ideology x black	0.16 (0.06)	0.15 (0.06)	0.15 (0.06)	0.15 (0.06)	0.15 (0.07)

(continued)

TABLE A14. (continued)

	Intermarriage (Close to Whites)	Intermarriage (Close to Blacks)	Intermarriage (Close to Hispanics)	Intermarriage (Close to Asians)	Intermarriage (Close to Caribbeans)
Ideology x Asian	-0.06 (0.09)	-0.07 (0.09)	-0.06 (0.09)	-0.06 (0.09)	-0.07 (0.09)
Ideology x Hispanic	0.14 (0.07)	0.15 (0.07)	0.14 (0.07)	0.14 (0.07)	0.12 (0.07)
Ideology x Caribbean	0.17 (0.08)	0.13 (0.08)	0.15 (0.08)	0.16 (0.08)	0.15 (0.08)
Close to group x black	0.07 (0.07)	-0.24 (0.07)	-0.21 (0.06)	-0.17 (0.06)	-0.13 (0.06)
Close to group x Asian	0.10 (0.09)	-0.28 (0.08)	-0.23 (0.07)	-0.22 (0.08)	-0.23 (0.07)
Close to group x Hispanic	-0.00 (0.07)	-0.12 (0.06)	-0.33 (0.06)	-0.18 (0.06)	-0.14 (0.06)
Close to group x Caribbean	0.01 (0.08)	-0.22 (0.08)	-0.26 (0.07)	-0.26 (0.07)	-0.24 (0.07)
N	2267	2268	2256	2216	2153

OLS models describing Approval of Interracial Marriage (0=strongly disagree, 1=strongly agree) as a function of Closeness to a racial group (0=not close at all, 1=very close) and personal attributes (NPS, Chapter 5, Figure 7).

228

TABLE AI5.

	Allies (Close to Whites)	Allies (Close to Blacks)	Allies (Close to Hispanics)	Allies (Close to Asians)	Allies (Close to Caribbeans)
Constant	0.76 (0.08)	0.71 (0.07)	0.70 (0.07)	0.72 (0.07)	0.72 (0.07)
Age	−0.22 (0.07)	−0.23 (0.07)	−0.23 (0.07)	−0.23 (0.07)	−0.22 (0.07)
Income	0.07 (0.22)	0.08 (0.22)	0.06 (0.22)	0.04 (0.22)	0.04 (0.23)
South	−0.02 (0.03)	−0.02 (0.03)	−0.03 (0.03)	−0.02 (0.03)	−0.03 (0.03)
Education	0.13 (0.05)	0.12 (0.05)	0.13 (0.05)	0.11 (0.05)	0.11 (0.05)
Female	0.06 (0.03)	0.05 (0.03)	0.06 (0.03)	0.06 (0.03)	0.06 (0.03)
Dem-Rep partisanship	−0.03 (0.04)	−0.04 (0.04)	−0.03 (0.04)	−0.02 (0.05)	−0.03 (0.05)
Lib-Con ideology	−0.12 (0.05)	−0.11 (0.05)	−0.10 (0.05)	−0.10 (0.06)	−0.09 (0.06)
Close to whites	0.05 (0.06)				
Close to blacks		0.16 (0.05)			
Close to Hispanics			0.17 (0.05)		
Close to Asians				0.14 (0.05)	
Close to Caribbeans					0.17 (0.05)
Black	−0.09 (0.11)	−0.15 (0.11)	−0.12 (0.11)	−0.13 (0.10)	−0.09 (0.10)
Asian	−0.19 (0.13)	−0.24 (0.13)	−0.27 (0.12)	−0.20 (0.13)	−0.25 (0.12)
Hispanic	−0.09 (0.11)	−0.11 (0.10)	0.02 (0.10)	−0.07 (0.09)	−0.06 (0.09)
Caribbean	−0.14 (0.13)	−0.15 (0.12)	−0.09 (0.13)	−0.07 (0.12)	−0.11 (0.13)
Age x black	0.12 (0.11)	0.16 (0.11)	0.16 (0.11)	0.15 (0.11)	0.12 (0.11)

(continued)

229

TABLE A15. *(continued)*

	Allies (Close to Whites)	Allies (Close to Blacks)	Allies (Close to Hispanics)	Allies (Close to Asians)	Allies (Close to Caribbeans)
Age x Asian	-0.07 (0.14)	-0.05 (0.14)	-0.08 (0.14)	-0.08 (0.14)	-0.13 (0.15)
Age x Hispanic	-0.21 (0.12)	-0.20 (0.12)	-0.20 (0.12)	-0.19 (0.12)	-0.23 (0.12)
Age x Caribbean	0.08 (0.14)	0.12 (0.13)	0.14 (0.13)	0.14 (0.13)	0.13 (0.14)
Income x black	-0.05 (1.11)	0.85 (1.20)	-0.02 (1.11)	0.12 (1.11)	-0.03 (1.12)
Income x Asian	-0.48 (0.34)	-0.51 (0.33)	-0.51 (0.33)	-0.48 (0.34)	-0.73 (0.44)
Income x Hispanic	0.08 (0.32)	0.06 (0.32)	0.09 (0.32)	0.11 (0.32)	0.09 (0.33)
Income x Caribbean	0.09 (0.43)	-0.00 (0.42)	0.08 (0.42)	0.12 (0.42)	0.09 (0.43)
South x black	-0.02 (0.04)	-0.02 (0.04)	-0.02 (0.04)	-0.03 (0.05)	-0.01 (0.05)
South x Asian	0.04 (0.06)	0.03 (0.06)	0.04 (0.06)	0.03 (0.06)	0.07 (0.07)
South x Hispanic	0.05 (0.05)	0.04 (0.05)	0.05 (0.05)	0.04 (0.05)	0.06 (0.05)
South x Caribbean	-0.09 (0.06)	-0.11 (0.06)	-0.07 (0.07)	-0.07 (0.07)	-0.07 (0.07)
Education x black	0.00 (0.07)	-0.01 (0.07)	0.00 (0.07)	0.02 (0.07)	0.01 (0.07)
Education x Asian	-0.02 (0.10)	-0.01 (0.10)	-0.01 (0.10)	0.01 (0.10)	0.02 (0.10)
Education x Hispanic	0.06 (0.07)	0.06 (0.07)	0.06 (0.07)	0.09 (0.07)	0.09 (0.07)
Education x Caribbean	0.08 (0.09)	0.02 (0.09)	0.06 (0.09)	0.07 (0.09)	0.07 (0.09)
Female x black	-0.03 (0.04)	-0.02 (0.04)	-0.03 (0.04)	-0.02 (0.04)	-0.02 (0.04)
Female x Asian	0.02 (0.05)	0.02 (0.05)	0.02 (0.05)	0.02 (0.05)	0.02 (0.05)
Female x Hispanic	-0.04 (0.04)	-0.04 (0.04)	-0.05 (0.04)	-0.05 (0.04)	-0.05 (0.04)
Female x Caribbean	-0.05 (0.05)	-0.06 (0.05)	-0.06 (0.05)	-0.04 (0.05)	-0.06 (0.05)

Party x black	0.06 (0.08)	0.06 (0.08)	0.06 (0.08)	0.04 (0.08)	0.06 (0.08)
Party x Asian	0.16 (0.08)	0.15 (0.08)	0.15 (0.08)	0.15 (0.08)	0.14 (0.09)
Party x Hispanic	0.03 (0.07)	0.05 (0.07)	0.05 (0.07)	0.02 (0.07)	0.05 (0.07)
Party x Caribbean	0.02 (0.09)	-0.01 (0.09)	0.01 (0.09)	-0.02 (0.09)	0.01 (0.09)
Ideology x black	0.08 (0.08)	0.08 (0.08)	0.07 (0.08)	0.07 (0.08)	0.06 (0.08)
Ideology x Asian	0.15 (0.11)	0.12 (0.10)	0.12 (0.10)	0.12 (0.11)	0.12 (0.11)
Ideology x Hispanic	0.08 (0.08)	0.08 (0.08)	0.06 (0.08)	0.06 (0.08)	0.06 (0.08)
Ideology x Caribbean	0.04 (0.09)	0.04 (0.09)	0.04 (0.09)	0.02 (0.09)	0.03 (0.09)
Close to group x black	-0.06 (0.08)	-0.04 (0.08)	-0.05 (0.07)	0.00 (0.07)	-0.09 (0.07)
Close to group x Asian	-0.18 (0.10)	-0.10 (0.09)	-0.03 (0.09)	-0.18 (0.09)	-0.08 (0.08)
Close to group x Hispanic	-0.05 (0.08)	-0.04 (0.07)	-0.25 (0.08)	-0.12 (0.07)	-0.18 (0.07)
Close to group x Caribbean	0.06 (0.09)	0.09 (0.09)	-0.07 (0.08)	-0.02 (0.08)	-0.06 (0.08)
N	2235	2236	2225	2184	2126

OLS models describing Racial Groups can be Political Allies (0=strongly disagree, 1=strongly agree) as a function of Closeness to a racial group (0=not close at all, 1=very close) and personal attributes (NPS, Chapter 5, Figure 8).

TABLE A16.

	Competition from Whites	Competition from Blacks	Competition from Hispanics	Competition from Asians	Competition from Caribbeans
Constant	0.36 (0.08)	0.18 (0.06)	0.21 (0.06)	0.19 (0.07)	0.19 (0.07)
Age	0.32 (0.07)	0.20 (0.05)	0.23 (0.05)	0.24 (0.05)	0.21 (0.05)
Income	0.20 (1.04)	-0.22 (0.17)	0.12 (0.17)	-0.18 (0.18)	-0.22 (0.17)
South	-0.00 (0.03)	0.03 (0.02)	0.05 (0.02)	0.02 (0.03)	0.04 (0.02)
Education	-0.12 (0.05)	-0.16 (0.03)	-0.20 (0.04)	-0.17 (0.04)	-0.18 (0.04)
Female	0.00 (0.03)	-0.01 (0.02)	-0.02 (0.02)	-0.02 (0.02)	-0.03 (0.02)
Dem–Rep partisanship	0.11 (0.06)	0.04 (0.03)	0.03 (0.04)	0.01 (0.04)	0.01 (0.04)
Lib-Con ideology	-0.06 (0.05)	0.11 (0.04)	0.08 (0.04)	0.07 (0.05)	0.05 (0.04)
Close to target group	-0.23 (0.05)	-0.23 (0.04)	-0.30 (0.04)	-0.22 (0.04)	-0.21 (0.04)
Close to ingroup	0.23 (0.06)	0.10 (0.05)	0.17 (0.05)	0.12 (0.05)	0.11 (0.05)
Black	0.10 (0.13)		0.16 (0.10)	0.05 (0.10)	0.01 (0.09)
Asian	0.12 (0.11)	0.14 (0.11)	0.09 (0.11)		0.09 (0.11)
Hispanic		0.18 (0.09)		0.21 (0.09)	0.16 (0.09)
Caribbean	0.02 (0.13)	0.20 (0.10)	0.28 (0.11)	0.21 (0.11)	
Age x black	-0.16 (0.13)		-0.01 (0.08)	-0.04 (0.09)	0.03 (0.08)
Age x Asian	-0.24 (0.11)	0.00 (0.11)	0.00 (0.11)		-0.06 (0.11)
Age x Hispanic		-0.10 (0.09)		-0.17 (0.10)	-0.08 (0.09)
Age x Caribbean	-0.02 (0.13)	0.05 (0.10)	0.04 (0.10)	-0.01 (0.11)	
Income x black	-0.45 (1.06)		-1.65 (0.95)	-0.19 (0.97)	-0.48 (0.91)
Income x Asian		0.23 (0.26)	-0.25 (0.26)		0.11 (0.33)

	(1)	(2)	(3)	(4)	(5)
Income x Hispanic	−0.41 (1.06)	0.21 (0.24)		0.11 (0.26)	0.07 (0.24)
Income x Caribbean	−0.01 (1.08)	0.43 (0.32)	0.35 (0.33)	0.29 (0.34)	
South x black	−0.04 (0.06)	−0.02 (0.05)	−0.04 (0.04)	−0.03 (0.04)	−0.01 (0.04)
South x Asian	−0.04 (0.04)	−0.09 (0.03)	−0.08 (0.05)		−0.06 (0.05)
South x Hispanic	0.01 (0.06)	−0.05 (0.05)	−0.09 (0.05)	−0.06 (0.04)	−0.06 (0.04)
South x Caribbean			0.06 (0.06)	−0.03 (0.05)	
Education x black	0.01 (0.09)	0.11 (0.08)	0.12 (0.08)	0.06 (0.06)	0.02 (0.06)
Education x Asian	0.02 (0.07)	0.01 (0.05)			0.11 (0.08)
Education x Hispanic	0.01 (0.08)	−0.09 (0.07)		−0.03 (0.06)	−0.04 (0.05)
Education x Caribbean			0.04 (0.07)	0.07 (0.07)	
Female x black	0.02 (0.04)	0.01 (0.04)	0.02 (0.03)	0.04 (0.03)	0.04 (0.03)
Female x Asian	0.04 (0.04)	0.04 (0.03)	0.02 (0.04)		−0.00 (0.04)
Female x Hispanic	0.05 (0.05)	0.03 (0.04)		0.07 (0.03)	0.06 (0.03)
Female x Caribbean			0.03 (0.04)	0.03 (0.04)	
Party x black	0.01 (0.08)	−0.08 (0.06)	−0.00 (0.06)	0.09 (0.06)	0.06 (0.06)
Party x Asian	0.08 (0.07)	0.01 (0.05)	−0.08 (0.07)		−0.07 (0.07)
Party x Hispanic	0.10 (0.09)	−0.01 (0.07)		0.02 (0.06)	0.02 (0.05)
Party x Caribbean			−0.02 (0.07)	0.04 (0.08)	
Ideology x black	0.05 (0.09)	−0.06 (0.08)	−0.06 (0.06)	−0.04 (0.06)	0.04 (0.06)
Ideology x Asian	0.03 (0.07)	−0.09 (0.06)	−0.03 (0.08)		0.00 (0.08)
Ideology x Hispanic	−0.01 (0.08)	−0.10 (0.07)		−0.10 (0.07)	−0.08 (0.06)
Ideology x Caribbean			−0.19 (0.07)	−0.14 (0.08)	
Close to target x black			0.21 (0.06)	0.12 (0.06)	0.17 (0.05)

(continued)

TABLE A16. *(continued)*

	Competition from Whites	Competition from Blacks	Competition from Hispanics	Competition from Asians	Competition from Caribbeans
Close to target x Asian	0.11 (0.08)	0.12 (0.07)	0.27 (0.07)		0.25 (0.06)
Close to target x Hispanic	0.06 (0.07)	0.06 (0.06)		0.16 (0.06)	0.26 (0.05)
Close to target x Caribbean	-0.04 (0.08)	0.14 (0.08)	0.16 (0.07)	0.02 (0.07)	
Close to ingroup x black	-0.12 (0.09)	-0.01 (0.08)	-0.12 (0.08)	-0.03 (0.08)	-0.06 (0.07)
Close to ingroup x Asian	-0.22 (0.08)	-0.03 (0.07)	-0.08 (0.08)		-0.02 (0.08)
Close to ingroup x Hispanic	-0.09 (0.08)	-0.08 (0.07)	-0.16 (0.08)	-0.09 (0.07)	-0.11 (0.07)
Close to ingroup x Caribbean				-0.05 (0.08)	
N	1556	1693	1721	1848	1810

OLS models describing Intergroup Competition (0=strongly disagree, 1=strongly agree) as a function of Closeness to a target group (0=not close at all, 1=very close), an ingroup (0=not close at all, 1=very close) and personal attributes (NPS, Chapter 5, Figure 9).

TABLE A17. *Affirmative Action*

	Close to Whites	Close to Blacks	Close to Hispanics	Close to Asians	Close to Caribbeans
Constant	0.54 (0.10)	0.46 (0.09)	0.55 (0.08)	0.57 (0.08)	0.53 (0.08)
Age	-0.06 (0.08)	-0.08 (0.08)	-0.08 (0.08)	-0.09 (0.08)	-0.06 (0.08)
Income	-0.41 (0.27)	-0.41 (0.26)	-0.40 (0.26)	-0.42 (0.26)	-0.42 (0.27)
South	-0.02 (0.04)	-0.04 (0.04)	-0.02 (0.04)	-0.03 (0.04)	-0.04 (0.04)
Education	-0.05 (0.06)	-0.05 (0.06)	-0.05 (0.06)	-0.08 (0.06)	-0.07 (0.06)
Female	0.12 (0.03)	0.11 (0.03)	0.12 (0.03)	0.12 (0.03)	0.14 (0.03)
Dem-Rep partisanship	0.30 (0.05)	0.28 (0.05)	0.31 (0.05)	0.29 (0.06)	0.25 (0.06)
Lib-Con ideology	-0.25 (0.07)	-0.23 (0.07)	-0.25 (0.07)	-0.26 (0.07)	-0.26 (0.07)
Close to racial group	0.05 (0.08)	0.22 (0.07)	0.06 (0.06)	0.11 (0.06)	0.21 (0.06)
Black	0.29 (0.14)	0.29 (0.14)	0.27 (0.13)	0.24 (0.13)	0.27 (0.13)
Asian	0.14 (0.17)	0.07 (0.16)	0.02 (0.15)	0.00 (0.16)	0.11 (0.15)
Hispanic	0.18 (0.13)	0.18 (0.12)	-0.03 (0.13)	0.09 (0.12)	0.09 (0.12)
Caribbean	0.08 (0.17)	0.15 (0.16)	0.07 (0.16)	0.14 (0.15)	0.08 (0.16)
Age x black	0.06 (0.13)	0.09 (0.13)	0.08 (0.13)	0.10 (0.13)	0.09 (0.13)
Age x Asian	0.04 (0.18)	0.07 (0.18)	0.06 (0.18)	0.06 (0.18)	0.10 (0.18)
Age x Hispanic	0.06 (0.15)	0.07 (0.15)	0.09 (0.15)	0.05 (0.15)	0.05 (0.15)
Age x Caribbean	0.21 (0.17)	0.24 (0.17)	0.25 (0.17)	0.27 (0.17)	0.24 (0.17)
Income x black	-1.39 (1.34)	-1.91 (1.45)	-1.36 (1.34)	-1.34 (1.34)	-1.53 (1.34)
Income x Asian	0.71 (0.40)	0.69 (0.40)	0.67 (0.40)	0.73 (0.40)	0.64 (0.52)
Income x Hispanic	0.69 (0.42)	0.69 (0.42)	0.71 (0.42)	0.74 (0.42)	0.69 (0.43)

(continued)

TABLE A17. (continued)

	Close to Whites	Close to Blacks	Close to Hispanics	Close to Asians	Close to Caribbeans
Income x Caribbean	0.64 (0.51)	0.63 (0.51)	0.62 (0.50)	0.67 (0.50)	0.64 (0.51)
South x black	0.00 (0.05)	0.02 (0.05)	0.00 (0.06)	0.00 (0.06)	0.03 (0.06)
South x Asian	0.05 (0.08)	0.03 (0.08)	0.05 (0.08)	0.04 (0.08)	0.10 (0.08)
South x Hispanic	0.03 (0.06)	0.04 (0.06)	0.02 (0.06)	0.03 (0.06)	0.06 (0.06)
South x Caribbean	-0.04 (0.08)	-0.03 (0.08)	-0.03 (0.08)	-0.04 (0.08)	-0.01 (0.08)
Education x black	0.11 (0.09)	0.12 (0.09)	0.10 (0.09)	0.14 (0.09)	0.13 (0.09)
Education x Asian	0.10 (0.12)	0.09 (0.12)	0.10 (0.12)	0.13 (0.12)	0.08 (0.13)
Education x Hispanic	-0.11 (0.09)	-0.13 (0.09)	-0.14 (0.09)	-0.10 (0.09)	-0.12 (0.09)
Education x Caribbean	0.18 (0.11)	0.17 (0.11)	0.17 (0.11)	0.22 (0.11)	0.18 (0.11)
Female x black	-0.15 (0.05)	-0.15 (0.05)	-0.15 (0.05)	-0.14 (0.05)	-0.17 (0.05)
Female x Asian	-0.05 (0.06)	-0.06 (0.06)	-0.04 (0.06)	-0.03 (0.06)	-0.06 (0.06)
Female x Hispanic	-0.01 (0.05)	-0.01 (0.05)	-0.01 (0.05)	-0.01 (0.05)	-0.03 (0.05)
Female x Caribbean	-0.14 (0.06)	-0.15 (0.06)	-0.16 (0.06)	-0.14 (0.06)	-0.16 (0.06)
Party x black	-0.12 (0.09)	-0.11 (0.09)	-0.11 (0.09)	-0.12 (0.09)	-0.09 (0.10)
Party x Asian	-0.17 (0.10)	-0.18 (0.10)	-0.20 (0.10)	-0.16 (0.10)	-0.15 (0.11)
Party x Hispanic	-0.14 (0.09)	-0.11 (0.09)	-0.18 (0.09)	-0.13 (0.09)	-0.08 (0.09)
Party x Caribbean	-0.11 (0.12)	-0.09 (0.12)	-0.10 (0.12)	-0.12 (0.12)	-0.07 (0.12)
Ideology x black	0.09 (0.09)	0.07 (0.09)	0.08 (0.09)	0.09 (0.09)	0.09 (0.10)
Ideology x Asian	0.06 (0.13)	0.03 (0.13)	0.03 (0.13)	0.07 (0.13)	0.06 (0.13)
Ideology x Hispanic	0.26 (0.10)	0.25 (0.10)	0.25 (0.10)	0.29 (0.10)	0.29 (0.11)

Ideology x Caribbean	0.22 (0.11)	0.19 (0.11)	0.20 (0.11)	0.21 (0.11)	0.24 (0.12)
Close to group x black	−0.07 (0.10)	−0.14 (0.10)	−0.06 (0.09)	−0.07 (0.09)	−0.16 (0.08)
Close to group x Asian	−0.16 (0.13)	0.02 (0.12)	0.10 (0.11)	−0.04 (0.12)	−0.11 (0.10)
Close to group x Hispanic	−0.18 (0.11)	−0.20 (0.10)	0.15 (0.10)	−0.08 (0.09)	−0.12 (0.08)
Close to group x Caribbean	−0.02 (0.12)	−0.18 (0.12)	−0.03 (0.10)	−0.24 (0.11)	−0.16 (0.11)
N	2065	2062	2053	2022	1969

OLS models describing Affirmative Action (0=a bad thing, 1=a good thing) as a function of Closeness to a racial group (0=not close at all, 1=very close) and personal attributes (NPS, Chapter 5, Figure 10).

References

Alba, Richard and Victor Nee. 2003. *Remaking the American Mainstream.* Cambridge, MA: Harvard University Press.

Aleinikoff, T. Alexander. 2002. *Semblances of Sovereignty: The Constitution, the State, and American Citizenship.* Cambridge, MA: Harvard University Press.

Aleinikoff, T. Alexander and Samuel Issacharoff. 1993. "Race and Redistricting: Drawing Constitutional Lines after Shaw v. Reno." *Michigan Law Review* 92(3): 588–651.

Alesina, Alberto and Eliana Ferrera. 2000. "Participation in Heterogeneous Communities." *The Quarterly Journal of Economics* 115: 847–904.

Alesina, Alberto, Edward Glaeser, and Bruce Sacerdote. 2001. "Why Doesn't the United States Have a European-Style Welfare State?" *Brookings Papers on Economic Activity 2001*: 187–254.

Allensworth, Elaine M. and Refugio I. Rochin. 1998. "Ethnic Transformation in Rural California: Looking beyond the Immigrant Farmworker." *Rural Sociology* 63(1): 26–51.

Allport, Gordon W. 1954. *The Nature of Prejudice.* New York: Addison-Wesley.

Anderson, Benedict. 1983. *Imagined Communities.* London: Verso.

Archibold, Randal C. 2006. "Arizona County Uses New Law to Look for Illegal Immigrants." *New York Times*, May 10, 2006, A19.

Aron, Arthur, Elaine N. Aron, Michael Tudor, and Greg Nelson. 1991. "Close Relationships as Including Other in the Self." *Journal of Personality and Social Psychology* 60: 241–253

Austin, Marsha. 2003. "Legal Immigrants' Loss of Medicaid Benefits 'Like End of Life.'" *The Denver Post*, March 9, 2003, A23.

Ayers, Edward L., Patricia Nelson Limerick, Stephen Nissenbaum, and Peter S. Onuf. 1996. *All Over the Map: Rethinking American Regions.* Baltimore: Johns Hopkins University Press.

Baldassare, Mark. 1992. "Suburban Communities." *Annual Review of Sociology* 18: 475–94.

————. 2003. Public Policy Institute of California March 2003 Survey Data.

Balin, Jane. 1999. *A Neighborhood Divided: Community Resistance to an AIDS Care Facility*. Ithaca, NY: Cornell University Press.

Batson, C.D., Chang, J., Orr, R., & Rowland, J. (2002). "Empathy, Attitudes, and Action: Can Feeling for a Member of a Stigmatized Group Motivate One to Help the Group?" *Personality and Social Psychology Bulletin* 28: 1656–66.

Beiner, Ronald. 1995. *Theorizing Citizenship*. Albany: State University of New York Press.

Bellah, Robert N., Richard Madsen, William N. Sullivan, Ann Swidler, and Steven M. Tipton. 1985. *Habits of the Heart: Individualism and Commitment in American Life*. Berkeley: University of California Press.

Berelson, Bernard R., Paul F. Lazarsfeld, and William N. McPhee. 1954. *Voting: A Study of Opinion Formation in a Presidential Campaign*. Chicago: University of Chicago Press.

Berscheid, Ellen, Mark Snyder, and Allen M. Omoto. 1989. "The Relationship Closeness Inventory." *Journal of Personality and Social Psychology* 57: 792–807.

Blakely, Edward James and Mary Gail Snyder. 1997. *Fortress America: Gated Communities in the United States*. Washington, D.C.: Brookings Institution Press.

Blalock, Hubert M. 1967. *Toward a Theory of Minority Group Relations*. New York: Wiley.

Blau, Peter and Joseph Schwartz. 1984. *Crosscutting Social Circles*. Orlando, FL: Academic Press.

Bobo, Lawrence and Frank Gilliam. 1990. "Race, Sociopolitical Participation, and Black Empowerment." *American Political Science Review* 84: 377–93.

Bobo, Lawrence and Vincent L. Hutchings. 1996. "Perceptions of Racial Group Competition: Extending Blumer's Theory of Group Position to a Multiracial Social Context." *American Sociological Review* 61: 951–72.

Bobo, Lawrence and James R. Kluegel. 1993. "Opposition to Race-targeting: Self-interest, Stratification Ideology, or Racial Attitudes?" *American Sociological Review* 58: 443–64.

Bobo, Lawrence, James R. Kluegel, and Ryan A. Smith. 1997. "Laissez-Faire Racism: The Crystallization of a Kinder, Gentler, Antiblack Ideology." In *Racial Attitudes in the 1990s: Continuity and Change*, eds. Steven A. Tuch and Jack K. Martin. Westport, CT: Praeger, 15–42.

Bobo, Lawrence D. and Mia Tuan. 2006. *Prejudice in Politics: Group Position, Public Opinion, and the Wisconsin Treaty Rights Dispute*. Cambridge, MA: Harvard University Press.

Bolan, Marc. 1997. "The Mobility Experience and Neighborhood Attachment." *Demography* 34(2): 225–38.

Borjas, George J. 1996. "The New Economics of Immigration: Affluent Americans Gain; Poor Americans Lose." *Atlantic Monthly* 278(5): 72–9.

Borjas, George J., Jeffrey T. Grogger, and Gordon H. Hanson. 2006. "Immigration and African-American Employment Opportunities: The Response of Wages,

Employment, and Incarceration to Labor Supply Shocks." NBER Working Paper No. W12518. Available at SSRN: http://ssrn.com/abstract=930608.

Brewer, Marilynn, and R. M. Kramer. 1985. "The Psychology of Intergroup Attitudes and Behavior." *Annual Review of Psychology* 36: 219–43.

———. 1991. "The Social Self: On Being the Same and Different at the Same Time." *Personality and Social Psychology Bulletin* 17: 475–82.

———. 1999. "The Psychology of Prejudice: Ingroup Love or Outgroup Hate?" *Journal of Social Issues* 55(3): 429–44.

Briggs, Xavier de Souza. 2007. "'Some of My Best Friends Are...': Interracial Friendships, Class, and Segregation in America." *City & Community* 6: 263–90.

Brimelow, Peter. 1995. *Alien Nation: Common Sense about America's Immigration Disaster*. New York: Random House.

Brown, Robert A. and Todd C. Shaw. 2002. "Separate Nations: Two Attitudinal Dimensions of Black Nationalism." *Journal of Politics* 64: 22–44.

Brown, Roger. 1986. *Social Psychology, Second Edition*. New York: The Free Press.

Brubaker, Rogers. 1992. *Citizenship and Nationhood in France and Germany*. Cambridge: Harvard University Press.

Buchanan, Patrick J. 2006. *State of Emergency: the Third World Invasion and Conquest of America*. New York: Thomas Dunne Books.

Caldwell, Christopher. 2006. "The Way We Live Now." *New York Times Magazine*, August 13, 2006, 13.

Calhoun, Craig. 1991. "The Problem of Identity in Collective Action." In *Macro-Micro Linkages in Sociology*, ed. Joan Huber. Newbury Park, CA: Sage, 51–75.

Carmines, Edward G. and James A. Stimson. 1989. *Issue Evolution: Race And The Transformation of American Politics*. Princeton, NJ: Princeton University Press.

Carroll, Joseph. 2006. "Public: National Anthem Should be Sung in English." http://www.gallup.com/poll/22639/Public-National-Anthem-Should-Sung-English.aspx.

"Census, Race and Science." 2000. *Nature Genetics* 24: 97–8 (editorial).

Chambers, John W. 1987. *To Raise an Army: the Draft Comes to Modern America*. New York: Free Press.

Chapman, John W. and Ian Shapiro, eds. 1993. *Democratic Community*. NY: New York University Press.

Chong, Dennis and Anna M. Marshall. 1999. "When Morality and Economics Collide (or Not) in a Texas Community." *Political Behavior* 21: 91–121.

Chugh, Dolly. 2006. "Bounded Ethicality." Presentation hosted by the Institute for Quantitative Social Science at Harvard University, Cambridge, MA.

Citrin, Jack, Beth Reingold, and Donald P. Green. 1990. "American Identity and the Politics of Ethnic Change." *Journal of Politics* 52(4): 1124–55.

Citrin, Jack, David O. Sears, Christopher Muste, and Cara Wong. 2001. "Multiculturalism in American Public Opinion." *British Journal of Political Science* 31: 247–75.

Citrin, Jack, Cara Wong, and Brian Duff. 2001. "The Meaning of American National Identity: Patterns of Ethnic Conflict and Consensus." In *Social Identity, Intergroup Conflict, and Conflict Resolution*, eds. Richard D. Ashmore, Lee Jussim, and David Wilder. Oxford: Oxford University Press, 71–100.

Citrin, Jack, Donald P. Green, Christopher Muste, and Cara Wong. 1997. "Public Opinion Toward Immigration Reform: The Role of Economic Motivations." *Journal of Politics* 59(3): 858–82.

Clark, Kenneth B. and Mamie P. Clark. 1958. "Racial Identification and Preference in Negro Children." In *Readings in Social Psychology, Third Edition*, eds. T. Newcomb and E. Hartley. New York: Holt, 602–11.

Clary, E. Gil and Mark Snyder. 1991. "A Functional Analysis of Altruism and Prosocial Behavior: The Case of Volunteerism." *Review of Personality and Social Psychology* 12: 119–48.

Clayton, Susan and Susan Opotow. 2003. *Identity and the Natural Environment: The Psychological Significance of Nature.* Cambridge, MA: MIT Press.

Conley, Dalton. 1999. *Being Black, Living in the Red: Race, Wealth, and Social Policy in America.* Berkeley, CA: University of California Press.

Connery, Brian A. 1997. "IMHO: Authority and Egalitarian Rhetoric in the Virtual Coffeehouse." In *Internet Culture*, ed. David Porter. New York: Routledge, 161–180.

Conover, Pamela Johnston. 1984. "The Influence of Group Identifications on Political Perceptions and Evaluations." *Journal of Politics* 46: 760–85.

———. 1987. "Approaches to the Political Study of Social Groups: Measures of Group Identification and Group Affect." Paper presented at the NES-sponsored conference on groups and American politics. Palo Alto, CA, January 16–17.

Converse, Philip. 1964. "The Nature of Belief Systems." In *Ideology and Discontent*, ed. David E. Apter. London: Free Press of Glencoe, 206–261.

Corlett, William S. 1989. *Community Without Unity: A Politics of Derridian Extravagance.* Durham, NC: Duke University Press.

Croal, N'Gai. 1999. "Long Live Rock 'n' Rap." *Newsweek*, July 19, 1999, 60.

Crosby, Faye J. and Elisabeth Pearsall Lubin. 1990. "Extending the Moral Community: Logical and Psychological Dilemmas." *Journal of Social Issues* 46: 163–72.

Cross, W.E., Jr. 1971. "The Negro-to-Black Conversion Experience." *Black World* 20: 13–27.

Crouch, Stanley. 1996. "Race Is Over: Black, White, Red, Yellow – Same Difference." *New York Times Magazine*, September 29, 1996, 170.

Cuba, Lee and David M. Hummon. 1993. "A Place to Call Home: Identification with Dwelling, Community, and Region." *Sociological Quarterly* 34(1): 111–22.

Dagger, Richard K. 1985. "Rights, Boundaries, and the Bonds of Community: A Qualified Defense of Moral Parochialism." *American Political Science Review* 79:436–47.

Dao, James. 2004. "Two States Trying to Keep Gambling Money At Home." *New York Times*, March 22, 2004, A16.

Darley, John M., and C D. Batson. 1973. "'From Jerusalem to Jericho': a Study of Situational and Dispositional Variables in Helping Behavior." *Journal of Personality and Social Psychology* 27: 100–108.

Davidson, W. and P. Cotter. 1986. "Measurement of Sense of Community Within the Sphere of City." *Journal of Applied Social Psychology* 16:608–19.

Davidson, William B. and Patrick R. Cotter. 1993. "Psychological Sense of Community and Support for Public School Taxes." *American Journal of Community Psychology* 21(1): 59–67.

Davies, Paul G., Claude M. Steele, and Hazel Rose Markus. 2008. "A Nation Challenged: The Impact of Foreign Threat on America's Tolerance for Diversity." *Journal of Personality and Social Psychology* 95: 308–18.

Davis, Darren W. and Ronald E. Brown. 2002. "The Antipathy of Black Nationalism: Behavioral and Attitudinal Implications of an African American Ideology." *American Journal of Political Science* 46: 239–52.

Davis, F. J. 1991. *Who Is Black?: One Nation's Definition.* Pennsylvania State University Press.

Davis, James Allan and Tom W. Smith. 2007. General Social Surveys, 1972–2006 (machine-readable data file). Chicago: National Opinion Research Center (producer); Storrs, CT: The Roper Center for Public Opinion Research, University of Connecticut (distributor).

Davis, Robert. 2005. "New Orleans Police Finally Arrive at Convention Center." *USA Today*, September 2, 2005. www.usatoday.com/news/nation/2005-09-02-neworleanspolice_x.htm.

Dawson, Michael C. 1994. *Behind the Mule: Race and Class in African-American Politics.* Princeton, NJ: Princeton University Press.

2001. *Black Visions.* Chicago: University of Chicago Press.

De Figueiredo, Rui J. P., Jr. and Zachary Elkins. 2003. "Are Patriots Bigots? An Inquiry into the Vices of Ingroup-Pride." *American Journal of Political Science* 47: 171–88.

De Vasconcelos Barros, Edgard. 1957. "Defining the Boundaries of a Brazilian Rural Community." *Rural Sociology* 22: 270.

Deaux, Kay. 1991. "Social Identities: Thoughts on Structure and Change." In *The Relational Self*, ed. Rebecca C. Curtis. New York: Guilford Press, 77–93.

———. 1993. "Reconstructing Social Identity." *Personality and Social Psychology Bulletin* 19: 4–12.

Deaux, Kay, Anne Reid, Kim Mizrahi, and Kathleen A. Ethier. 1995. "Parameters of Social Identity." *Journal of Personality and Social Psychology* 68: 280–91.

Decker, Cathleen. 1995. "Faith in Justice System Drops." *Los Angeles Times*, October 8, 1995, S2.

Delli-Carpini, Michael X. and Scott Keeter. 1996. *What Americans Know About Politics and Why It Matters.* New Haven: Yale University Press.

Deutsch, Karl Wolfgang. 1953. *Nationalism and Social Communication: An Inquiry into the Foundations of Nationality.* New York: Technology Press of the Massachusetts Institute of Technology and Wiley.

Devos, Thierry and Mahzarin R. Banaji. 2005. "American = White?" *Journal of Personality and Social Psychology* 88: 447–466.

Dewan, Shaila. 2006. "In Georgia County, Divisions of North and South Play Out in Drives to Form New Cities." *New York Times,* June 13, 2006, A16.

DeWolfe Howe, M. A. 1924. *Barrett Wendell and His Letters.* Boston: Atlantic Monthly Press.

Diamond, Jared. 1994. "Race Without Color." *Discover* 15: 82–89.

Dixon, Travis L. 2008. "Network News and Racial Beliefs: Exploring the Connection Between National Television News Exposure and Stereotypical Perceptions of African Americans." *Journal of Communication* 58: 321–337.

Driehaus, Bob. 2007. "Audit Finds Many Faults in Cleveland's 06 Voting." *New York Times,* April 20, 2007, A16.

Du Bois, W. E. B. 1968 [1903]. *The Souls of Black Folk.* New York: Johnson Reprint Corp.

Duany, Andres, Elizabeth Plater-Zyberk, and Jeff Speck. 2000. *Suburban Nation: The Rise of Sprawl and the Decline of the American Dream.* New York: North Point Press.

Duster, Troy. 2005. "Race and Reification in Science." *Science* 307: 1050–51.

Edgell, Penny, Joseph Gerteis, and Douglas Hartmann. 2006. "Atheists as 'Other.' " *American Sociological Review* 71: 211–34.

Egan, Timothy. 2003. "Vanishing Point." *New York Times* (December 1, 2003), A1.

Elkins, Zachary and John Sides. 2007. "Can Institutions Build Unity in Multiethnic States?" *American Political Science Review* 101: 693–708.

Elster, Jon. 1995. *Local Justice in America.* Russell Sage Foundation.

Espenshade, Thomas J. and Charles A. Calhoun. 1993. "An Analysis of Public Opinion Toward Undocumented Immigration." *Population Research and Policy Review* 12: 189–224.

Ethier, Kathleen A. and Kay Deaux. 1994. "Negotiating Social Identity when Contexts Change: Maintaining Identification and Responding to Threat." *Journal of Personality and Social Psychology* 67(2): 243–52.

Etzioni, Amitai. 2002. "Are Particularistic Obligations Justified? A Communitarian Examination." *Review of Politics* 64: 573–98.

Farley, Reynolds. 1999. "Racial Issues: Recent Trends in Residential Patterns and Intermarriage." In *Diversity and Its Discontents: Cultural Conflict and Common Ground in Contemporary American Society,* eds. Neil J. Smelser and Jeffrey C. Alexander. Princeton, NJ: Princeton University Press, 85–128.

Feagin, Joe R., and Eileen O'Brien. 2003. *White Men on Race: Power, Privilege, and the Shaping of Cultural Consciousness.* Beacon Press.

Feldman, Roberta M. 1990. "Settlement-Identity: Psychological Bonds with Home Places in a Mobile Society." *Environment and Behavior* 22: 183–229.

Feldman, Stanley, and Marco R. Steenbergen. 2001. "The Humanitarian Foundation of Public Support for Social Welfare." *American Journal of Political Science* 45: 658–77.

Feldman, Stanley, and Karen Stenner. 1997. "Perceived Threat and Authoritarianism." *Political Psychology* 18: 741–70.

Fernandez, R.R. and D.A. Dillman. 1979. "The Influence of Community Attachment on Geographic Mobility." *Rural Sociology* 44 (2): 345–60.

Fessler, D.R. 1952. "The Development of a Scale for Measuring Community Solidarity." *Rural Sociology* 17: 144–52.

Fischel, William A. 2001. *The Homevoter Hypothesis.* Cambridge: Harvard University Press.

Fischer, Claude S. 2002. "Ever-More Rooted Americans." *City & Community* 1: 177–98.

———. 1982. *To Dwell Among Friends: Personal Networks in Town and City.* Chicago: University of Chicago Press.

Foley, D. 1952 *Neighbors or Urbanites.* Rochester: University of Rochester

Fossett, Mark A. and K. Jill Kiecolt. 1989. "The Relative Size of Minority Populations and White Racial Attitudes." *Social Science Quarterly* 70: 820–35.

Fowler, James H. and Cindy D. Kam. 2007. "Beyond the Self: Social Identity, Altruism, and Political Participation." *Journal of Politics* 69: 813–27.

FOX News. 2005. "Half Katrina Refugees Have Records." September 22, 2005. http://www.foxnews.com/story/0,2933,170134,00.html.

Freie, John F. 1998. *Counterfeit Community: The Exploitation of Our Longings for Connectedness.* New York: Rowman & Littlefield.

Friedrich, Carl J. 1959. "The Concept of Community in the History of Political and Legal Philosophy." In *Nomos II: Community*, ed. Carl J. Friedrich, 3–24.

Frohnen, Bruce. 1996. *The New Communitarians and the Crisis of Modern Liberalism.* Lawrence, KS: University Press of Kansas.

Frug, Jerry. 1996. "The Geography of Community." *Stanford Law Review* 48: 1047–1108.

Frymer, Paul. 1999. *Uneasy Alliances: Race and Party Competition in America.* Princeton, NJ: Princeton University Press.

Furia, Peter. 2001. "Global Citizenship, Anyone?" Paper prepared for the 2001 annual meeting of the American Political Science Association, San Francisco, CA.

Gaertner, Lowell and Chester A. Insko. 2000. "Intergroup Discrimination in the Minimal Group Paradigm: Categorization, Reciprocation, or Fear?" *Journal of Personality and Social Psychology* 79: 77–94.

Gainsborough, Juliet F. 2001. *Fenced Off: The Suburbanization of American Politics.* Washington, DC: Georgetown University Press.

Galpin, Charles J. 1915. "The Social Anatomy of an Agricultural Community." *Research Bulletin* 34. Madison: University of Wisconsin Agricultural Experiment Station.

Gamson, William. 1971. "Political Trust and Its Ramifications." In *Social Psychology and Political Behavior*, eds. Gilbert Abcarian and John W. Soule. New York: Charles E. Merrill, 40–55.

Garrison, Marsha. 1998. "Autonomy or Community? An Evaluation of Two Models of Parental Obligation." *California Law Review* 86: 41–117.

Gay, Claudine. 2006. "Seeing Difference: The Effect of Economic Disparity on Black Attitudes toward Latinos." *American Journal of Political Science* 50: 982–97.

Gay, Claudine and Katherine Tate. 1998. "Doubly Bound: The Impact of Gender and Race on the Politics of Black Women." *Political Psychology* 19: 169–84.

Gerson, Kathleen, C. Ann Stueve, and Claude Fischer. 1977. "Attachment to Place." In *Networks and Places*, eds. Claude Fischer, et al. New York: The Free Press, 139–61.

Gerstle, Gary. 2001. *American Crucible: Race and Nation in the Twentieth Century*. Princeton, NJ: Princeton University Press.

Gilens, Martin. 1999. *Why Americans Hate Welfare: Race, Media, and the Politics of Antipoverty Policy*. Chicago: University of Chicago Press.

Gilliam, Frank D., Jr. and Shanto Iyengar. 2000. "Prime Suspects: The Influence of Local Television News on the Viewing Public." *American Journal of Political Science* 44: 560–573.

Gitlin, Todd. 1995. *The Twilight of Common Dreams: Why America is Wracked by Culture Wars*. New York: Henry Holt and Company.

Glaeser, E. L., D. I. Laibson, J. A. Scheinkman, and C. L. Soutter. 2000. "Measuring Trust." *Quarterly Journal of Economics* 115: 811–46.

Glaser, James. 1994. "Back to the Black Belt: Racial Environment and White Racial Attitudes in the South." *Journal of Politics* 56: 21–41.

———. 2002. "White Voters, Black Schools: Structuring Racial Choices with a Checklist Ballot." *American Journal of Political Science* 46: 35–46.

Glazer, Nathan. 1997. *We Are All Multiculturalists Now*. Cambridge: Harvard University Press.

Gleason, Philip. 1980. "American Identity and Americanization." *Harvard Encyclopedia of American Ethnic Groups*. Cambridge, MA: Harvard University Press.

Glynn, Thomas J. 1981. "Psychological Sense of Community: Measurement and Application." *Human Relations* 34: 789–818.

Gorman, Anna. 2008. "Immigration Debate Hits Home for Liver Transplant Patients." *Los Angeles Times*, April 13, 2008.

Goudy, Willis J. 1982. "Further Considerations of Indicators of Community Attachment." *Social Indicators Research* 11: 181–92.

Green, Donald Phillip, Dara Strolovich, and Janelle S. Wong. 1998. "Defended Neighborhoods, Integration, and Hate Crime." *American Journal of Sociology* 104: 372–403.

Greenfeld, Liah. 1992. *Nationalism: Five Roads to Modernity*. Cambridge, MA: Harvard University Press.

Greenhouse, Linda. 2006. "Justices Express Concern Over Aspects of Some Texas Redistricting." *New York Times*, March 2, 2006, A24.

Grimes, William. 1997. "Face-to-Face Encounter on Race in the Theater." *New York Times*, January 29, 1997, B1.

Guest, Avery M. and Barrett A. Lee. 1984. "How Urbanites Define Their Neighborhoods." *Population and Environment* 7: 32–56.

Guest, Avery M. and Susan K. Wierzbicki. 1999. "Social Ties at the Neighborhood Level." *Urabn Affairs Review* 35: 92–111.

Gurin, Patricia and Edgar Epps. 1975. *Black Consciousness, Identity and Achievement*. New York: John Wiley.

Gurin, Patricia, Shirley Hatchett, and James S. Jackson. 1989. *Hope and Independence: Blacks' Response to Electoral and Party Politics.* New York: R. Sage Foundation.

Gurin, P., T. Peng, G. Lopez, and B.R. Nagda. 1999. "Context, Identity, and Intergroup Relations." In *Cultural Divides: The Social Psychology of Intergroup Contact,* eds. D. Prentice and D. Miller. New York: Russell Sage Foundation.

Gustafson, Per. 2001. "Roots and Routes: Exploring the Relationship Between Place Attachment and Mobility." *Environment and Behavior* 33: 667–86.

Guterbock, Thomas M. and Bruce London. 1983. "Race, Political Orientation, and Participation: An Empirical Test of Four Competing Theories." *American Sociological Review* 48: 439–53.

Habyarimana, James, Macartan Humphreys, Daniel N. Posner, and Jeremy M.Weinstein. 2007. "Why Does Ethnic Diversity Undermine Public Goods Provision?" *American Political Science Review* 101: 709–725.

Hacker, Andrew. 1995. *Two Nations: Black and White, Separate, Hostile, Unequal. Expanded and Updated.* New York: Ballantine Books.

Haga, W.J. and C.L. Folse. 1971. "Trade Patterns and Community Identity." *Rural Sociology* 36: 42–51.

Halter, Marilyn. 2000. *Shopping for Identity: the Marketing of Ethnicity.* Schocken Books.

Haney-Lopez, Ian F. 1996. *White by Law: The Legal Construction of Race.* New York: New York University Press.

Hanson, Sandra L., William J. Sauer, and Wayne C. Seelbach. 1983. "Racial and Cohort Variations in Filial Responsibility Norms." *The Gerontologist* 23: 626–31.

Harmon, Amy. 2005. "Blacks Pin Hope on DNA to Fill Slavery's Gaps in Family Trees." *New York Times,* July 25, 2005, A1.

Harris, David R., and Jeremiah J. Sim. 2002. "Who Is Multiracial? Assessing the Complexity of Lived Race." *American Sociological Review* 67: 614–27.

Harris, David R. 2001. "Why are Whites and Blacks Averse to Black Neighbors?" *Social Science Research* 30: 100–16.

Hartigan, John. 1999. *Racial Situations: Class Predicaments of Whiteness in Detroit.* Princeton, NJ: Princeton University Press.

Hatamiya, Leslie. 1993. *Righting a Wrong: Japanese Americans and the Passage of the Civil Liberties Act of 1988.* Stanford, CA: Stanford University Press.

Healy, David. 1997. "Cyberspace and Place: The Internet as Middle Landscape on the Electronic Frontier." In *Internet culture,* ed. David Porter. New York: Routledge, 55–68.

Hero, Rodney E. 1992. *Latinos and the U.S. Political System: Two-Tiered Pluralism.* Philadelphia, PA: Temple University Press.

Herring, Mary, Thomas B. Jankowski, and Ronald E. Brown. 1999. "Pro-Black Doesn't Mean Anti-White: The Structure of African-American Group Identity." *Journal of Politics* 61: 363–86.

Herszenhorn, David M. 2001. "Greenwich Says Law Allows Bans on Beach Use." *New York Times,* March 16, 2001, B4.

Herting, Jerald R., David B. Grusky, and Stephen E. Van Rompaey. 1997. "The Social Geography of Interstate Mobility and Persistence." *American Sociological Review* 62: 267–87.

Higginbotham, Evelyn B. 1993. *Righteous Discontent:The Women's Movement in the Black Baptist Church, 1880–1920*. Cambridge, MA: Harvard University Press.

Higham, John. 1988. *Strangers in the Land: Patterns of American Nativism, 1860–1925*. 2d ed. New Brunswick, NJ: Rutgers University Press.

Highton, Benjamin. 1997. "Easy Registration and Voter Turnout." *Journal of Politics* 59 (2): 565–77.

Hillery, George A., Jr. 1955. "Definitions of Community: Areas of Agreement." *Rural Sociology* 20: 111–23.

———. 1959. "A Critique of Selected Community Concepts." *Social Forces* 37: 237–42.

Hirschman, Albert O. 1970. *Exit, Voice, and Loyalty: Responses to Decline in Firms, Organizations, and States*. Cambridge, MA: Harvard University Press.

Hirschman, Charles, Richard Alba, and Reynolds Farley. 2000. "The Meaning and Measurement of Race in the U.S. Census: Glimpses into the Future." *Demography* 37: 381–93.

Hochschild, Jennifer L. 1981. *What's Fair?: American Beliefs about Distributive Justice*. Cambridge, MA: Harvard University Press.

Hoffmann, Stanley. 1981. *Duties Beyond Borders: On the Limits and Possibilities of Ethical International Politics*. Syracuse, NY: Syracuse University Press.

Hollinger, David A. 1995. *Postethnic America: Beyond Multiculturalism*. New York: Basic Books.

Hopkins, Daniel J. 2009. "Politicized Places: Explaining Where and When Immigrants Provoke Local Opposition. Unpublished manuscript. Washington, D.C.

Huckfeldt, Robert, Paul Allen Beck, Russell J. Dalton, and Jeffrey Levine. 1995. "Political Environments, Cohesive Social Groups, and the Communication of Public Opinion." *American Journal of Political Science* 39 (4): 1025–55.

Huckfeldt, Robert, Eric Plutzer, and John Sprague. 1993. "Alternative Contexts of Political Behavior: Churches, Neighborhoods, and Individuals." *Journal of Politics* 55 (2): 365–381.

Huckfeldt, Robert and John Sprague. 1991. "Discussant Effects on Vote Choice: Intimacy, Structure, and Interdependence." *Journal of Politics* 53(1): 122–59.

Huckfeldt, Robert. 1986. *Politics in Context: Assimilation and Conflict in Urban Neighborhoods*. New York: Agathon Press.

Huddy, Leonie and Nadia Khatib. 2007. "American Patriotism, National Identity, and Political Involvement." *American Journal of Political Science* 51: 63–77.

Hunter, Albert. 1975. "The Loss of Community: An Empirical Test Through Replication." *American Sociological Review* 40: 537–52.

Huntington, Samuel P. 2004. *Who Are We?: The Challenges to America's National Identity*. New York: Simon and Schuster.

———. 1981. *American Politics: The Promise of Disharmony*. Cambridge, MA: Harvard University Press.

Ignatiev, Noel. 1995. *How the Irish Became White*. New York: Routledge.

Ignatiev, Noel, and John Garvey. 1996. *Race Traitor*. New York: Routledge.

Jackson, Byran O. 1987. "The Effects of Racial Group Consciousness on Political Mobilization in American Cities." *Western Political Quarterly* 1: 631–46.

Jackson, James S., Patricia Gurin, and Shirley J. Hatchett. National Black Election Study, 1984. Sponsored by the Ford Foundation, Rockefeller Foundation, and Carnegie Corporation. Ann Arbor, MI: Inter-university Consortium for Political and Social Research [distributor]. ICPSR Study No. 8938.

Jackson, James S., Vincent L. Hutchings, Ronald Brown, and Cara Wong. National Politics Study, 2004. Sponsored by the National Science Foundation, Carnegie Corporation, and the University of Michigan Office of the Vice President of Research. Ann Arbor, MI: Inter-university Consortium for Political and Social Research [distributor]. ICPSR Study No. 24483.

Jackson, Kenneth. 1995. *Crabgrass Frontier: The Suburbanization of the United States*. New York: Oxford University Press.

Jacobson Matthew Frye. 1998. *Whiteness of a Different Color: European Immigrants and the Alchemy of Race*. Cambridge, MA: Harvard University Press.

Jacoby, Tamar. 2006. "Immigration Nation." *Foreign Affairs* 85: 50–65.

Jefferson, Margo. 1997. "Arguing Culture and Identity." *New York Times*, February 4, 1997, B1.

Jeske, Diane. "Special Obligations," *The Stanford Encyclopedia of Philosophy* (Fall 2008 Edition), Edward N. Zalta (ed.), http://plato.stanford.edu/archives/fall2008/entries/special-obligations/.

Johnson, Kevin R. 2005. "The Forgotten 'Repatriation' of Persons of Mexican Ancestry and Lessons for the 'War on Terror'." UC Davis Legal Studies Research Paper Series. http://ssrn.com/abstract=862905.

Jones, Jeffrey M. 2007. "Some Americans Reluctant to Vote for Mormon, 72-Year-Old Presidential Candidates." http://www.gallup.com/poll/26611/some-americans-reluctant-vote-mormon-72yearold-presidential-candidates.aspx.

Junn, Jane and Krista Jenkins. 1997. "Explaining Trends in Black Electoral Participation." Paper presented at the 1997 annual meeting of the Midwest Political Science Association, Chicago, IL.

Kahn, Jonathan. 2005. "Misreading Race and Genomics After Bi Dil." *Nature Genetics* 37: 655–656.

Karst, Kenneth L. 1989. *Belonging to America: Equal Citizenship and the Constitution*. New Haven, CT: Yale University Press.

Katz, Michael B. 2001. *The Price of Citizenship*. New York: Henry Holt and Company.

Keller, Suzanne. 2003. *Community: Pursuing the Dream, Living the Reality*. Princeton, NJ: Princeton University Press.

Kelly, Wendy. 2004. Letter from the Editor. *Porch Magazine 1*.

Kelman, Herbert C., and V. Hamilton. 1990. *Crimes of Obedience: Toward a Social Psychology of Authority and Responsibility*. New York: Yale University Press.

Kettner, James H. 1978. *The Development of American Citizenship, 1608–1870.* Chapel Hill, NC: University of North Carolina Press.

Key, V. O. 1949. *Southern Politics in State and Nation.* New York: Knopf.

Kim, Claire Jean. 2000. *Bitter Fruit: The Politics of Black-Korean Conflict in New York City.* New Haven, CT: Yale University Press.

Kinder, Donald R. and Lynn M. Sanders. 1996. *Divided by Color: Racial Politics and Democratic Ideal.* Chicago: University of Chicago Press.

Kinder, Donald R. and Nicholas Winter. 2001. "Exploring the Racial Divide: Blacks, Whites, and Opinion on National Policy." *American Journal of Political Science* 45: 439–56.

Kirp, David L. 2000. *Almost Home: America's Love-Hate Relationship with Community.* Princeton, NJ: Princeton University Press.

Klosko, George. 2004. "Multiple Principles of Political Obligation." *Political Theory* 32: 801–824.

Koch, Jeffrey W. 1993. "Is Group Membership a Prerequisite for Group Identification?" *Political Behavior* 15: 49–60.

Koerner, Brendan I. 2005. "Blood Feud." *Wired* Sept. 2005. http://www.wired.com/wired/archive/13.09/seminoles.html.

Kosterman, Rick and Seymour Feshbach. 1989. "Toward a Measure of Patriotic and Nationalistic Attitudes." *Political Psychology* 10: 257–274.

Krupat, E. 1985. *People in Cities: The Urban Environment and Behavior.* New York: Cambridge University Press.

Krysan, Maria and Reynolds Farley. 2002. "The Residential Preferences of Blacks: Do They Explain Persistent Segregation?" *Social Forces* 80: 937–80.

Ladd, John. 1959. "The Concept of Community: A Logical Analysis." In *Nomos II: Community*, ed. Carl J. Friedrich. New York: Liberal Arts Press, 269–93.

Lamont, Michelle. 2002. "Working Men's Imagined Communities." In *The Postnational Self: Belonging and Identity*, eds. Ulf Hedetoft and Mette Hjort. Minneapolis, MN: University of Minnesota Press, 178–197.

Lamont, Michelle and Virag Molnar. 2002. "The Study of Boundaries in the Social Sciences." *Annual Review of Sociology* 28: 167–195.

Lang, Robert E., and Karen A. Danielsen. 1997. "Gated Communities in America: Walling Out the World." *Housing Policy Debate* 8: 867–899.

Latané, B, and John Darley. 1969. "Bystanders 'Apathy'." *American Scientist* 57: 244–268.

Lau, Richard R. 1989. "Individual and Contextual Influences on Group Identification." *Social Psychology Quarterly* 52: 220–31.

Lazarsfeld, Paul Felix, Bernard Berelson, and Hazel Gaudet. 1944. *The People's Choice: How the Voter Makes Up His Mind in a Presidential Campaign.* New York: Duell, Sloan and Pearce.

Leach, William. 1999. *Country of Exiles: The Destruction of Place in American Life.* New York: Pantheon Books.

Lee, Barrett A., R. S. Oropesa, and James W. Kanan. 1994. "Neighborhood Context and Residential Mobility." *Demography* 31: 249–270.

Leighley, Jan. 2001. *Strength in Numbers?: The Political Mobilization of Racial and Ethnic Minorities.* Princeton, NJ: Princeton University Press.

Lelieveldt, Herman. 2004. "Helping Citizens Help Themselves: Neighborhood Improvement Programs and the Impact of Social Networks, Trust, and Norms on Neighborhood-Oriented Forms of Participation." *Urban Affairs Review* 39: 531–51.

Lemann, Nicholas. 1992. *The Promised Land: The Great Black Migration and How It Changed America*. New York: Vintage Books.

Levine, Robert A. and Donald T. Campbell. 1972. *Ethnocentrism: Theories of Conflict, Ethnic Attitudes, and Group Behavior*. Hoboken, NJ: John Wiley & Sons.

Lewin, Kurt. 1948. *Resolving Social Conflicts: Selected Papers on Group Dynamics 1935–1946*. New York: Harper.

Lichter, Daniel T., Domenico Parisi, Steven M. Grice, and Michael Taquino. 2007. "Municipal Underbounding: Annexation and Racial Exclusion in Small Southern Towns." *Rural Sociology* 72: 47–68.

Lieberman, Evan S. 2003. *Race and Regionalism in the Politics of Taxation in Brazil and South Africa*. New York: Cambridge University Press.

Lilli, Waldemar and Michael Diehl. 1999. "Measuring National Identity." *Mannheim Centre for European Social Research, Working Paper 10*.

Lippmann, Walter. 1965. *Public Opinion*. New York: The Free Press.

Liptak, Adam. 2008. "Power to Build Border Fence Is Above U.S. Law." *New York Times*, April 8, 2008, A1.

Logan, John, Deirdre Oakley, Polly Smith, Jacob Stowell, and Brian Stults. 2001. "Separating the Children." Report by the Lewis Mumford Center, May 4, 2001. Updated December 28, 2001.

Lollock, Lisa. 2001. "The Foreign-Born Population in the United States: March 2000." *Current Population Reports*, 20–534. Washington, DC: Bureau of the Census.

Long, Larry H. 1972. "The Influence of Number and Ages of Children on Residential Mobility." *Demography* 9: 371–82.

Lorde, Audre. 1984. *Sister Outsider: Essays and Speeches*. Trumansburg, NY: Crossing Press.

Lynd, Robert Staughton and Helen Merrell Lynd. 1929. *Middletown: A Study in American Culture*. New York: Harcourt, Brace and Co.

MacDonald, Karin. 1998. "Preparing for Redistricting in 2001 – Communities Define their Interests." Paper prepared for the 1998 annual meeting of the American Political Science Association, Boston, MA.

Macedo, Stephen. 2008. "When and Why Should Liberal Democracies Restrict Immigration?" Paper presented at the 2008 annual meeting of the American Political Science Association, Boston, MA.

MacIver, R.M. and Charles H. Page. 1952. *Society: An Introductory Analysis*. London: MacMillan & Co., Ltd.

Malik, Kenan. 2005. "Is This the Future We Really Want? Different Drugs for Different Races." www.timesonline.co.uk/article/0,,1072-1658766,00.html.

Marcus, George E., John L. Sullivan, Elizabeth Theiss-Morse, and Sandra L. Wood. 1995. *With Malice Toward Some: How People Make Civil Liberties Judgments*. NY: Cambridge University Press.

Marklein, Mary B. 2006. "Are Out-of-State Students Crowding Out In-Staters?: Smaller States Such as Vermont Often Must Choose Between Greater Tuition Income and Admitting Local Students; In Many Cases, the Local Students Lose." *USA Today*, August 31, 2006, A1.

Marshall, T. H. 1973. *Class, Citizenship and Social Development*. Westport, CT: Greenwood Press.

Massey, Douglas S. 2000. "The Residential Segregation of Blacks, Hispanics, and Asians, 1970–90." In *Immigration and Race: New Challenges for American Democracy*, ed. Gerald D. Jaynes. New Haven, CT: Yale University Press, 44–73.

Massey, Douglas S. and Nancy A. Denton. 1993. *American Apartheid: Segregation and the Making of the Underclass*. Cambridge, MA: Harvard University Press.

McClosky, Herbert and John Zaller. 1984. *The American Ethos: Public Attitudes Toward Capitalism and Democracy*. Cambridge, MA: Harvard University Press.

McDermott, Monica and Frank L. Samson. 2005. "White Racial and Ethnic Identity in the United States." *Annual Review of Sociology* 31: 245–61.

McDonnell, Patrick J. 1997. "Judge Upholds Wilson Ban on Prenatal Care." *Los Angeles Times*, December 18, 1997, A3.

McGuire, William J., Claire V. McGuire, P. Child, and T. Fujioka. 1978. "Salience of Ethnicity in the Spontaneous Self-Concept as a Function of One's Ethnic Distinctiveness in the Social Environment." *Journal of Personality and Social Psychology* 36: 511–520.

McMillan, David W. and David M. Chavis. 1986. "Sense of Community: A definition and theory." *Journal of Community Psychology* 14: 6–23.

Merelman, Richard M., Greg Streich, and Paul Martin. 1998. "Unity and Diversity in American Political Culture: An Exploratory Study of the National Conversation on American Pluralism and Identity." *Political Psychology* 19: 781–807.

Merton, Robert K. 1968. *Social Theory and Social Structure, 1968 Enlarged Edition*. NY: The Free Press.

Merton, Robert K. and Alice S. Rossi. 1968. "Contributions to the Theory of Reference Group Behavior." In Robert K. Merton, *Social Theory and Social Structure, 1968 Enlarged Edition*. New York: The Free Press, 279–334.

Mertz, Elizabeth. 1994. "Legal Loci and Places in the Heart: Community and Identity in Sociolegal Studies." *Law & Society Review* 28:971–92.

Meyrowitz, Joshua. 1985. *No Sense of Place: The Impact of Electronic Media on Social Behavior*. New York: Oxford University Press.

Miller, Arthur H., Patricia Gurin, Gerald Gurin, and Oksana Malanchuk. 1981. "Group Consciousness and Political Participation." *American Journal of Political Science* 25: 494–511.

Miller, David. 1995. *On Nationality*. Oxford: Oxford University Press.

Montgomery, David. 2006. "An Anthem's Discordant Notes." *Washington Post*, April 28, 2006, A1.

Molnar, Joseph J., Sally Purohit, Howard A. Clonts, and V. Wilson Lee. 1979. "A Longitudinal Analysis of Satisfaction with Selected Community Services in a Nonmetropolitan Area." *Rural Sociology* 44: 401–19.

Morse, Rob. 1997. "We in the Community Community." *San Francisco Chronicle*, July 6, 1997, A2.

Muller, Eric L. 2001. *Free to Die for Their Country: The Story of the Japanese American Draft Resisters in World War II*. New York: University of Chicago Press.

Myrdal, Gunnar. 1944. *An American Dilemma; The Negro Problem and Modern Democracy*. New York: Harper & Brothers.

Navarro, Mireya. 2006. "For Latinos, Familiar Faces May Not Be Friendly Bosses." *New York Times*, October 22, 2006, section 9, 6.

Nelson, Thomas E. and Donald R. Kinder. 1996. "Issue Frames and Group-Centrism in American Public Opinion." *Journal of Politics* 58: 1055–78.

Niebuhr, Reinhold. 1960. *Moral Man and Immoral Society*. New York: Scribner.

Nobles, Melissa. 2004. "The Other Side of American Exceptionalism: The Comparative Study of Racial Politics." *APSA-CP Newsletter* 15: 13–15.

Noe, Raymond A. and Allison E. Barber. 1993. "Willingness to Accept Mobility Opportunities: Destination Makes a Difference." *Journal of Organizational Behavior* 14: 159–75.

Nossiter, Adam. 2006. "Bit by Bit, Some Outlines Emerge for a Shaken New Orleans." *New York Times*, August 27, 2006, A1.

Nussbaum, Martha. 1996. *For Love of Country: Debating the Limits of Patriotism*. Boston: Beacon Press.

Ogden, Christopher. 1996. "President Buchanan and the World." *TIME International* 147 (March 4, 1996).

Oliver, J. Eric. 2001. *Democracy in Suburbia*. Princeton, NJ: Princeton University Press.

Oliver, J. Eric and Tali Mendelberg. 2000. "Reconsidering the Environmental Determinants of White Racial Attitudes." *American Journal of Political Science* 44(3): 574–89.

Oliver, Melvin L. and Thomas M. Shapiro. 1995. *Black Wealth/White Wealth: a New Perspective on Racial Inequality*. NY: Routledge.

Olsen, Laurie. 1997. *Made in America: Immigrant Students in Our Public Schools*. New York: The New Press.

Olzak, Susan, and Suzanne Shanahan. 2003. "Racial Policy and Racial Conflict in the Urban United States, 1869–1924." *Social Forces* 82: 481–517.

Olzak, Susan. 1992. *The Dynamics of Ethnic Competition and Conflict*. Stanford, CA: Stanford University Press.

Omi, Michael and Howard Winant. 1986. *Racial Formation in the United States: From the 1960s to the 1980s*. New York: Routledge & Kegan Paul.

Onishi, Norimitsu. 2006. "Village Writes Its Epitaph: Victim of a Graying Japan." *New York Times*, April 30, 2006, A18.

Opotow, Susan. 1990. "Moral Exclusion and Injustice." *Journal of Social Issues* 46: 1–20.

———. 1993. "Animals and the Scope of Justice." *Journal of Social Issues* 49 (1):71–86.

———. 2008. "'Not So Much as Place to Lay Our Head...': Moral Inclusion and Exclusion in the American Civil War Reconstruction." *Social Justice Research* 21: 26–49.

Orfield, Gary, and John C. Boger, eds. 2006. *School Resegregation: Must the South Turn Back?* Chapel Hill, NC: University of North Carolina Press.

Oyserman, Daphna, Izumi Sakamoto, and Armand Lauffer. 1998. "Cultural Accommodation." *Journal of Personality and Social Psychology* 74: 1606–1618.

Pear, Robert. 2006. "White House to Ease Medicaid Rule on Proof of Citizenship." *New York Times,* July 7, 2006, A15.

Perea, Juan F. 1998. *Immigrants Out!: The New Nativism and the Anti-Immigrant Impulse in the United States.* New York: New York University Press.

Pettigrew, Thomas F. 1998. "Intergroup Contact Theory." *Annual Review of Psychology* 49: 65–86.

Pickus, Noah. 1998. *Immigration and Citizenship in the Twenty-First Century.* Rowman & Littlefield.

———. 2005. *True Faith and Allegiance: Immigration and American Civic Nationalism.* Princeton, NJ: Princeton University Press.

Pitkin, Hanna. 1972. *Wittgenstein and Justice.* Berkeley: University of California Press.

Piven, Frances Fox and Richard Cloward. 1971. *Regulating the Poor.* New York: Vintage.

Posner, Daniel N. 2004. "The Political Salience of Cultural Differences: Why Chewas and Tumbukas are Allies in Zambia and Adversaries in Malawi." *American Political Science Review* 98: 529–45.

Pretty, G. 1990. "Relating Psychological Sense of Community to Social Climate Characteristics." *Journal of Community Psychology* 18: 60–5.

Putnam, Robert D. 1993. *Making Democracy Work.* Princeton, NJ: Princeton University Press.

———. 2000. *Bowling Alone: The Collapse and Revival of American Community.* New York: Simon & Schuster.

———. 2007. "E Pluribus Unum: Diversity and Community in the Twenty-first Century, The 2006 Johan Skytte Prize Lecture." *Scandinavian Political Studies* 30: 137–74.

Quillian, Lincoln. 1995. "Prejudice as a Response to Perceived Group Threat: Population Composition and Anti-Immigrant and Racial Prejudice in Europe." *American Sociological Review* 60: 586–611.

Rankin, Tom. 2000. *Local Heroes Changing America.* NY: W. W. Norton & Company.

Reid, Anne and Kay Deaux. 1996. "Relationship between social and personal identities: segregation or integration." Special Issue: The Self and Social Identity. *Journal of Personality and Social Psychology* 71 (6):1084–92.

Reynolds, Katherine J., John C. Turner, and S. Alexander Haslam. 2000. "When Are We Better than Them and They Worse Than Us? A Closer Look at Social Discrimination in Positive and Negative Domains." *Journal of Personality and Social Psychology* 78: 64–80.

Rich, Frank. 1997. "Two Mouths Running." *New York Times,* February 1, 1997, A19.

Robinson, Deborah Marie. 1987. *The Effect of Multiple Group Identity Among Black Women on Race Consciousness.* Unpublished Ph.D. dissertation, University of Michigan.

Rosenberg, Seymour and Michael A. Gara. 1985. "The Multiplicity of Personal Identity." *Review. of Personality and Social Psychology* 6: 87–113.

Rosenstone, S. J., and J. M. Hansen. 2003. *Mobilization, Participation, and Democracy in America.* New York: Longman.

Rosenstone, Steven J., Donald R. Kinder, Warren E. Miller, and the National Election Studies. American National Election Study, 1996: Pre- and Post-Election Survey [computer file]. ICPSR06896-v5. Ann Arbor, MI: University of Michigan, Center for Political Studies [producer], 2003. Ann Arbor, MI: Inter-university Consortium for Political and Social Research [distributor], 2005–05–23. doi:10.3886/ICPSR06896.

Rosenstone, Steven J., Virginia Sapiro, Warren E. Miller, Donald R. Kinder, and the National Election Studies. American National Election Study: 1997 Pilot Study [computer file]. ICPSR02282-v2. University of Michigan, Center for Political Studies [producer], 1999. Ann Arbor, MI: Inter-university Consortium for Political and Social Research [distributor], 1999. doi:10.3886/ICPSR02282.

Ross, Dalton. 2006. "'Survivor' Race Battle." *Entertainment Weekly* 2006. http://www.ew.com/ew/article/0,,1279451,00.html.

Saguaro Seminar. 2000. The Social Capital Community Benchmark Survey. Storrs, CT: The Roper Center for Public Opinion Research, University of Connecticut [distributor].

Sampson, Robert J. 1988. "Local Friendship Ties and Community Attachment in Mass Society: a Multilevel Systemic Model." *American Sociological Review* 53: 766–79.

Sandalow, Marc. 1994. "Lawmaker Wants No Quake Aid For Undocumented Immigrants." *San Francisco Chronicle*, January 27, 1994, A3.

Sandel, Michael J. 1982. *Liberalism and the Limits of Justice.* Cambridge, UK: Cambridge University Press.

Sanderson, John P. 1856. *Republican Landmarks: The Views and Opinions of American Statesmen on Foreign Immigration.* Philadelphia: J. B. Lippincott and Co.

Santos, Fernanda. 2006. "Reverberations of a Baby Boom." *New York Times,* August 27, 2006, A23.

Savelle, Max. 1962. "Nationalism and Other Loyalties in the American Revolution." *The American Historical Review* 67: 901–23.

Schaar, John H. 1981. *Legitimacy in the Modern State.* New Brunswick, NJ: Transaction Books.

Schachter, Jason. 2001. "Geographical Mobility: March 1999 to March 2000." *Current Population Reports.* Washington, DC: Bureau of the Census, 20–538.

Scheffler, Samuel. 2001. *Boundaries and Allegiances: Problems of Justice and Responsibility in Liberal Thought.* NY: Oxford University Press.

Scherzer, Kenneth A. 1992. *The Unbounded Community: Neighborhood Life and Social Structure in New York City.* Durham, NC: Duke University Press.

Schildkraut, Deborah J. 2007. "Defining American Identity in the Twenty-First Century: How Much 'There' is There?" *Journal of Politics* 69: 597–615.

Schlesinger, Arthur Meier. 1992. *The Disuniting of America.* New York: Norton.

Schmitt, Eric. 2001. "Segregation Growing among U.S. Children." *New York Times,* May 6, 2001, A20, A28.

Schrag, Peter. 1999. *Paradise Lost.* Berkeley: University of California Press.

Schuck, Peter H. and Rogers M. Smith. 1985. *Citizenship Without Consent: Illegal Aliens in the American Polity.* New Haven, CT: Yale University Press.

Schuman, Howard, Charlotte Steeh, Lawrence Bobo, and Maria Krysan. 1997. *Racial Attitudes in America: Trends and Interpretations. Revised Edition.* Cambridge, MA: Harvard University Press.

Schwartz, Amy E. 1994. "Satire, Stereotype, Schwarzenegger." *Washington Post,* July 22, 1994, A23.

Schwartz, Roberts. 2001. "Racial Profiling in Medical Research." *New England Journal of Medicine* 344: 1392–1393.

Sears, David, and Jack Citrin. 1985. *Tax Revolt: Something for Nothing in California.* Cambridge, MA: Harvard University Press.

Sears, David O. and Leonie Huddy. 1986. "Social Identities and Political Disunity Among Women." NES 1985 Pilot Study Report.

Sears, David O., Richard R. Lau, Tom R. Tyler, and Harris M. Allen, Jr. 1980. "Self-Interest vs. Symbolic Politics in Policy Attitudes and Presidential Voting." *American Political Science Review* 74: 670–84.

Seelbach, Wayne C. and William J. Sauer. 1977. "Filial Responsibility Expectations and Morale among Aged Parents." *The Gerontologist* 17: 492–99.

Seiler, Lauren H. and Gene F. Summers. 1974. "Locating Community Boundaries: An Integration of Theory and Empirical Techniques." *Sociological Methods & Research* 2: 259–80.

Sellers, Robert M., Stephanie A. J. Rowley, Tabbye M. Chavous, J. Nicole Shelton, Mia A. Smith. 1997. "Multidimensional Inventory of Black Identity: A Preliminary Investigation of Reliability and Construct Validity." *Journal of Personality and Social Psychology* 73: 805–15.

Sellers, Robert M., Mia A. Smith, J. Nicole Shelton, Stephanie A. J. Rowley, and Tabbye M. Chavous. 1998. "Multidimensional model of racial identity: A reconceptualization of African American racial identity." *Personality & Social Psychology Review* 2 (1): 18–39.

Shaw, Daron, Rodolfo O. De La Garza, and Jongho Lee. 2000. "Examining Latino Turnout in 1996: a Three-State, Validated Survey Approach." *American Journal of Political Science* 44: 338–46.

Sherif, Muzafer and Carolyn W. Sherif. 1979. "Research on Intergroup Relations." In *The Social Psychology of Intergroup Relations,* eds. William G. Austin and Stephen Worchel. Monterey, CA: Brooks/Cole Publishing Co., 7–18.

Shingles, Richard D. 1981. "Black Consciousness and Political Participation: The Missing Link." *American Political Science Review* 75: 76–91.

Shklar, Judith N. 1998. *Redeeming American Political Thought.* eds. Stanley Hoffmann and Dennis F. Thompson. Chicago: University of Chicago Press.

———. 1998. *Political Thought and Political Thinkers.* ed. Stanley Hoffmann. Chicago: University of Chicago Press.

————. 1991. *American Citizenship: The Quest for Inclusion.* Cambridge, MA: Harvard University Press.

Shue, Henry. 1979. "Rights in the Light of Duties." In *Human Rights and U.S. Foreign Policy*, eds. Peter G. Brown and Douglas MacLean. Lanham, MD: Lexington Books.

————. 1988. "Mediating Duties." *Ethics* 98: 687–704.

Sidanius, Jim and Felicia Pratto. 1999. *Social Dominance: An Intergroup Theory of Social Hierarchy and Oppression.* New York: Cambridge University Press.

Sigelman, Lee and Susan Welch. 1993. "The Contact Hypothesis Revisited: Interracial Contact and Positive Racial Attitudes." *Social Forces* 71: 781–95.

Sigelman, Lee, Steven A. Tuch, and Jack K. Martin. 2005. "What's in a Name? Preference for 'Black' versus 'African American' Among Americans of African Descent." *Public Opinion Quarterly* 69: 429–38.

Simmel, Georg. 1955. *Conflict and the Web of Group-Affiliations.* Free Press.

Singer, Peter. 2002. *One World: The Ethics of Globalization.* New Haven, CT: Yale University Press.

Skerry, Peter. 2000. *Counting on the Census?: Race, Group Identity, and the Evasion of Politics.* Washington, DC: Brookings Institution Press.

Skitka, Linda J. 1999. "Ideological and Attributional Boundaries on Public Compassion: Reactions to Individuals and Communities Affected by a Natural Disaster." *Personality & Social Psychology Bulletin* 25 (7):793.

Skitka, Linda J. and Philip Tetlock. 1992. "Allocating Scarce Resources: A Contingency Model of Distributive Justice." *Journal of Experimental Social Psychology* 28: 491–522.

————. 1993. "Providing Public Assistance: Cognitive and Motivational Processes Underlying Liberal and Conservative Policy Preferences." *Journal of Personality and Social Psychology* 65: 1205–23.

Smith, Marc A. and Peter Kollock. 1999. *Communities in Cyberspace.* New York: Routledge.

Smith, Rogers M. 1993. "Beyond Tocqueville, Myrdal, and Hartz: the multiple traditions in America." *American Political Science Review* 87 (3): 549–67.

————. 1997. *Civic Ideals: Conflicting Visions of Citizenship in U.S. History.* New Haven, CT: Yale University Press.

————. 2003. *Stories of Peoplehood: The Politics and Morals of Political Membership.* New York: Cambridge University Press.

Sniderman, Paul M., Gretchen C. Crosby, and William G. Howell. 2000. "The Politics of Race." In *Racialized Politics: The Debate about Racism in America*, eds. David O. Sears, Jim Sidanius, and Lawrence Bobo. Chicago: University of Chicago Press, 236–79.

Sniderman, Paul M. and Louk Hagendoorn. 2007. *When Ways of Life Collide.* Princeton: Princeton University Press.

Sonenshein, Raphael J. 1993. *Politics in Black and White: Race and Power in Los Angeles.* Princeton, NJ: Princeton University Press.

Song, Sarah. 2008. "Three Models of Civic Solidarity." Paper presented at the 2008 annual meeting of the Western Political Science Association, San Diego, CA.

South, Scott J. and Kyle D. Crowder. 1997. "Residential Mobility Between Cities and Suburbs: Race, Suburbanization, and Back-to-the-City Moves." *Demography* 34: 525–38.

Soysal, Yasemin Nuhoglu. 1994. *Limits of Citizenship: Migrants and Postnational Membership in Europe*. Chicago: University of Chicago Press.

Speare, Alden, Jr. 1974. "Residential Satisfaction as an Intervening Variable in Residential Mobility." *Demography* 11: 173–88.

Staub, Ervin. 1992. *Roots of Evil: The Origins of Genocide and Other Group Violence*. New York: Cambridge University Press.

Stedman, Richard C. 2002. "Toward a Social Psychology of Place: Predicting Behavior from Place-Based Cognitions, Attitudes, and Identity." *Environment and Behavior* 34: 561–81.

Stein, Catherine H., Virginia A. Wemmerus, Marcia Ward, Michelle E. Gaines, Andrew L. Freeberg, and Thomas C. Jewell. 1998. "'Because They're My Parents': An Intergenerational Study of Felt Obligation and Parental Caregiving." *Journal of Marriage and the Family* 60: 611–22.

Steinhauer, Jennifer. 2006. "Storm Evacuees Placing Strains on Texas Hosts." *New York Times*, April 20, 2006, A1.

Sterngold, James. 1998. "A Racial Divide Widens on Network TV." *New York Times*, December 29, 1998, A1.

Stoker, Laura. 1996. "Racial Groups and Interested Political Reasoning." Unpublished manuscript. University of California, Berkeley.

Stolle, Dietlind, Stuart Soroka, and Richard Johnston. 2008. "When Does Diversity Erode Trust? Neighborhood Diversity, Interpersonal Trust and the Mediating Effect of Social Interactions." *Political Studies* 56: 57–75.

Stout, David. 2006. "Bush, Signing Bill for Border Fence, Urges Wider Overhaul." *New York Times*, October 27, 2006, A16.

Strom, Stephanie. 2005. "Figures Reveal Dynamics of Disaster Giving." *New York Times*, October 23, 2005, A18.

Tajfel, Henri. 1970. "Experiments in Intergroup Discrimination." *Scientific American* 223: 96–102.

———. 1981. *Human Groups and Social Categories*. Cambridge, UK: Cambridge University Press.

———. 1982. *Social Identity and Intergroup Relations*. Cambridge, UK: Cambridge University Press.

Takaki, Ronald. 1989. *Strangers From a Different Shore: A History of Asian Americans*. New York: Little, Brown and Company.

Tamir, Yael. 1993. *Liberal Nationalism*. Princeton, NJ: Princeton University Press.

Tamir, Yael. 1995. "The Enigma of Nationalism." *World Politics* 47: 418–40.

Tate, Katherine. 1993. *From Protest to Politics: The New Black Voters in American Elections*. New York: Russell Sage Foundation.

Taylor, Marylee C. 1998. "How White Attitudes Vary with the Racial Composition of Local Populations: Numbers Count." *American Sociological Review* 63: 512–35.

Thernstrom, Abigail and Stephan Thernstrom. 1999. *America in Black and White: One Nation, Indivisible*. New York: Simon and Schuster.

Thompson, Chalmer E. and Robert T. Carter. 1997. "An Overview and Elaboration of Helms' Racial Identity Development Theory." In *Racial Identity Theory: Applications to Individual, Group, and Organizational Interventions*, eds. Chalmer E. Thompson and Robert T. Carter. Mahwah, NJ: Lawrence Erlbaum Associates, Inc., 15–32.

Tichenor, Daniel J. 2002. *Dividing Lines: The Politics of Immigration Control in America*. Princeton, NJ: Princeton University Press.

Tobey, Ronald, Charles Wetherell, and Jay Brigham. 1990. "Moving Out and Settling In: Residential Mobility, Home Owning, and the Public Enframing of Citizenship, 1921–1950." *American Historical Review* 95: 1395–1422.

Tocqueville, Alexis de. 1969. *Democracy in America*. J. P. Mayer, ed., George Lawrence, trans. Garden City, NY: Anchor Books.

Toennies, Ferdinand. 1957. *Community and Society – Gemeinschaft und Gesellschaft*. trans. and ed. Charles P. Loomis. East Lansing: Michigan State University Press.

Transue, John E. 2007. "Identity Salience, Identity Acceptance, and Racial Policy Attitudes: American National Identity as a Uniting Force." *American Journal of Political Science* 51: 78–91.

Truman, David B. 1951. *The Governmental Process: Political Interests and Public Opinion*. New York: Knopf.

Ture, Kwame and Charles Hamilton. 1992 (1967). *Black Power: The Politics of Liberation*. New York: Vintage Books.

Turner, John C. 1982. "Towards a Cognitive Redefinition of the Social Group." In *Social Identity and Intergroup Relations*, ed. Henri Tajfel. Cambridge, UK: Cambridge University Press, 15–40.

Turner, J. C., P. J. Oakes, H. A. Haslam, and C. McGarty. 1994. "Self and Collective: Cognition and Social Context." *Personality and Social Psychology Bulletin* 20: 454–63.

Tyler, Tom R. and E. Allan Lind. 1992. "A Relational Model of Authority in Groups." In *Advances in Experimental Social Psychology* 25: 115–91. New York: Academic Press.

Van de Kragt, Alphons J.C., Robyn M. Dawes, and John M. Orbell. 1988. "Are People Who Cooperate 'Rational Altruists'?" *Public Choice* 56: 233–47.

Varshney, Ashutosh. 2002. *Ethnic Conflict and Civic Life: Hindus and Muslims in India*. New Haven, CT: Yale University Press.

Verba, Sidney, Kay Lehman Schlozman, and Henry E. Brady. 1995. *Voice and Equality: Civic Voluntarism in American Politics*. Cambridge, MA: Harvard University Press.

Verba, Sidney, Kay Lehman Schlozman, Henry E. Brady, and Norman Nie. American Citizen Participation Study, 1990 [computer file]. ICPSR version. Chicago, IL: University of Chicago, National Opinion Research Center (NORC) [producer], 1995. Ann Arbor, MI: Inter-university Consortium for Political and Social Research [distributor], 1995. doi:10.3886/ICPSR06635

Waldron, Jeremy. 1993. *Liberal Rights: Collected Papers, 1981–1991*. New York: Cambridge University Press.

Walsh, Katherine Cramer. 2003. *Talking About Politics: Informal Groups and Social Identity in American Life*. Chicago: University of Chicago Press.

———. 2007. *Talking about Race: Community Dialogues and the Politics of Difference*. Chicago: University of Chicago Press.

Walsh, Katherine Cramer, M. Kent Jennings, and Laura Stoker. 2004. "The Effects of Social Class Identification on Participatory Orientations Towards Government." *British Journal of Political Science* 34: 469–95.

Walzer, Michael. 1981. "Philosophy and Democracy." *Political Theory* 9: 379–99.

———. 1983. *Spheres of Justice: A Defense of Pluralism and Equality*. New York: Basic Books.

———. 1990. "What Does It Mean to Be an American?" *Social Research* 57:591–614.

———. 1996. "Spheres of Affection." In *For Love of Country: Debating the Limits of Patriotism*, ed. Joshua Cohen. Boston: Beacon Press, 125–27.

Waters, Mary C. 1998. "Multiple Ethnic Identity Choices." In *Beyond Pluralism: The Conceptions of Groups and Group Identities in America*, eds. Wendy F. Katkin, Ned Landsman, and Andrea Tyree. Urbana: University of Illinois Press, 28–45.

———. 1990. *Ethnic Options: Choosing Identities in America*. Berkeley: University of California Press.

White, Constance C. R. 1997. "Invoking Tribal Spirits as 90's Muses." *New York Times*, November 7, 1997, A13.

Wiebe, Robert H. 1980. *The Search for Order, 1877–1920*. Westport, CT: Greenwood Press.

Wilder, Thornton. (1938) 2003. *Our Town: A Play in Three Acts*. New York: Harper Perennial Classics.

Williams, Gregory H. 1995. *Life on the Color Line: The True Story of a White Boy Who Discovered He Was Black*. New York: Dutton.

Williams, Juan and Julian Bond. 1992. *Eyes on the Prize: America's Civil Rights Years, 1954–1965*. New York: Penguin Group Australia.

Wolfe, Alan. 1998. *One Nation, After All: What Middle-Class Americans Really Think About: God, Country, Family, Racism*. New York: Viking.

Wong, Cara. 1998. "Group Closeness." NES 1997 Pilot Study Report.

———. 1999. "Blurring the Color Line: The Effects of Ingroup Identity and Outgroup Affinity on Redrawing Community Boundaries." Presented at the 1999 annual meeting of the American Political Science Association, Atlanta, Georgia.

———. 2007. "'Little' and 'Big' Pictures in Our Heads: Race, Local Contexts and Innumeracy about Racial Groups in the U.S." *Public Opinion Quarterly* 71: 392–412.

Wong, Cara and Grace E. Cho. 2005. "Two-Headed Coins or Kandinskys: White Racial Identification." *Political Psychology* 26: 699–720.

———. 2006. "*Jus Meritum*: Citizenship for Service." In *Transforming Politics, Transforming America*, eds. Taeku Lee, Karthick Ramakrishnan, Ricardo Ramírez. Charlottesville, VA: University of Virgina Press, 71–88.

Wong, Cara, Jake Bowers, and Katherine W. Drake. 2005. "Maps and 'Pictures in Our Heads': Testing the Assumptions of Power Threat Theory." Paper presented at the annual meeting of the Midwest Political Science Association. April 2005, Chicago.

Wood, Alastair J. J. 2001. "Racial Differences in the Response to Drugs – Pointers to Genetic Differences." *New England Journal of Medicine* 344: 1393–1396.

Wright, Gerald C. 1977. "Contextual Models of Electoral Behavior: The Southern Wallace Vote." *American Political Science Review* 71: 497–508.

Yack, Bernard. 1993. *The Problems of a Political Animal: Community, Justice, and Conflict in Aristotelian Political Thought*. Berkeley, CA: University of California Press.

———. 1996. "The myth of the civic nation." *Critical Review* 10: 193–211.

Yang, Alan S. 1997. "Trends: Attitudes Toward Homosexuality." *Public Opinion Quarterly* 61: 477–507.

Yoshino, Kenji. 2006. *Covering: The Hidden Assault on Our Civil Rights*. New York: Random House.

Zakaria, Fareed. 2006. "The Enemy Within." *New York Times*, December 17, 2006, F8.

Zangwill, Israel. 1909. *The Melting Pot*. New York: MacMillan.

Zhou, Min. 1997. "Segmented Assimilation: Issues, Controversies, and Recent Research on the New Second Generation." Special Issue: Immigrant Adaptation and Native-Born Responses in the Making of Americans. *International Migration Review* 31 (4): 975–1009.

Index

Books in the Series